Communication in Organizations

Communication in Organizations

Everett M. Rogers
and Rekha Agarwala-Rogers

THE FREE PRESS
A Division of Macmillan Publishing Co., Inc.
NEW YORK

The Free Press
A Division of Macmillan Publishing Co., Inc.
866 Third Avenue, New York, N.Y. 10022

Library of Congress Catalog Card Number: 75-32368

Printed in the United States of America

printing number

10

Library of Congress Cataloging in Publication Data

Rogers, Everett M
    Communication in organizations.

    Bibliography: p.
    Includes index.
    1. Communication in organizations. 2. Technological innovations. I. Rogers, Rekha Agarwala, joint author.
II. Title.
HD38.R578   658.4'5   75-32368
ISBN 0-02-926710-2

The sketch on page 105 is reproduced from *Interiors*, January 1968, page 97, by permission. It is based on a plan drawn by the German office of the Schelle Organization, inventors of office landscaping.

In memory of
Amar N. Agarwala

Contents

* *Titles shown in this typeface indicate readings to illustrate the text.*

Preface

We teach a course on communication and innovation in organizations. Closely related at our university are eighteen courses on organizational behavior in the departments of psychology, sociology, business management, industrial engineering, public health, political science, education, and industrial relations. All of these courses emphasize how organizational structure affects human behavior; most of them have a unit on organizational communication. All of the professors in these courses that we have talked to agree that communication is the most vital ingredient in an organization. Without it, in fact, there would be no organization.

Most of these professors are also unhappy with the textbooks available on the topic of communication in organizations. Most of them are "how-to" manuals dealing with business communication, focusing on how to write better letters or clearer memos and how to "solve" problems of organizational communication (often without fully understanding their causes). "Better" communication is prescribed as the panacea for all ills in an organization. Such how-to books are seldom appropriate for advanced undergraduate or graduate-level courses, where students expect a more theoretical treatment of the topic. They want to know why communication problems occur and, more generally, understand the functioning of communication in organizations.

Among the conceptual works in this field, we regard *The Social Psychology of Organizations*, by Daniel Katz and Robert L. Kahn (1966), which has several sections dealing with communication and information, as excellent. We have used this fine book, based on open system theory, as one of our texts in courses on communication in organizations at Eastern Michigan University, Michigan State University, the University of Allahabad (India), and the University of Michigan since the 1960s. But it is now rather dated; a huge volume of researches on organizational communication has appeared in the past decade. And the Katz and Kahn volume has little to say about innovation in organizations. In fact, this important issue has not been handled very adequately in any existing text on organizational behavior, despite its obvious importance.

A concise synthesis of the conclusions drawn by the hundreds of available research reports, articles, dissertations, and monographs dealing with organizational communication has not appeared to date. We feel that such a synthesis—which we seek to provide in this book—is needed to give this field coherence and to provide common definitions and a conceptual framework.

We generally utilize open system theory in this book, as did some of the investigators whose work we seek to summarize in this volume. But our approach is distinctive in that we give emphasis, especially in Chapter 6, to innovation in organizations, stressing the dynamic aspects of organizational structure and functioning. Although many organizational behaviorists have stressed that organizations are almost continuously in a state of change, few have focused explicitly on innovation in organizations.

This book is about two interrelated concepts: *communication* and *organizations*. Chapters 1, 2, and 3 (on the nature of organizational communication and theories of organizational behavior and environments) are prerequisite to Chapters 4, 5, and 6, which deal with the heart of the book's topic: communication *in* organizations. The reader is urged therefore, not to become impatient while perusing the first three chapters; their content is essential to a full grasp of what comes later.

Even though this book is mainly about organizational behavior in the United States, we shall bring in examples and research findings from our work, and that of others, in different national settings, believing that: "the only way to understand the organizational features which are specific in our society is to compare them with the organizational features in other societies" (Mouzelis 1967, p. 179). Our intent throughout this volume is to search for what is generally true about organizational communication, across cultures and across organizations within a culture.

In writing this book, we have kept three main audiences in mind:
1. students in courses on organizational behavior who want a succinct treatment of communication in order to aid their understanding of human behavior and change in organizational settings;
2. students in courses on organizational communication who seek to learn how communication patterns and the innovation process are distinctive when they take place in the highly structured setting of an organization; and
3. everyone who engages in communication in industry, business, government, education, and other organizations and wishes to gain an improved understanding of the process in which they are participants, which they observe at close range but do not always completely comprehend.

Our research and teaching on communication and innovation in organizations have been much influenced by Professors Larry Mohr and Jack Walker and by our colleague J. D. Eveland (a co-author of Chapter 6), all of the University of Michigan; by Professor Eugene Jacobson of Michigan State University, by Professor Jerry Zaltman of the University of Pittsburgh; and by William Richards and Georg Lindsey of Stanford University. In addition, we are grateful to the National Science Foundation, the Exxon Education Foundation, and the National Institute of Education for their sponsorship of our recent researches on communication and innovation in organizations.

Stanford University   EMR
Applied Communication Research   RAR
Stanford, California

1. The Nature of Organizational Communication

"In any exhaustive theory of organization, communication would occupy a central place."
—*Chester I. Barnard*

"All human action takes place in a cross-fire of information."
—*Torsten Hägerstrand*

"Communication is a good deal more talked about than understood."
—*Lee Thayer*

The purpose of this book is to familiarize the reader with the main concepts, viewpoints, and research findings and applications in the field of organizational communication. Our focus in this book is on the ways in which organizational structure affects communication behavior, and vice versa.

We discuss, for example, how structure can restrict communication flows, leading to problems of distortion and omission, and how solutions to these difficulties can in turn lead to information overload. The existence of informal communication behavior, typified by rumors, and of informal communication roles, such as liaisons and gatekeepers in communication networks, suggests that the formal structure in an organization far from completely determines communication behavior. Furthermore, such approaches as "office landscaping" imply that communication behavior can occasionally determine organizational structure. Instead of viewing an organization as a completely stable structure, we show how external communication across its boundary with the environment is essential to its functioning, and especially to the innovation process. Our use of open system theory directs us to emphasize information exchange with the organization's environment, as well as communication flows within the organization.

1

So this book is about communication, but about a rather special kind of communication, viz., that occurring in highly structured settings. Generally, communication scholars have avoided studying the way in which structure affects human interaction. Perusal of communication research literature, at least prior to the 1970s, would almost lead one to assume that social structure does not affect human communication. For example, communication theorists who postulated the S–M–C–R (Source–Message–Channel–Receiver) model and similar models of communication did not accord much importance to the nature of the social relationships between source and receiver. Perhaps this shortcoming stems from the largely psychological backgrounds of early communication scientists, who emphasized intraindividual aspects of human communication in their choice of concepts, units of analysis, and paradigms. In any case, most communication research has been conducted in a way that artificially "destructures" human behavior. The present volume seeks to correct this bias by summarizing what is presently known about communication in organizations.

The research approach of communication scientists in the past has seriously underestimated the impact of social structure on communication behavior. Social structure has often been regarded as an extraneous, bothersome influence in studies of communication behavior, and structural variables have simply been ignored. For example, in most laboratory experiments relative strangers are brought together in a transitory and artificial setting for a brief encounter. The full impact of the social relationships among participants in more real-life communication exchanges is hardly replicated. The effects of social structure on communication that were observed in laboratory studies need to be tested in organizational settings before they can be accepted as appropriate principles of organizational communication (Chapter 5).

In survey research on communication, the role of structure is usually depreciated by the research methods used. The individual is usually the unit of response and is often the unit of analysis (Coleman 1958). Such an atomistic approach ignores the relational nature of human behavior. Most communication is reciprocal and transactional, not a unidirectional flow, as most overly simplified models of human communication would seem to imply (Rogers and Bhowmik 1971).

Organization scholars, for their part, have recognized the crucial significance of communication in understanding organizational behavior, but they are more expert in studying organizational structure itself than in understanding the effects of this structure on communication (or vice versa).[1] The intellectual separateness of communication and organization

[1] Probably because of the difficulties involved in investigating the effects of organizational structure on communication behavior, especially in operationalizing variables measuring the relational nature of communication in organizations.

scientists has discouraged the development of organizational communication as an integrated mode of inquiry.

Our purpose here is to accord organizational communication its rightful place as a serious field of study after many years of "stepchild" treatment by communication, as well as organization, scholars. Our assumption throughout this work is that *the behavior of individuals in organizations is best understood from a communication point of view.*

Communication behavior has been investigated in many kinds of organizations, ranging from industrial plants to government agencies to universities and military units, and we shall draw on research findings from these various studies in the present book. We also present a series of illustrative readings about communication behavior in organizations. The following reading shows how inadequate communication between officials and resident families helped contribute to the failure of a showcase housing project. The Pruitt–Igoe project constituted an organization by the definition we present in a following section: it was a stable system of individuals working together through a hierarchy of ranks and division of labor, and with common goals. We feel it is useful to analyze the following case from the viewpoint of communication in an organization.

THE RISE AND FALL OF THE PRUITT-IGOE PROJECT

Public housing for the poor is one of the most controversial social issues in the United States, ranking in the same category as racial busing of school children and welfare programs. Nowhere is the controversy better illustrated than in St. Louis's massive Pruitt-Igoe public housing project.

The project was initially conceived in the 1950s as a means of removing the poor blacks of St. Louis from their vicious cycle of unemployment, crime, poverty, disease, and rundown housing. The federal government gave $20 million toward the $36 million cost of providing the finest low-rent housing that money could buy. Minoru Yamasaki, one of America's most promising architects, was employed to design the massive project of thirty-three apartment buildings, each eleven stories high. Pruitt–Igoe (named after a black war hero and a local congressman) was hailed as the most progressive poor people's housing project in the United States.

Yamasaki designed the project as a series of tall brick apartment buildings with 200 feet of open space between each of them, in which children could play and adults could stroll. Each building had a series of elevators that were designed to stop only at the fourth, seventh, and tenth stories, where long galleries or walkways were located. The architect expected that these galleries would be used as community centers, for lounging and socializing and for children to play inside.

A manager/mayor was appointed who had been an army psychologist. Pruitt–Igoe was ready for business.

In October 1954, the first family, a Mr. and Mrs. Green and their four children, took up their residence. Monthly rental was only $37. Mr. Green told a newspaper reporter: "Pruitt Homes will be a swell place to live." More of the 12,000 residents began to move in. Each apartment came equipped with electric refrigerator, gas stove, and lavatory, "luxuries" unavailable to most of the new residents in their previous dwellings.

The central assumption of Pruitt–Igoe was that if an individual's environment were changed from slum conditions to a new, modern apartment complex, the individual's behavior would change accordingly.

Architect Yamasaki began to win lavish praise for his design. *Architectural Forum* predicted that Pruitt–Igoe would change the public housing pattern in all other cities. The skip-floor elevators and the galleries were lauded as creating "vertical neighborhoods." In the face of such praise, it was easy to forget that the residents had not been consulted at any stage in the architectural planning.

Actually, some residents, especially women, were beginning to see the galleries as "gauntlets" through which they had to pass from the elevator to their apartment door. Housewives had to survive a torrent of abuse, spitting, touching, teasing, and taunting. It was an intimidating experience for the toughest of women.

The elevators started to become very dirty. A lack of public bathrooms on the ground floor prompted hundreds of children to have "accidents" in the elevators. Youths would follow old men onto the elevators and rob and beat them, leaving their bleeding victims inside.

Rent collection became a dangerous calling, and so rents went uncollected. By 1960, St. Louis department stores refused to deliver purchases to Pruitt–Igoe residents. Western Union also refused to deliver telegrams in the project, the only address in America to be so treated. City policemen were ordered not to use their sirens in Pruitt–Igoe out of fear of a violent reaction. The open spaces between the buildings began to fill up with broken glass and abandoned cars. Bands of razor-wielding youths roamed the area. Delivery men were fatal victims; nurses and welfare workers were raped and brutalized. Hundreds of windows were smashed, but city workmen dared not venture to repair them. During one typical 180-day period in 1968, the project had 2 murders, 10 rapes, 50 robberies, 45 cases of aggravated assault, and 103 burglaries.

Junkies tore the copper sheeting from the building roofs to sell it to scrap dealers in order to support their drug habit. In the winter of 1971, rain from the leaking roofs froze the pipes, which then burst, leaving hundreds of apartments inches deep in ice. The stairwells became so slippery that residents had to tie ropes around their waists to keep from falling down the stairs.

Under these conditions, more and more of the project families began moving out. As more units became vacant, and the remaining families seldom paid their rent, project operating funds became very tight. The city administration responded by raising the rent. Rents were raised twice in 1968, and a third increase was announced for early 1969. The residents rebelled, as many of them found it difficult to pay the new rent on their low incomes. They began a rent strike that lasted nine months, toppled the city housing administration, and all but bankrupted the public housing authority. But the new administrators were as far removed from the people in Pruitt–Igoe as those they replaced, and equally unable to cope with the project's problems.

Finally, in 1974, the city government reluctantly announced that it was calling in the heavy iron ball and the dynamite charge. The first two buildings were brought down in only ten seconds with hundreds of pounds of gelignite charges. By the end of the year, all thirty-three buildings had been destroyed. And the only remaining residents of the Pruitt–Igoe public housing project were the thousands of rats who flourished in the piles of bricks and rubble.

Instead of the new environment changing the residents' behavior, the residents had destroyed the new environment. One resident commented: "It was a luxury apartment, but it ended up being a penitentiary!"

What lesson can be learned from the rise and fall of Pruitt–Igoe? In hindsight, observers concluded that the main problem, in addition to architectural blunders, was the lack of participation afforded residents in designing and governing their "city." Accordingly, the St. Louis administration now allows the residents of two new projects, Carr Square and Darst, self-government in running these projects. Modest salaries are paid to certain tenants to serve as liaisons between tenants and project management. An elected board of directors hires all staff, from the overall manager to custodians. Improvements in the buildings can now be made, as rent collections average over 100 percent, with many tenants paying off back rent. Through participatory management, many problems are being solved. The Darst project does lack residents in about one-third of its apartments owing to a lack of funds to make them livable again; thirty million dollars are needed for repairs. But the experience of the Darst project suggests that the debacle of Pruitt–Igoe was unnecessary. And it suggests that participatory management can be a vital force in organizational effectiveness.

The Pruitt–Igoe project illustrates many other principles of organizational communication. By the time you are finished with this book, you will hopefully be able to recognize these other communication concepts.

We aim to provide you with some of the tools for analyzing communication problems in various types of organizations.

The Importance of Organizational Communication

Most of one's daily life is spent in organizations: schools, businesses, factories, hospitals, the military services, churches, social clubs.[2] We live in an organizational society. Imagine that you had the task of collecting a dime each week from your four best friends. Easy, you say. Quite right —no organization is needed to accomplish the task. But now suppose your responsibility is to collect income taxes from the millions of individuals in your nation. Obviously, an organization would be necessary (Blau and Meyer 1971, p. 3).

Almost everyone belongs to one or more organizations. And most would agree that it is communication that gives life to an organizational structure. One of the early scholars of organizational behavior, Chester Barnard, recognized that "in any exhaustive theory of organization, communication would occupy a central place, because the structure, extensiveness, and scope of organizations are almost entirely determined by communication technique" (Barnard 1938, p. 8). More recently, Katz and Kahn (1966, p. 224) noted that "communication is . . . a social process of broadest relevance in the functioning of any group, organization, or society." It is "the very essence of a social system or an organization" (Katz and Kahn 1966, p. 223). Herbert Simon (1956, p. 109) probably stated it most sweepingly: "The question to be asked of any administrative process is: How does it influence the decisions of the individual? Without communication, the answer must always be: It does not influence them at all."

An *organization* is a stable system of individuals who work together to achieve, through a hierarchy of ranks and division of labor, common goals.[3] The relationships among the members of an organization are relatively stable; this structural stability enables an organization to function effectively in accomplishing certain objectives. *Organizational structure lends predictability and stability to human communication, and thus facilitates the accomplishment of administrative tasks.*

How different is human behavior in organizations from that occurring in other, less structured situations? "The behavior of people in organiza-

---

[2] Much of this section is adapted from Rogers and Agarwala–Rogers (1975a), and is used with permission.

[3] We contend that an individual's goals and those of an organization are not always in harmony. The formal and informal communication systems in an organization are often manifestations of such conflict between individuals and their organizations.

tions is still the behavior of individuals, but it has a different set of determinants than behavior outside organizational roles" (Katz and Kahn 1966, p. 391). Most of these distinctive determinants are variables that involve organizational structure. For instance, assume that individual A is trying to persuade individual B to use a new reporting form that B does not feel is necessary. Ordinarily, we would not expect B's behavior to change. But what if A were company president and B a lathe operator? Structural variables like hierarchical status and authority make a difference!

A critical reason for studying organizational communication is that it occurs in a highly structured context. An organization's structure tends to affect the communication process: thus, communication from a subordinate to a superior is very different from communication between equals.

Communication is the lifeblood of an organization; if we could somehow remove communication flows from an organization, we would not have an organization. Communication pervades all activities in an organization, represents an important work tool through which individuals understand their organizational role, and integrates organizational subunits. From an open system perspective, an organization is an elaborate set of interconnected communication channels designed to import, sort, and analyze information from the environment and export processed messages back to the environment. Communication provides a means for making and executing decisions, obtaining feedback, and correcting organizational objectives and procedures as the situation demands.

One usually thinks of industrial production, for example, as compromising the application of heat, chemicals, and other materials to an input in order to create an output, but communication is seldom counted as a crucial element. The physical transformation is important, of course, but communication is also very much involved. Communication is a thread that holds the various interdependent parts of an organization together. The functions of planning, coordination, and control are very important processes. If communication were somehow removed from industry, it would collapse instantly. "When communication stops, organized activity ceases to exist. Individual uncoordinated activity returns" (Hicks 1967, p. 130).

Not only is communication an essential ingredient in the internal functioning of an organization, but, as we noted, it is also vital in the organization's information exchanges with its environment. "*The communication system serves as the vehicle by which organizations are embedded in their environments*" (Guetzkow 1965, p. 534; emphasis added).

The tools of communication research are useful in seeking to understand organizational behavior. "If we can map the pathways by which communication is communicated between different parts of an organization and by which it is applied to the behavior of the organization in relation to the outside world, we will have gone far toward understanding that organization" (Deutsch 1952). We proceed, then, under the assumption that *communication is an indispensable element in an organization's functioning.*

THE HOSPITAL AS AN
INFORMATION SYSTEM

A perceptive visitor to a hospital would observe that a great deal of staff activity is devoted to information processing activities.

At the nursing station are several nurses filling up patient record forms, talking on the telephone, or discussing the coordination of their day's schedule. A doctor is being paged on the P.A. system. Food trays are being wheeled down the corridor to patients' rooms, each tray supposedly assigned to a particular patient on the basis of particular dietary needs, as indicated on a form that was sent previously to the hospital kitchen. At bedside, a doctor is obtaining information from a patient about symptoms, information that will then be entered in the patient's record file.

It would be hard to overestimate the importance of this file to the hospital. If the record file were ever lost or misplaced, as sometimes happens, the hospital would be at an almost complete loss as to how to treat the patient. The file is begun when the patient enters the hospital's door, and it must accompany the patient wherever he or she goes: to X-ray or to surgery, for example. Upon discharge, the file, by this time an inch or two thick with forms, charts, and notes (and representing hundreds of hours of skilled expertise worth thousands of dollars), goes permanently to the hospital records department. The record file is so sacred to the hospital that the patient is not allowed to see it, except in very unusual cases, and then only with the permission of the doctor. The file can be so thick that it represents an information overload problem. One solution is to computerize the file data; another approach is to utilize a "problem-oriented" record system, in which essential data are isolated and instantly accessible.

Great effort is expended by the hospital to ensure that the patient record file contains adequate and accurate information. Each entry in the file must be signed and initialed, so that responsibility for it is precisely fixed. Every bit of information about the patient must be recorded: every bowel movement, every medication that is administered, every rise in temperature. The cost of an error in the patient file is awesome: each year one or more patients' lives in a typical hospital may be lost owing to errors in information processing or transmittal. Because of the cost of such errors, most hospitals expend great effort on continually redesigning their communication system, on training and retraining the hospital staff to use it properly, and on checking on its accuracy and adequacy through various feedback devices.

Despite such extensive precautions, however, embarrassing communication breakdowns still occur. One spectacular example is the case of a patient in the Chicago-area Veterans Administration hospital, Erwin Pawelski, who was "lost" for twenty-seven hours.

Pawelski, a patient who could not speak, was strapped onto a wheel chair by an attendant and wheeled out of his ward to receive occupational therapy at 9:30 A.M. on May 1, 1975. What happened next is anybody's guess. The patient's record file shows a twenty-seven-hour blank. A hospital spokesman later told newspaper reporters: "There's a presumption that he arrived in the basement for therapy. But we are not positive."

At 7:00 A.M. on May 2nd, Pawelski's wife was called by the hospital to ask if she had removed him from the hospital. When she rushed to the hospital, she found that another patient had moved into his bed. Pawelski's effects had been shoved into a closet.

Pawelski was found by a therapy supervisor who stepped into an elevator in the hospital basement at 1:10 P.M. on May 2nd. The hospital has 3,000 employees, 1,295 patients, and about 700 visitors daily. Pawelski was in one of the main banks of elevators, ridden each day by hundreds of doctors, nurses, attendants, patients, and visitors. "It's unbelievable that there wouldn't be one person during those twenty-seven hours offering to help this man slumped over in a wheelchair. It's a mystery what happened," stated the hospital spokesman.

Twenty days after Pawelski was "misplaced" for twenty-seven hours, he died from cerebral hemorrhage after undergoing brain surgery. The hospital claimed that his death was not connected with any ill effects sustained from the incident.

A hospital can best be viewed, then, as an organization that devotes much of its activity to processing information. So, in fact, do most other types of organizations.

Studying Communication in Organizations

This book is about communication in organizations. What is communication? We define *communication* as the process by which an idea is transferred from a source to a receiver with the intention of changing his or her behavior. Such behavior may encompass a change in knowledge or attitude as well as in overt behavior. An *organization* was previously defined as a stable system of individuals who work together to achieve, through a hierarchy of ranks and a division of labor, common goals. Thus, when an organization executive issues an order to a subordinate, he expects it to be obeyed; the purpose may be carried out, or it may not be. But our point here is that the communication was made with the intention of achieving a certain result.

This book is concerned with communication within organizations and that between an organization and its environment—which together make up what we call *organizational communication*. Most of the present chapter is devoted to elucidating the concepts we use to describe the process of human communication. Most of what we say in this chapter applies to all types of communication, not only that in organizations. When the communication process occurs in organizations, however, it is highly structured and geared toward formalization and predictability. In succeeding chapters, we shall detail what is distinctive about communication when it occurs in organizations.

MAIN ELEMENTS IN THE COMMUNICATION PROCESS[4]

The four main components in the communication model are the source, the message, the channel, and the receiver. Because these elements are almost always present in every communication act, this simple conception of communication is often referred to as the "S–M–C–R" model (Berlo 1960).[5] It is a much oversimplified conception of communication, but it will be useful to us in our discussion here as a starting point. In the

[4] Many of the ideas in this section are taken from Rogers (1973a, pp. 43–61), and are used by permission.

[5] Various models of communication have been proposed which attempt to explain what communication is. A *model* is an attempt to represent real-world phenomena in terms of abstract theory. Probably the earliest communication model was proposed by Aristotle, who specified the speaker, the speech, and the audience as the constituent elements of the communication act. In the late 1940s, Harold Lasswell, Claude E. Shannon, and Warren Weaver proposed models of communication which reigned as the dominant paradigms of communication until the 1960s, and which continue to affect our conception of communication today. Lasswell pointed out that *who* says *what*, in *which channel*, *to whom*, and with *what effect* are the main elements in communication (Bryson 1948). Shannon, a mathematician, and Weaver, an electrical engineer, analyzed human communication in terms of five components: (1) a source, (2) a transmitter, (3) a signal, (4) a receiver, and (5) a destination (Shannon and Weaver 1949). Wilbur Schramm (1955) described communication as an act of establishing contact between a sender and a receiver, with the help of a message; the sender and receiver have some common experience which lends meaning to the message encoded and sent by the sender, and received and decoded by the receiver. Westley and MacLean (1957) postulated a more sophisticated model of the communication act: they distinguished various communication roles, emphasized feedback, and placed the communication act in the wider framework of an external environment. This was the backdrop for David Berlo's S–M–C–R model of the communication act, which was an attempt to synthesize previously described models.

presentation that follows, we define each of these four elements (S, M, C, R) plus two others, effects and feedback (Figure 1-1).

1. *Source*: The *source* is the originator of the message. It may be an individual or several individuals working together, such as a television news team. A source may also be an institution or an organization, although even then individuals are ultimately the sources, even though they are acting in an organizational role. The main responsibility for preparing the messages lies with the source.

2. *Message*: The *message* is the stimulus that the source transmits to the receiver. It's what the act of communication is all about; it's the idea that is communicated.

Messages are composed of symbols having (for the source and the receiver) a certain meaning. *Encoding* is the translation by the source of an already conceived idea into a message appropriate for transmission. To encode is thus to change a meaning into a symbol. *Decoding* is the translation of received stimuli into an interpreted meaning. Receivers thus decode messages by changing the symbol into a meaning. In order to give meaning to stimuli, individuals classify phenomena in categories and give them labels (called "codes").

Many messages are expressed in the form of language symbols, but the symbols may also be nonverbal, such as hand or facial gestures, other body movements, or pictures. Language distinguishes man from other creatures; dolphins and chimpanzees, for example, may have rough communication systems, but they have no true language.

Meanings are references such as ideas, images, and thoughts that are expressed in symbols (that is, in language). For communication to occur at all, the source and the receiver must have at least some minimum degree of prior common experience, some level of shared meanings. At the other extreme, no two individuals have exactly the same experiences; hence the language used (the message symbols) has somewhat different meanings for the receiver and the source. Furthermore, an individual's experience is continuous, so that the meaning of the same message sym-

FIGURE 1-1. The Source–Message–Channel–Receiver (S–M–C–R) Model of the Communication Process, Also Showing Effects and Feedback

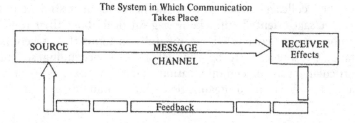

The System in Which Communication
Takes Place

bols will change over time. Many failures to communicate are due to mistaken assumptions by source or receiver about the meaning of a symbol they have exchanged.

Meanings are relative and open to subjective interpretation. This fact led Berlo (1960) to state: "Meanings are in people, not in the message." He meant that words have no meanings in themselves; their meanings are assigned by the source and the receiver.

Messages contain *information*, defined as a change in the probability that some alternative will occur in a given situation (Miller 1955, 1965, and 1972). Conveying information thus reduces the receiver's uncertainty about some phenomenon. An example of information is a market research report to an executive that shows that consumer demand for a product will drop 20 percent in the next three months.

Some messages are new to the receiver, and hence represent a stimulus of a kind different from that contained in ordinary messages. An *innovation* is an idea, practice, or object perceived as new by the receiver. When the message is an innovation to the receiver, such an act of communication is called *diffusion*, the process by which innovations are communicated to the members of a social system over time (Chapter 6).

3. *Channel*: A *channel* is the means by which a message travels from a source to a receiver. It is the path through which the message is physically transmitted. Channels may be classified into mass media or interpersonal channels.

Mass media channels are those means of transmitting messages, such as newspapers, magazines, films, radio and television, that enable a source to reach many receivers. *Interpersonal* channels are those that involve a face-to-face exchange between a source and a receiver.

One of the most important differences between mass media and interpersonal communication is that feedback is facilitated in the latter. As we indicated in our diagram of a communication event (Figure 1–1), communication is not a one-way flow of a message from a source to a receiver. The receiver also generates information and messages for the source, and, in fact, such interaction is necessary for communication to thrive. We shall have more to say, later, about feedback.

4. *Receivers*: The most important single element in the communication process is the *receiver*. Communicators (sources) often forget him. Some sources are source-oriented; an example is textbook authors who write for their colleagues, and go over the heads of their student readers. Some are message-oriented: they know a great deal about their topic, but they do not express (encode) it meaningfully in terms their receivers can understand. Or sources may be channel-oriented, depending so entirely on a particular means of communication that the receiver is ignored. An example is the official in an organization who communicates solely by the

distribution of written memos to his receivers; he never uses a staff meeting, even when it would be more effective, or a combination of a written memo plus a staff meeting.

5. *Effects*: Communication *effects* are the changes in receiver behavior that occur as a result of the transmission of a message. Hence when we speak of "effective communication," we mean communication that results in those changes in receiver behavior that were intended by the source. There are three main types of communication effects:

1. Changes in receivers' *knowledge*.
2. Changes in receivers' *attitudes*, defined as the relatively enduring organization of an individual's beliefs about an object that predisposes his actions. That is, an attitude often (though not always) predicts the action that an individual may take.
3. Changes in receivers' *overt behavior*, such as voting, purchasing of products, or coming to work on time.

These three changes usually, but not always, occur in sequence; that is, a change in knowledge usually precedes a change in attitude, which precedes a change in overt behavior.

The purpose of most communication, as we have said previously, is to bring about certain intended effects in receivers. Most communication research by social scientists seeks to study the effects of communication, with the aim of making possible more effective communication. A kind of "component approach" is used, in which one (or more) of the elements in the communication process is manipulated to induce greater effects. We shall have more to say later about this predominant approach in communication studies, and much of it will be critical.

6. *Feedback*

Feedback is a response by the receiver to the source's message. The source may take account of feedback in modifying subsequent messages; thus feedback makes communication a dynamic, two-way process.

Feedback may be thought of as messages to the source conveying knowledge of the effectiveness of a previous communication. *Positive feedback* informs the source that the intended effect of a message was achieved; *negative feedback* informs the source that the intended effect of a message was *not* achieved. As such, negative feedback is disruptive of the source-receiver relationship, and it can generate hostility between source and receiver.

From the viewpoint of achieving effective communication, negative feedback is more important than positive feedback. Yet it is more likely to be unrewarded or even punished, because of its disruptive nature. Ever try to tell the boss that his pet idea is not working? More on this in Chapter 6.

In general, the more feedback-oriented a communication process, the more effective it is. Attention to feedback implies an orientation to the receiver, a concern with whether he or she is "getting the message." Such an orientation requires for its implementation some *feed forward*, information about the receivers that is gained by the source prior to initiating communication with them, and that is used to design communication messages for maximum effectiveness. It is important to know one's audience. If a source has false assumptions about his receivers, his efforts to communicate are likely to be less effective.

False assumptions are more likely to be made when the receivers and the source are dissimilar. If the two are highly similar, communication is easier and more effective, for the source only has to know himself in order to know his receiver. *Homophily* is the degree to which a source–receiver pair are similar in certain attributes, such as beliefs, education, or social status; *heterophily* is the degree to which a source–receiver pair are different in certain attributes. Communication within a heterophilous source–receiver pair is generally less effective than that within a homophilous pair; when source and receiver share meanings, communication is more facile. Heterophilous communication, on the other hand, often leads to message distortion, delayed transmission (because of longer reaction time), restricted channels, and cognitive dissonance (when the receiver is exposed to messages that are inconsistent with his existing beliefs). Yet, while heterophilous communication is more difficult, it also has the potential of conveying new information to the receiver, and hence instigating behavior change. We shall have more to say about heterophily in Chapter 5.

We apply the word *noise* to disturbances in the communication process that interfere with the intended effects of the communication. An example is trying to talk with someone while a radio is playing loud music. One way to reduce noise is to increase *redundancy*, the repetition of the message or of some part of it. Redundancy is a kind of "noise insurance" in that, while it does not remove the noise, it reduces the disturbing influence of the noise on communication effectiveness. At least half of typical conversation may be redundant.

THE NATURE OF COMMUNICATION RESEARCH

We seek to utilize a communication point of view in this book. Such an approach implies that human behavior change is not capricious or random, if it can be understood from the receiver's viewpoint. Through social scientific methods we hope to be able to gain this viewpoint, to see the communication event through the receiver's eyes (rather than just from the source's viewpoint). Our scientific approach, however, does not have as its sole purpose accumulating an abstract fund of knowledge about human communication; usually, our objective is also to facilitate the solution of important social problems. So communication research is a highly applied type of social science.

Modern scientific approaches to defining communication can be traced back to the 1940s. Prior to that time, communication as an academic field was mainly a matter of teaching the skills of message production. Human communication was considered an art, a practice. The fields of speech, journalism, education, advertising, marketing, literature, and broadcasting, among others, exemplified this approach. But some leaders in these fields saw that mastering the skills of message production, as important as that was, could not guarantee effective communication. Prior to the development of communication as a science, the effects of messages, however well designed or elegant they might be, could seldom be predicted for a given audience.

The application of social science methods and concepts to human communication promised to help improve our understanding of the likely effects of a communication message to a given audience. Among the pioneers in the new field of communication science were the sociologist Paul Lazarsfeld, the political scientist Harold Lasswell, and the social psychologists Kurt Lewin and Carl Hovland. Their work, and that of their students, began to provide a basis for an empirically based and theoretically integrated understanding of communication.

But communication science is a relatively recent intellectual enterprise, and it still has a long way to go. Presently, there are several hundred university departments of communication in the United States and abroad, of which perhaps fifty award the highest academic degree, the Ph.D. The scientific approach to human communication is also taught within most of the behavioral sciences and their applied fields.

So the communication approach to human behavior change seeks to understand the effects of communication from the receiver's viewpoint, as well as the source's, through the application of social science methods and concepts.

THE COMPONENT APPROACH IN
PAST COMMUNICATION RESEARCH

Most communication research in the past was oriented to studying the effects of communication on the receivers. A communication scholar using this approach would alter one of the components in the S–M–C–R communication model (Figure 1–1) in order to determine its effects. Thus, a mass medium might be contrasted with an interpersonal channel to assess which is more effective in bringing about behavioral effects among a particular audience of receivers. For example if the message conveyed is an order, it is more likely to be carried out if it is communicated in written rather than oral form. One large American automobile manufacturer instructs its supervisors to give no verbal orders and each is provided with a memo pad on which is stamped "NVO." Employees are instructed not to accept an order unless it is in written form. Why? Verbal messages are impermanent and less accountable, although they may be more appropriate in a crisis.

The communication researcher may experimentally alter some *source* variable such as the credibility[6] of the source as perceived by the receiver. An identical message about future employment trends, for example, may be attributed with one set of receivers to the company president, and, with another (but similar) audience of receivers to the president of a competitor; the two messages are printed as articles in two different forms of the company's house organ. Communication theory would lead us to predict that the message attributed to the higher-credibility source (that is, presumably, the company president) will have greater effects in changing attitudes toward the issue.

In yet other communication researches, *message* variables may be altered to test the different effects on receivers. For example, a similar message may be presented so as to involve fear appeals in the case of one group of receivers, but not another. Thus, employees may be told that unless their output increases the company will enter bankruptcy and they will lose their jobs. Another audience of employees might be told of a new bonus for higher production.

In all of these illustrations, one of the variables S, M, C, or R is experimentally altered in order to determine the differential effectiveness of these variables on the receivers. Effects-oriented research of this kind treats communication essentially as something that one person does *to* another. Such investigations use an audience of receivers as respondents, and their behavior is studied largely for the benefit of the sources.

Such an approach may present serious ethical problems: for example, why shouldn't the researchers study how receivers can *immunize* themselves from the source's message, so as to *prevent* its intended effect? Worse, the overwhelming focus on effects in communication research is often antithetical to our theoretical conception of the process of communication. It implies a linear, left-to-right, one-way aspect to the communication event, which is incompatible with our conception of communication as a two-way, reciprocal-exchange process. Despite these serious limitations, the component approach has been a predominant one in past

---

[6] *Credibility* is defined as the degree to which a communication source or channel is perceived by a receiver as trustworthy and competent.

communication research. But in recent years, an intellectual revolt against this dominant approach has begun.

FROM LINEAR MODELS TO A SYSTEMS APPROACH

Communication is a *process*—that is, a continuous sequence of actions through time. It is not meaningful to talk about a beginning or an end of communication, because, like all other processes, communication flows like a stream through time. Someone has suggested that all processes should always begin and end with the word "and."

Our paradigm (Figure 1–1) of the communication process is a linear, left-to-right model. As such, it is a great oversimplication of reality. Conveying the notion of communication as process is helped somewhat when we add feedback to the model. Now our model better reflects a concern with events occurring over time, and hence begins to imply process.

Communication is a multivariable, dynamic interplay of numerous elements. Its complexity can hardly be expressed in a linear model with the channel carrying messages from the source to the receiver, like a bucket carries water (Diaz–Bordenave 1972). Such a transmission approach to communication implies taking a message from one place and reproducing it in another, as a telephone company does.

The black-and-white oversimplification involved in communication models like S–M–C–R led to growing interest in conceptualizing communication as a *system*. This theoretical view put the multivariable complexity back in communication models, and emphasized the synergistic interdependence of the elements in the communication process. The theoretical shift from linear models to a systems approach happened in the late 1960s, at the same time that most social science disciplines were adopting a systems view of human behavior (see Chapter 2).

The linear models imply a mechanistic concept of the communication act, which facilitates understanding because of its simplicity but profoundly distorts reality. Worse, they may imply an autocratic, one-sided vision of human relationships. "[The linear model] assumes an active source operating on a passive receiver via the persuasive monologue. It thus suggests a vertical relationship in which the source will tend to direct or dominate the behavior of the receiver" (Beltrán 1972). Communication according to this model, would therefore amount to a special type of receiver manipulation by a source.

On the other hand, the systems model of human communication assumes a greater degree of equality between the participants in the communication event. Communication is conceived of as a dialogue, in which source manipulation of the receiver may be counterbalanced by receiver influence on the source. The receiver, in any event, is largely free to determine the meaning of the source's message for himself.

The purpose of communication is to commune with, rather than just to persuade or command. Significantly, the words "common," "commune," and "communication" have the same etymological root. Communication is the sharing of information. And sharing implies that two or more people do something together, not that one individual does something to another. In this sense, rather than saying that an individual "communicates," it is more meaningful to say that he *engages in* communication and becomes part of a communication *system*. So communication is not simply a matter of action and reaction; it is a transactional exchange between two or more individuals (Watzlawick and others, 1967). Communication occurs as a series of exchanges of messages, with each subsequent message building on the previous one. The roles of source and receiver are reversed with each sequential exchange. Thus, once we bring in the process and systems aspects of communication, the linear and unidirectional S–M–C–R model no longer is adequate to describe the multidirectional, transactional nature of the communication act. Then it is appropriate for communication research to ask not, "What does communication do to individuals?" but rather, "What do people do with communication?"

At many points in this book we are forced to follow an implicitly linear and unidirectional model of communication in order to facilitate understanding. But we wish to stress that this one-way, "timeless" conception of human communication is adopted by us for heuristic purposes only. Communication is in reality a synergistic process in which the elements operate in an interdependent and intricate fashion.

BIASES IN PAST COMMUNICATION RESEARCH

There have been, in our view, three important conceptual/methodological biases in past communication research:

1. the lack of a process orientation
2. associated with this, an ignoring of mutual causality among the elements in the communication process
3. a psychological orientation, leading to the shortchanging of structure in the communication process

THE LACK OF A PROCESS ORIENTATION

Every textbook definition of communication either states or implies that it is a *process*.[7] Thus one might expect an overwhelming emphasis in

[7] This section and the two that follow are adapted from Rogers (1975).

research and theory on the conceptualization of communication as process. A recent content analysis of communication research, however, shows that existing research designs and measurements almost never allow analysis of communication as it occurs over time, which would be necessary to adequately explore its nature as process (Arundale 1971). Very few communication researches include data gathered at more than one point in time, and almost none at more than two such points. Hence almost all communication research is unable to trace the change in a variable over time; it deals only with the "present tense" of behavior. Communication thus becomes, in prevailing communication research, an artificially halted "snapshot" rather than a continuous "film" or moving picture.

Why has communication research not dealt more adequately with the change-over-time aspects of the communication process?

1. We lack concepts and propositions which truly reflect a process orientation.
2. Time-series data are expensive to gather, unless one depends on respondent recall, a methodological procedure that is often less than satisfactory.
3. Repeated data gathering over time leads to problems of respondent sensitization (unless one uses unobtrusive and nonreactive measurement methods), as the research itself is a communication process between respondent and researcher.
4. Communication researchers are often pressured by research sponsors, limited funds, doctoral dissertation requirements, and other factors to produce immediate results; this strongly discourages research over time.

So, unfortunately, we define communication as a process, but then proceed to treat it, in communication research, as a one-shot affair. Most communication research designs allow for only cross-sectional data analysis; such designs cannot tell us very much about the *process* of communication over time.

Future research ought to emphasize such improved methods as field experiments[8] and panel studies (repeated surveys of the same audience), which, by their research designs, are better able to take "moving pictures" of the communication process as it occurs over time.

---

[8] A field *experiment* is an active intervention by an experimenter who administers a treatment (in the form of a program, project, or activity) to randomly selected respondents arranged in groups that are equivalent in the way they were chosen, with at least one treatment and one control group (who do not receive the treatment). More detail on field experiments in communication may be found in Rogers and Agarwala–Rogers (1975b), and we previously illustrated several possible field experiments in our discussion of the component approach in communication research.

THE BIAS AGAINST MUTUAL CAUSALITY

Previously, we described the component approach in past communication research, in which a source, message, channel, or receiver variable is experimentally varied in order to test the consequence of this manipulation for the effects of communication. Changes in the source, message, channel, or receiver thus constitute the "independent" variables in such research; the "dependent" variable consists of communication effects which are caused by the change in the independent variable.

In order for independent variable X to be the cause of dependent variable Y: (1) X must precede Y in time; (2) they must be associated; and (3) X must have a "forcing quality" on Y. Most past communication researches have determined only that various independent variables are associated or correlated with a dependent variable; correlational analysis of one-shot survey data does not allow the determination of time order. So again we see the importance of research designs that allow us to learn the over-time aspects of communication. Field experiments are ideally suited to the purpose of assessing the effect of various antecedent independent variables on the consequent dependent variable.

In order for X to cause Y, they must at least be associated, or vary together. If such covariance is very low, X is probably not a cause of Y. If their common variance is high, X may be a cause of Y.

Forcing quality, the way in which the cause X acts on the result Y, is a theoretical rather than empirical issue, which rests on the inherent nature of the X and Y variables. Much greater attention needs to be given in communication research to the theoretical reasoning of why certain variables might have a forcing quality on others. And the systems perspective in communication research (elaborated later in Chapters 2, 3, and 5) implies that the search for independent and dependent varables in communication research is often futile. The pertinent variables may be interdependent; each is a cause as well as a consequent of the others. They are in reality a *system* of variables in mutual interaction.

Implementation of the systems approach in communication research would entail abandoning reliance of the past on the component approach of varying a source, message, channel, or receiver variable to determine its communication effects. Rather, the communication process would be conceived of as a holistic system in dynamic interplay.

THE PSYCHOLOGICAL BIAS

The psychological bias in communication research stems (1) from its historical roots as an academic field, and (2) from researchers' acceptance of how social problems are defined. Several early communication scholars came from backgrounds in psychology, where at the time an individual-centered perspective was dominant. It was only natural that their models of communication largely ignored social structural variables that affect communication. The transactional and relational nature of human communication tended to be overlooked, at least until fairly recently.

One manifestation of the psychological bias in communication research is the overwhelming focus on the *individual* as the unit of analysis, while the importance of communication *relationships* between sources and receivers is largely ignored. This distorted approach is often due to the assumption that if the individual is the unit of response, he must consequently be the unit of analysis (Coleman 1958)[9]. Coleman (1958) goes on to note that "the kinds of substantive problems on which such research focuses [tend] to be problems of 'aggregate psychology,' that is, within-individual problems and never problems concerned with relations between people."

The use of survey methods in communication research has "destructured" behavior. "Using random sampling of individuals, the survey is a sociological meat-grinder, tearing the individual from his social context and guaranteeing that nobody in the study interacts with anyone else in it" (Barton 1968). The parallel is to "a biologist putting his experimental animals through a hamburger machine and looking at every hundredth cell through a microscope; anatomy and physiology get lost; structure and function disappear and one is left with cell biology" (Barton 1968).

Only recently has the focus in communication research on the individual as the unit of analysis shifted to the dyad, the clique, the network, or the system of individuals; that is, to the communication relationships between individuals rather than the individuals themselves. Examples of new approaches seeking to overcome the psychological bias in communication research are the coorientation model, relational analysis,[10] network analysis, and the systems approach (all of which are detailed in Chapter 2 and 5).

These conceptual/methodological approaches assume that even when the individual is the unit of response, the communication relationship can be the unit of analysis via some type of sociometric measurement (Chapter 5). Sampling and data-analysis procedures for relational analysis are being worked out, but we still lack relational concepts, and theories linking these concepts. Until communication scholars begin to think in relational terms, there will not be much relational analysis.

A second manifestation of the psychological bias in communication

---

[9] In reality, we can study (1) *individuals* as units of analysis, (2) *system effects* on individuals, and (3) *systems* as units of analysis. We illustrate each of these three methodological approaches in the chapters that follow.

[10] *Relational analysis* is a research approach in which the unit of analysis is a relationship between two or more individuals (Rogers and Bhowmik 1971).

research is the acceptance of a *person-blame* definition or *causal attribution* of social problems. *Person blame* is the tendency to hold an individual responsible for his or her problems. Clearly, what is done about a social problem, including research, depends on how it is defined. Seldom do communication scientists participate in the identification and definition of social problems; so they borrow or accept these definitions from alarmists, government officials, or other scientists.[11]

Many illustrations of person blame can be cited in behavioral research. Caplan and Nelson (1973) find a high degree of person blame in psychological research on such social problems as highway safety and race relations. Dervin (1971, p. xiii) noted that person-blame assumptions affected communication research on the problem of poverty:

> Only very recently have some students of the poor come to see that it is the social structure, not the poor as individuals, that needs change. It is incomplete, for instance, to say that the poor lack knowledge where the system does not make information available to them.[12]

Person blame rather than system blame permeates most definitions of social problems. The definers are seldom able to change the system (or so they think), so they accept it. Such acceptance encourages a distorted focus on psychological variables in communication research. Often, the problem definer's individual-level cause becomes the researcher's main independent variable.

How can the person-blame bias be overcome? By keeping an open mind about the causes of a social problem, at least until exploratory data are gathered. By involving the participants in a social problem, rather than just those persons who are seeking its amelioration, in the definition of the problem. And especially, in research on communication in organizations, by considering structural variables, as well as intraindividual variables.

Using a systems point of view in research on communication in organizational structures is a step toward coping with each of the three biases in past communication research. First of all, a systems viewpoint (elucidated in Chapter 2) assumes a concern with process; it orients the researcher toward gathering data at more than one point in time so as to take moving pictures instead of snapshots of human behavior. Furthermore, from a systems viewpoint, there is no simple cause-and-effect; all the variables indexing a system are thought to be in mutual interaction.

[11] Sometimes (probably rarely) an alarmist argues for redefining a social problem in system-blame terms. An illustration is the efforts by Ralph Nader (1966) in the mid-1960s, especially through his book *Unsafe at Any Speed*, to redefine the problem of highway safety in terms of safer automobiles and highways, rather than just reckless driving.

[12] Similarly, Caplan and Nelson (1973) ask: "Why do we constantly study the poor rather than the nonpoor in order to understand the origins of poverty?"

Finally, the systems approach considers the effects of organizational structure on communication behavior, and vice versa (Chapter 4).

RESEARCH ON COMMUNICATION IN ORGANIZATIONS

Much attention in the literature about organizations has been given to communication *problems*; in fact, reading these publications gives one the impression that insufficient communication is frequently the main cause of difficulties in organizations. We dispute this overly simplified picture of organizational communication problems (in Chapter 4), and, furthermore, we doubt the intellectual usefulness of the past focus on communication problems in organizations. More important is the ability to understand the factors causing such problems. We agree with Thayer (1967, p. 80), who observed: "Perhaps more has been 'communicated' about 'communication problems' in organizations than [about] any other single topic in the field. Yet this plethora of commentary has not been conducive either to theory-building or to theory-validation."

Most early communication research in organizations consisted of case studies of a single organization. Researchers immersed themselves for a considerable period of time in one organization, observing what went on in its everyday activities and perhaps administering questionnaires to the organization's members or personally interviewing them. The researchers might focus on one department within an organization or even on a small work group within a department. This intensive approach enabled the researchers to learn a lot about very little. But it did not provide a very sound basis for generalization of the research results. For example, how was one to know whether the communication behavior of the fourteen workers in, say, the Bank Wiring Room of the Western Electric Hawthorne plant was at all representative of the thousands of employees in the Hawthorne plant, let alone of all assembly-line workers in all factories in the United States?

Organization scholars subsequently began to conduct comparative studies in two or more organizations. In order to handle the larger amounts of data now involved, researchers were forced to learn less about more, and to convert their impressions into statistical data that could be punched onto IBM cards and analyzed with computers.

Finally, communication researchers began to gather data from larger samples of perhaps a hundred or more organizations. This approach provided a more solid basis for generalization of the research findings, but it usually necessitated knowing very little about any one organization in the sample that was studied. Frequently, a questionnaire was sent to the chief executive of each organization sampled, so that only the view from the top was obtained. This extensive, quantitative approach essentially destructured the organization, in that relatively little about the internal nature of each organization could be measured.

One problem in generalizing the results of scientific research in organizations was that in the past, such studies were mainly concerned with a rather narrow range of industrial, business, and governmental organizations. Modern organizations have certain similarities whether they are concerned with the production of a product for profit, the conduct of governmental business, a charitable enterprise, the education of students, the treatment of the ill, or the defense of a country. Now attention is also being given in organizational communication research to such other kinds of organizations as schools, hospitals, prisons, labor unions, cities, voluntary organizations, and political parties. Nevertheless and regrettably, we know a great deal more today about organizational behavior in business firms and governmental bureaucracies than we do about other kinds of organizations. "The literature leaves one with the impression that after all not a great deal has been said about organizations, but it has been said over and over in a variety of languages" (March and Simon 1958, p. 5).

"Organization theory . . . has been altogether too accommodating to organizations and their power" (Perrow 1972, p. iii). Most research in this field has undoubtedly benefited management more than it has lower-level workers, and members of the organization more than its clients. There are many reasons for the pro-organization orientation in research on organizational behavior, including who sponsors the research, for whose benefit it is conducted, and what methods of study are used. In this book we seek to evaluate research on organizational communication with an objectivity that will hopefully make our findings equally helpful to the executives, the workers, and the clients of an organization.

TOWARD NETWORK ANALYSIS

The general trend in research on organizational communication behavior has been toward greater quantification, toward reducing human behavior to variables that can assume numerical values. This use of highly quantitative measures in social science research may be deceitfully reassuring to the researcher. This may be one reason why questionnaires and survey interviews have been so widely utilized in studies of organizational behavior. Writing in 1934, a leading social psychologist warned that "the questionnaire is cheap, easy, and mechanical. . . . Quantitative measurements are quantitatively accurate. . . . Yet it would seem far more worthwhile to make a shrewd guess regarding that which is essential, than to accurately measure that which is likely to prove quite irrelevant" (La-Piere 1967, p. 31).

Unfortunately, survey research methods are not entirely satisfactory for studying communication in organizations. One reason is that interviews or questionnaires tend to isolate the respondent as an atomistic entry, at least in a heuristic research sense, while the very nature of organizational communication is relational, holistic, and structured. Survey data can, of course, be gathered from individuals in an organization, but how does one take into account the position of the individual respondents in the organizational structure? In a random sample of 100 respondents from among the 1,000 members of an organization, what if the organization's president is randomly selected? Should his responses be weighted equally with the janitor's? And how are such relational phenomena as communication flows and patterns measured when the data represent only individual responses?

One important modification in survey research procedures is to ask sociometric questions about communication behavior. An example would be: "With which other individuals in this organization have you talked within the last day?" The responses lend themselves to such types of relational analysis as communication network analysis. Thus, even though the individual remains the unit of response, he need not always be the unit of analysis.

One approach to research on organizational communication has been to discover and analyze the interpersonal communication patterns within an organization (or within some section of an organization) with network analysis procedures, and then to compare these patterns with the formal communication patterns that would be expected on the basis of the organizational structure. Network analysis is an essential research tool in analyzing the existing reality; specifically it is used to identify cliques within the organization and to isolate such key communication roles as liaisons and opinion leaders (Chapter 5). In the case of *bürolandschaft* or "landscaped offices," network analysis is utilized to guide the physical arrangement of individuals and hence indirectly to reorganize the formal structure of the organization so that it is more closely in line with the reality of the informal communication structure.

In any event, comparison of the informal communication patterns with the formal structure illuminates the discrepancies between the two, and this procedure can be a useful diagnostic tool, leading to suggesting changes (1) in the formal structure, to bring it more into line with the interpersonal communication patterns, or (2) in the physical layout of the organization, so as to indirectly change the informal and/or formal communication patterns.

We return in Chapter 5 to a more detailed discussion of how network analysis procedures can be used to understand and improve communication behavior within organizational structures.

Summary

This books aims to familiarize the reader with the main concepts, viewpoints, and research findings and applications in the field of organizational communication. Organizational communication is distinct from other types of human communication in that it occurs in highly structured settings. In the past, organization scholars focused mainly on structure rather than communication behavior, while communication scholars generally neglected communication in organizational structures.

Communication is defined as the process by which an idea is transferred from a source to a receiver with the intention of changing his or her behavior. An *organization* is a stable system of individuals who work together to achieve, through a hierarchy of ranks and a division of labor, common goals. Communication is the lifeblood of an organization; it pervades all activities in an organization. *Organizational communication* is that which occurs within an organization and between an organization and its environment.

The six main elements of the communication process are: source, message, channel, receiver, effect, and feedback. Unfortunately, oversimplified models of communication led to a component approach in communication research, in which one of these elements is manipulated in order to determine its influence on effects. Almost all past communication research was of this kind.

Recently, linear models of communication have given way to a systems approach, in which communication is studied as a continuing process through time entailing a mutual exchange between the participants. One does not "communicate"; one *engages in* communication. The shift to the systems approach in communication research may help overcome three conceptual/methodological biases: (1) lack of a process orientation; (2) ignoring mutual causality among the elements in the communication process; and (3) a psychological orientation that shortchanges structure.

2. Three Schools of Organizational Behavior

"The Scientific . . . Management [School] is in bad repute these days. The principles and rules which earlier in the century marked the beginning of the management movement today appear to many, in the light of our present knowledge of human relations, as a hopelessly inadequate guide to organization and management."
— *John T. Diebold*

"Too often it is assumed that the organization of a company corresponds to . . . an organization chart. Actually, it never does."
— *Fritz J. Roethlisberger and William J. Dickson*

"The open system does not run down, because it can import energy from the world around it."
— *Daniel Katz and Robert Kahn*

There is a tremendous volume of books and other literature published on the topic of organizations, and even the specialty of communication in organizations is represented by over 1,200 books and articles in a recent bibliography (Carter 1972). In dealing with this enormous volume of literature, it is useful to describe the three theoretical viewpoints that have predominated in the study of organizational behavior. These three "schools"—groups of scholars who shared a common viewpoint about organizational behavior—go by the names of Scientific Management, Human Relations, and Systems. The Scientific Management School originated in 1911 and was popular until the 1930s; the Human Relations School then predominated until the 1960s, when the Systems School became preeminent. While each of the first two approaches to organizational theory had its "day," neither has faded completely from sight nor been completely replaced by the school that followed it. In fact, there are still followers of the Scientific Management School today, and the Human Relations School has by no means been made completely obsolete

27

by the Systems viewpoint. Indeed, each of the earlier schools had a strong influence on the now-dominant Systems School. So it will be useful to understand each of these theoretical positions in order to have a complete grasp of how organizations function, and of the role of communication in organizations.[1]

Revolutionary Paradigms and Invisible Colleges

Any given field of scientific research begins with a major breakthrough of reconceptualization which provides a new way of looking at some phenomenon (Kuhn 1970). This so-called "revolutionary paradigm" is often a universally recognized scientific achievement that for a time provides model problems and solutions to a community of scholars. Famous examples are associated with names like Copernicus, Newton, Darwin, Pasteur, and Freud. The paradigm typically sets off a furious amount of intellectual effort as promising young scientists are attracted to the field, either to advance the new conceptualization with their research or to disprove certain of its aspects. Gradually, a scientific consensus about the field is developed.

An "invisible college" forms around the revolutionary paradigm, consisting of "an unofficial establishment based on fiercely competitive excellence. [The members] send each other duplicated preprints of papers yet to be published, and for big things they telephone and telegraph in advance. . . . They keep warm the seats of jet planes and commune with each other at small select conferences and seminars" (Price 1970).

Why do scientists band together in invisible colleges? Because science is a puzzle-solving process, and each scientist is faced with a tremendous amount of uncertainty in seeking to cope with the unknown in his or her discipline. A revolutionary paradigm provides a temporary sense of order, and a starting place for empirical investigation.

Furthermore, scientists are faced with an information explosion of books, journal articles, and research reports in their field (Price 1963). It is impossible for them to keep abreast of all of this scientific literature unless they somehow narrow it down. The invisible college, centering around a revolutionary paradigm, provides a means for doing so. It defines for the scientist what is relevant, and irrelevant, to his or her special research interests.

Research studies of invisible colleges in several fields show that they provide a structure and continuity to scientists with like interests (Crane

[1] The story of the passing intellectual prominence enjoyed by the three schools of organizational behavior is related in numerous books, among them Etzioni (1964), Mouzelis (1967), Perrow (1972), and Pugh and others (1971). For a review by a Russian author, see Gvishiani (1972).

1972). There are respected leaders within an invisible college; usually they are the high producers of scholarly publications in the field.

The history of scientific research on organizational behavior presents a good illustration of the formation of an invisible college—or, more accurately, of three subcolleges. Each centered around a revolutionary paradigm that was initially proposed by one or more founders. The Scientific Management School was launched by Frederick W. Taylor in 1911; many books and other publications soon appeared dealing with his paradigm of human behavior in organizations. But in the 1930s, Chester Barnard and Elton Mayo found Taylor's paradigm unsatisfactory in explaining the nature of organizational behavior as they understood it—from Barnard's personal experience as a business executive and Mayo's empirical research at the Western Electric Company's Hawthorne plant near Cicero, Illinois. So Barnard and Mayo set forth a new paradigm, around which the invisible college that we call the Human Relations School grew.

An intellectual watershed occurred in the 1960s, when growing dissatisfaction with the Human Relations paradigm, along with the attractive alternative of general systems theory, led to the formation of the Systems School of organization theorists.

The main elements of each of these three viewpoints are set forth in Table 2–1.

Scientific Management School

This school is sometimes called the "machine-theory" school, and is also known as "Taylorism" (after its founder), but it is usually called "Scientific Management" because it marked the introduction of scientific methods into the managing of organizations.

The Scientific Management School was preceded by the development of a body of management principles by the managers of businesses and industries and by professors at the business schools in U.S. universities, influenced somewhat by European authors like Henri Fayol.[2] Most of these principles were very simple by today's standards, such as the admonition to "plan ahead." There was almost no social science component

---

[2] Fayol was a French engineer who had managed Commentary–Fourchamboult–Decazeville, a giant mining and metallurgical company, taking it almost from bankruptcy to where it had become one of the most powerful concerns in France by the time of his retirement in 1918. His theory of management was based upon fourteen administrative principles, presumably derived mainly from his personal experience. His book *General and Industrial Management* was published in French in 1916, although it was not available in English until thirty-three years later (Fayol 1949).

TABLE 2-1. The Three Main Schools of Organizational Behavior

	1. SCIENTIFIC MANAGEMENT SCHOOL	2. HUMAN RELATIONS SCHOOL	3. SYSTEMS SCHOOL
1. Basic principles and assumptions about human behavior	A mechanistic view of behavior: man is economically motivated, and will respond with maximum performance if material rewards are closely related to work efforts. Favors human engineering of worker effort and time in order to achieve maximum production, efficiency, and profit for the managers/owners.	A social view of man: informal groups affect production rates; attention to workers' needs and job satisfaction can motivate higher performance; worker participation in decision making; realization that the individual's goals may differ from the organization's goals; workers motivated by social needs and by their peer relationships.	The organization is an open system in continuous interaction with its environment; the system and its environment co-determine each other. The system must be analyzed as a whole in order to be understood properly. The organization is composed of subsystems, which are interdependent; individuals are the carriers of the organization.
2. Main research methods used	Observation (including time-and-motion studies); participation; some surveys.	Survey interviews and questionnaires; observation; participation; diary keeping; sociometric analysis of leadership and communication patterns.	Network analysis of sociometric data from survey interviews and questionnaires; systems analysis; computer simulation.
3. Main types of organizations studied	Industrial firms and public utilities.	Manufacturing plants (especially assembly-line operations), including some outside of the U.S.	Industrial, military, and government organizations; hospitals; educational and mental institutions; prisons.
4. Bias of the school	Pro-management; "management knows best."	Pro-workers; sympathetic to them. Attempts to help employers and employers solve their problems through understanding.	Pro-"organization"; the organization exists as an entity that consists of more than just its present individual members.

TABLE 2-1. (continued)

5. *View of organizational communication*	Emphasis on written, formal channels of communication: impersonal, work-related messages initiated by higher-ups and sent down the chain of command. The role of communication is not considered especially important.	Informal communication as well as formal; stress on interpersonal channels, especially with peers. Rumor and the grapevine exist.	Communication is crucial, as it holds the organization together and interrelates the subsystems. Communication across organization's boundary with its environment is also important.
6. *Founder or dominant figures*	Frederick W. Taylor.	Chester I. Barnard; Elton Mayo.	Herbert A. Simon; Daniel Katz and Robert L. Kahn; James G. Miller
7. *Landmark books*	Frederick W. Taylor (1911), *Scientific Management.* Henri Fayol (1949), *General and Industrial Management.* Luther Gulick and Lyndall F. Urwick (1937), *Papers on the Science of Administration.*	Chester I. Barnard (1938), *The Functions of the Executive.* Fritz Roethlisberger and William Dickson (1939), *Management and the Worker.* Elton Mayo (1960), *The Social Problems of an Industrial Civilization.* Rensis Likert (1961), *New Patterns of Management;* (1967), *The Human Organization.* George C. Homans (1950), *The Human Group.*	Daniel Katz, and Robert L. Kahn (1964), *The Social Psychology of Organizations.* James G. Miller (1972), *Living Systems: The Organization.* Joan Woodward (1958), *Management and Technology;* (1965), *Industrial Organization: Theory and Practice.* Paul R. Lawrence and Jay W. Lorsch (1967), *Organization and Environment: Managing Differentiation and Integration.* Herbert A. Simon (1947), *Administrative Behavior;* (1956), *Models of Man.*

in this early period, as social scientists were not much interested in studying organizations in general, or business firms in particular. Social science thinking had not yet begun to invade the fledgling business schools. In fact, there was very little science of any kind in the study of organizational behavior in this era; it was a time of learning mainly from experience. Management principles were pragmatic, and they seemed to work.

But all that changed in 1911, when Frederick W. Taylor published his influential book, *Scientific Management*. Taylor's basic approach to organizational research was extremely atomistic and mechanical: he analyzed each job in terms of its smallest aspect. For instance, Taylor would observe a work task in great detail by measuring and timing (with a stopwatch) each of the worker's movements that were involved. Repeated time-and-motion studies would be made of each action required to complete the task. Then Taylor would analyze the capacities of the worker as a "human machine" just as carefully, and seek to fit the worker and the task together.[3] The assumption of the Scientific Management School was that work operations could best be understood by breaking the whole down into its basic parts, and then aggregating these tiny bits and pieces back together into the whole system. This assumption was strongly challenged by the Systems School over fifty years later.

Taylor was able to achieve some spectacular results with his method. For example, he studied coal shoveling at the Bethlehem Steel Works, where he was employed for many years. His time-and-motion studies indicated that the average weight of coal scooped by a shovel ranged from 16 to 38 pounds. His experiments showed that a good worker could load twice as much coal in one work shift if he used a relatively small shovel holding 21 to 22 pounds. Fifteen different types of shovels were provided for loading different kinds of materials; workers were issued written instructions as to which shovel to use for each purpose. Within a few years, 140 workers were doing the same work that previously had required 400 to 600 workers (Gvishiani 1972, p. 179).

These time-and-motion experiments soon created considerable interest in the scientific management approach on the part of industrial managers and owners. But Taylor advocated far more than just efficiency studies such as these. He claimed that every worker should be paid according to his individual output, rather than that of the gang or shop of which he was a part. That is, the reward system should be tied to individual, not group, performance. So Taylor's approach was actually a combination of

---

[3] Among the followers of Frederick W. Taylor were Frank and Lillian Gilbreth (of *Cheaper by the Dozen* fame). Frank Gilbreth had been a brickwork contractor, who became interested in scientific management about 1906 when he read some of Taylor's early writings. Gilbreth specialized in time-and-motion studies, often using motion pictures of a worker performing a task in order to break it down into its basic parts.

(1) studying the physical capabilities of workers, and (2) designing industrial reward systems around a conception of "economic man."[4]

The main tenets of Taylorism were summed up as: "Science, not rule of thumb. Harmony, not discord. Cooperation, not individualism. Maximum output, in place of restricted output. The development of each man to his greatest efficiency and prosperity" (Taylor 1911, p. 140). This approach assumed that the worker was deeply irrational if left on his own, but would respond properly to money rewards. Man was made for the organization, and through cooperation with its objectives his maximum productivity could be achieved. Thus the worker was essentially perceived as a human appendage to the industrial machine (Etzioni 1964, p. 21).

CRITICAL REACTIONS TO TAYLORISM

"Scientific management will mean, for the employers and the workmen who adopt it, the elimination of almost all causes of dispute and disagreement between them" (Taylor 1911). Unfortunately, this sanguine vision of mutual worker–employer benefits from scientific management was not appreciated by the workers, who reacted bitterly to what they perceived as the inhumanity of Taylor's system. They did not like being reduced to the level of efficiently functioning machines. Scientific management was thus bitterly opposed by labor unions in the 1920s and 1930s.[5] The unions saw it as a means of employer exploitation of workers, leading to higher unemployment as a result of the greater efficiency that was attained. "All the time study in the world could not say how much ought to be paid for a job; it can only show the length of time a job ought to take" (Cole 1917, p. 13).

Today, we know the Scientific Management School best as a set of principles of management that grew out of the work of Taylor, Fayol, and other representatives of the school: span of control (each supervisor should manage the work of only a handful of subordinates, usually five or six at most), unity of command (each individual should have only one direct boss), and delegation of authority to subordinates. The Taylor School denied the importance of noneconomic motivations and discounted the influence of informal work groups.[6] The organization's formal structure

[4] The Taylorist spirit of rationalization was extended from the individual worker to the organization as a whole through the influence of Henri Fayol (Mouzelis 1967, p. 2).

[5] As depicted in the play and film *The Pajama Game*, about the introduction of Taylorism in a pajama factory in Dubuque, Iowa.

[6] In fact, it tended to deal with worker behavior as if it did not occur within an organizational context. Taylorism was "more concerned with the worker as an isolated unit . . . than as an organizational member" (Mouzelis 1967, p. 79).

was the main tool for achieving maximum performance and efficiency. People were adapted to this structure; organizations hired only the parts of people that related to their task.

Today, the shortcomings of Taylorism are thought to outweigh its strong points. "This school of thought is fighting a rear-guard action in the groves of academe, if not in the stony field of actual organization" (Perrow 1970a, p. 16). Few advocates of the Scientific Management School can be found to trumpet its principles today, although certain vestiges of its thinking may be seen in assembly-line production and in military organizations.

TAYLORISM AND COMMUNICATION

Frederick Taylor actually had little to say about communication in his book *Scientific Management*. His emphasis was on organizational structure and on individual behavior. Communication was to be formal, hierarchical, and planned; its purpose was to get the work done, to increase productivity and efficiency. In sum, Taylorism viewed communication as one-sided and vertical (top–down) and task-related.

Henri Fayol (1949) most clearly elaborated the role of communication flows in organizations, and the restrictions placed on communication by the organizational structure. Fayol illustrated this problem of restricted communication flows, and suggested a solution. If communication is required between individuals L and M (see Figure 2–1), who are at the same hierarchical level but in two different departments, they can formally contact each other only by sending a message up and down the long, twelve-step ladder of command. It is obviously much more sensible, and much quicker, for L and M to communicate directly, even though this action bypasses their eleven superiors. Fayol argued that such direct, horizontal communication ought to be allowed in an organization, at least in crisis situations when rapid action is essential. His special-purpose bypassing device today bears the name of "Fayol's Bridge"; it represents recognition by the Scientific Management School that the formal structure may unduly impede useful communication flows, and that special exceptions ought to be allowed (we return to this point in Chapter 4).

The Scientific Management School recognized that communication problems occurred in organizations, at least when certain management "principles" were not followed correctly. For instance, if the span of control of a manager became too wide because he or she had more than five or six subordinates, ability to communicate effectively with underlings was likely to suffer (Gulick and Urwick 1937; Mooney and Reiley 1939). The solution to this problem, the Taylorists claimed, was the delegation

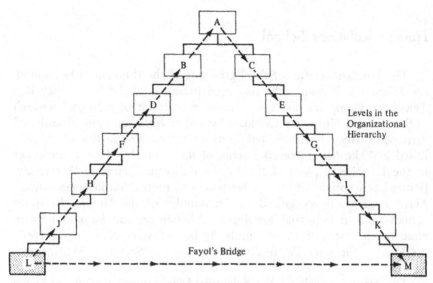

FIGURE 2-1. Diagram of Fayol's Bridge, Providing for Direct Horizontal Communication Between Individuals L and M

of authority by the manager to lower levels in the hierarchy, with an accompanying decrease in the span of control.[7]

Scientific Management also distinguished between the communication functions of "line" and "staff." Staff officials were usually specialists in certain matters (like personnel, accounting, and supply), and their communication function was thought to consist in persuading their executive head to accept their advice. Line officials were cogs in the chain of command, and so their function was to communicate orders from their boss to their subordinates, and to see that such instructions were properly carried out.

Overall, *the Scientific Management School did not accord a very significant role to communication, and it conceived of communication as limited to command and control through vertical, formal channels.* This viewpoint assumed that those at the top possessed all the relevant information, and the function of communication was to disseminate their knowledge.

We know today that communication operates in many ways in an organization. But it was not until the 1940s that these came to be more fully realized with the advent of the Human Relations School.

[7] More recently, it has been recognized that the span of control may include more or less than five to seven individuals, depending on such factors as the nature of the organizational task and the capacity of the leader.

Human Relations School

The Human Relations School grew out of the thinking of two founders: Chester I. Barnard, who had been president of the New Jersey Bell Telephone Company, and Elton Mayo, a professor of industrial research in the Harvard University Graduate School of Business. Barnard authored a tremendously influential book, *The Functions of the Executive*, published in 1938; Mayo headed a series of researches by Harvard professors in the Hawthorne plant of the Western Electric Company that revolutionized conceptions of human behavior and motivation in organizations. Mayo is generally recognized as the founder of the Human Relations School (and of industrial sociology), although he and Barnard were in close touch at the time, and probably both deserve about equal credit for leading the scientific revolution against the Scientific Management School.

The frontal attack on the Scientific Management School reached a peak in the late 1940s and 1950s. Barnard's book and the findings from the Hawthorne studies (see below) were crucial, but changes in the industrial landscape were also involved. The proportion of white-collar workers in the work force increased tremendously during the economic boom following World War II; these professionals at lower- and middle-management levels were not hired because they were a relative of the owner, nor did most of them rise through the ranks. Rather, they were flowing out of engineering and business schools into the corporations. Government and other nonindustrial organizations had also begun to hire large numbers of professionals. The cost of hiring these well-educated employees helped make organizations more aware of employees' needs; they were treated with consideration in order to keep them in the organization. No longer were workers viewed by management as quiescent extensions of the company's machines.

The studies that were most important in rediscovering human motivation at work, and which became a cornerstone of organizational behavior theory, are known as the Hawthorne studies.

ILLUMINATION AT THE HAWTHORNE PLANT

In the mid-1920s, the National Research Council's Illuminating Engineering Society conducted a series of industrial lighting studies. The results were rather surprising, as they indicated that "it was clear that a direct relationship between illumination and production was non-existent" (Snow 1927). Additional studies were planned on the relationship between illumination on the job and workers' productivity. One of the participating firms was the Western Electric Company.

In the late 1920s, that firm, in collaboration with the Committee on Work in Industry of the National Research Council, initiated a series of such studies at the Western Electric Hawthorne plant in Cicero, Illinois, outside of Chicago. These researches were begun by William J. Dickson, a Western Electric manager. The Hawthorne plant employed about 4,000 workers in manufacturing equipment for the telephone industry. Its name was to become famous as the site of a classic social science investigation that was to revolutionize conceptions of organizational behavior.

The research at the Hawthorne plant began with a number of field experiments on improved illumination,[8] all of which ended in surprising and intellectually frustrating results. In one experiment, for example, workers were divided into two groups: a control group in which the regular level of lighting was maintained, and an experimental group in which the lighting was increased, first from 24 to 46, and then to 70 footcandles. As expected, production increased under these brighter conditions. But, amazingly, production also increased by about the same amount in the control group!

Then the lighting was diminished in the experimental room, first to 10 and then to 3 footcandles. Production went up, not down (as expected). In the control room, where lighting remained constant, production went up.

In yet another experiment, the illumination was reduced to .06 of a footcandle, approximately equivalent to moonlight; not until this very dim condition was reached did production begin to decrease.

Something very strange was going on, and the researchers tried to figure out exactly what it was. Clearly they could not conclude from their investigations that illumination was directly related to the level of production of the workers. Rather, production seemed to be related to the workers' perception of the special attention they were getting from the investigators. Whether they were in the experimental or in the control group, the workers knew they were respondents in a research study, and this realization apparently inspired them to greater production. In honor of the study in which this effect was first noticed and so dramatically demonstrated, social scientists have called it the "Hawthorne effect" (defined as the tendency for individuals to behave in an artificial way when they know they are subjects in an experiment).

One of the Hawthorne researchers, Fritz J. Roethlisberger (1941, p. 15), an industrial psychologist from Harvard University, concluded that "in most work situations the meaning of a change is likely to be as important, if not more so, than the change itself. This was . . . the new illumination

---

[8] A research approach that was initially quite in line with the Taylor approach of the Scientific Management School.

that came from the research. It was an illumination quite different from what . . . had [been] expected from the illumination studies."

ENTER THE PROFESSORS

When the results of the illumination experiments appeared mysterious to the investigators, they called in Professor Elton Mayo from the Harvard University Business School, an industrial sociologist who had had previous research experience in studying workers' productivity. Professor Mayo and his colleagues, Fritz Roethlisberger and William Dickson, along with several others carried out a series of researches between 1927 and 1932 that are today referred to as the "Hawthorne studies."

In one experiment, the researchers set up a small work room called the Relay Assembly Test Room. Six female workers were assigned to assemble telephone relays. A variety of experimental treatments were introduced: a group payment incentive, rest pauses, shorter working hours, and refreshments. Production increased with each of these treatments. Then the Relay Assembly Test Room reverted to a 48-hour, six-day week, with no incentives, no rest pauses, and no refreshments. Production went up to the highest level yet recorded!

Next, Mayo and his research group set up the Bank Wiring Observation Room, in which the researchers could closely observe and record the behavior of the workers. The latter constituted a highly integrated group, with their own norms and code of behavior. The production rate of this work group seldom varied, and the social scientists soon learned why: the work group had its own standards of production, and group pressure was exerted to achieve and maintain this standard, despite the efforts of management to increase production.

REDISCOVERING INFORMAL COMMUNICATION

This serendipitous rediscovery of the roots of worker motivation in informal social relationships was to become the most famous product of the Hawthorne studies.[9] In their review of social science research literature, Katz and Lazarsfeld (1955, pp. 33–42) consider the Hawthorne studies one of the main empirical investigations leading to the "rediscovery" of the primary group (a relatively small-sized group of individuals in intimate relationships, such as a family or a friendship network): a belated recogni-

[9] The main book reporting the results of the Hawthorne studies is Roethlisberger and Dickson (1939); other publications about this investigation are Mayo (1933), Roethlisberger (1941), Whitehead (1938), Landsberger (1958), and Homans (1950).

tion of the importance of informal interpersonal relationships in situations formerly conceptualized as strictly formal and atomistic.[10]

The Hawthorne studies marked an important intellectual watershed in conceptions of organizational behavior, leading to an entire recasting of assumptions about human behavior in organizations. The resulting new paradigm was called the "Human Relations" School, because of its emphasis on employee relationships as the determining factor in production. Concepts like worker satisfaction and morale rose to the fore in this school, which was individual-centered rather than organization-oriented.

In contrast to the Scientific Management School's conception of the worker as an economic man who responded directly to monetary incentives, the Human Relations School preceived the worker as a *social* man, responding to the interpersonal influences of the informal work group. "The emotional, unplanned, nonrational elements in organizational behavior" were stressed (Etzioni 1964, p. 20). One noted example of such group influence on worker productivity was observed in the Bank Wiring Observation Room of the Hawthorne plant. The workers produced at a rate established not by their supervisors, nor by time-and-motion experts, but *by themselves as a group*. If a worker did not produce up to this standard, the group would exert pressure on him to work harder, and they might even pitch in to help the slow producer (thus confounding the official work production records kept on the individual). At the same time, an overproducer (called a "speed king" or "ratebuster") was also pressured by his peers, and might even be physically assaulted until his work output returned to the group-sanctioned norm.

CHANGING ORGANIZATIONAL BEHAVIOR THROUGH THE HUMAN RELATIONS APPROACH

Clearly, the Human Relations scholars argued, conducting time-and-motion studies of individual workers and offering them cash incentives as individuals would, in such a group-centered work situation, be futile. A more appropriate strategy would be to assess the workers' needs and then seek to satisfy them; the increased job satisfaction would presumably lead

[10] Other "rediscoveries" of the importance of informal communication included (1) the Erie County study in which Lazarsfeld and others (1948) found that the effects of the mass media in a political election campaign were mediated by opinion leaders in a two-step flow of communication, thus destroying the "hypodermic needle" model of mass media effects, and (2) *The American Soldier* studies in World War II by Stouffer and others (1949), which found that soldiers were motivated in combat not by the coercion of discipline and of formal orders from above, but by loyalty to a peer group of buddies. In each of the three investigations, informal communication had to be rediscovered because more formal and atomistic conceptualizations left too much unexplained.

to higher production. The message of the Human Relations School was that "tender loving care" of the workers by their supervisors, and by higher management, would pay off in higher production. The Human Relations viewpoint ultimately led organizational scholars to focus on leadership as a means of attaining greater job satisfaction and thus greater productivity.

Organizational researchers at the Institute for Social Research at the University of Michigan, one of the academic centers for Human Relationists in the 1950's and 1960's, were generally not able to prove that satisfied workers produce more than dissatisfied workers (Tannenbaum and Seashore, no date).[11] In fact, sometimes the least satisfied workers are the highest producers. This unreasonable finding led researchers to investigate supervisory leadership, and a common research finding was that style of supervision (such as showing a concern for subordinates as human beings) was related to production. Training programs for work leaders were subsequently designed, emphasizing the human relations approach, as a means of raising production.

The Human Relations School advocated the use of such training programs to change human behavior and thus solve organizational problems. This approach amounts to altering individual behavior in order to bring about change in the system. An alternative approach would, of course, be to change the organizational structure or goals (Perrow 1970b). In many cases, both individual training programs and changing the organizational structure are needed. In fact, a common experience is that a new trainee, when returned to his or her old job in an existing structure, quickly slides back into his or her old behavior.

THE SCANLON PLAN: AN OPERATIONALIZATION OF THE HUMAN RELATIONS APPROACH

The most famous participation and incentive system growing out of the Human Relations movement is called the Scanlon Plan, after its founder, Joseph N. Scanlon. Scanlon was a laborer in the 1930s on an open-hearth blast furnace in a steel company that was rapidly slipping into bankruptcy. Its equipment was obsolete, its profits were nil, and the labor union was demanding higher wages. Scanlon was a union leader in this steel mill, and he convinced the company executives and his fellow workers to try a co-

---

[11] Vroom (1964) found a consistent but weak correlation between worker satisfaction and performance. Lawler and Porter (1967) concluded that satisfaction might be a consequence, rather than a cause, of high performance. There are hundreds of other investigations of job satisfaction and its correlates in organizational settings. Most such studies do not find strong evidence for the satisfaction–production hypothesis of the Human Relationists.

operative work–management productivity plan to meet the immediate financial crisis. Thus was born the Scanlon Plan (Lesieur 1958).

The employees agreed to make an all-out effort to improve production, and offered numerous suggestions for reducing costs, decreasing waste, and improving efficiency and quality. Management agreed to grant the union's demands for higher wages as soon as improved production made such increases possible.

The story ended happily, as the steel company pulled out of its financial nose dive and the workers soon received their salary boost. Joe Scanlon became famed as a consultant who could rescue failing companies with his radical plan for labor–management cooperation. He took a staff position with the United Steelworkers Union, where he promoted the Scanlon Plan, and then he joined the faculty of MIT, although he still continued his consulting activities in the field of labor-management relations.

At the heart of the Scanlon Plan are two essential elements: (1) that all members of the organization participate in improving productivity by offering suggestions, and (2) that all members are rewarded equitably for improving productivity (Frost and others, 1974, p. 5). The first tenet of the plan is achieved by utilizing an open suggestion system, with a set of "production committees" throughout the organization (composed of one manager and a small number of representatives elected by the workers) to screen the suggestions. For example, in the Atwood Vacuum Machine Company of Rockford, Illinois, over 28,000 suggestions were received from its 2,000 employees during the first fourteen years of the Scanlon Plan (Lesieur and Puckett 1969). At the Stromberg–Carlson Company, 1,300 suggestions were received during the first eighteen months of the plan; half of these suggestions were accepted and implemented in order to improve production. The suggestion system provides a means for upward feedback from the workers to management; the fact that these messages get through and are acted upon encourages the feeling that making suggestions is worthwhile. From time to time, special campaigns are organized in order to obtain even more suggestions, sometimes by offering prizes and other benefits.

Each production committee has the authority to immediately implement in its shop or division any suggestions it considers reasonable, except for relatively high-cost suggestions, which are passed on to the company's "screening committee" (composed equally of top executives and elected workers) for action. This committee also computes and allocates a monthly bonus to all employees on the basis of the current increase in total company productivity as compared with a previous time period, which implements the second element of the plan. The bonus is not an *individual worker* incentive, as the Scientific Management school advocated, but a *group* incentive, paid on the basis of the performance of the total organization; the purpose of this bonus system is to encourage all parts of the organization to work together cooperatively for higher performance. Thus the employee suggestions and the extensive committee work that is required by the Scanlon Plan pay off in improved welfare for all.

For example, the Parker Pen Company of Janesville, Wisconsin, initiated the Scanlon Plan among its 1,000 workers in 1955. Monthly bonuses, ranging from 6 to 20 per cent, have been earned in about 85 percent of the months since (Lesieur and Puckett 1969). Today, a number of North American and European companies use some version of the Scanlon Plan. It is not always successful, and it has failed in some organizations.

The Scanlon Plan operationalizes in a specific and useful form many of the key tenets of the Human Relations school: a participatory management style in which the workers are involved,[12] bottom–up communication flows in the form of employee suggestions about how to improve organizational performance, and a bonus system that encourages cooperative activities by groups of workers and managers. Its relative success to date is one evidence that the Human Relations viewpoint has some validity, at least in certain organizations.

CRITICISMS OF THE HAWTHORNE STUDIES

The data base from the Hawthorne studies was actually rather inadequate for the broad assumptions and claims of the Human Relations School, and a number of scholarly criticisms along this line have appeared in recent years.[13] These criticisms claim that the methodology of the Hawthorne studies was inadequate or defective (for example, they cite faulty sampling as a basis for generalization of the research results), and question the resulting philosophy of the Human Relations School, such as that satisfying workers' needs leads to higher production.

Some critics of the Human Relations School have charged that it is manipulative, in that involving the workers in participatory decision making may be used by management only to gain the facade of democracy, while in fact the decisions have already been made. "It has been charged that providing workers with 'gripe sessions' and suggestion boxes . . . may reduce their alienation without improving their lot" (Etzioni 1964, p. 45).

Other critics object to the purpose of management's ostensible concern for, and communication with, workers. "Those who favor the syrupy form of human relations—being friendly, knowing each worker's name and how

---

[12] Research studies in several companies that have adopted the Scanlon Plan show that their management style is indeed highly participatory (Likert 1967, p. 40).

[13] Some of the most penetrating criticisms of the Hawthorne studies—and, more broadly, of the Human Relations School—are: Argyle (1953), Carey (1967), Mouzelis (1967), Perrow (1972), Cook (1967), Baritz (1961), and Sykes (1965).

many children he has, distributing selectively a little bag of rewards—have done a great disservice to management by obscuring its real responsibilities and the real needs of workers" (Mott 1972, p. 183).

Managers and work supervisors became the focus of interest of the Human Relations School and the vehicles for changing worker behavior, as we showed previously. To maximize production, they needed to pay attention to employees' social needs. "In effect, they took a bagful of cookies along when they took the child to the dentist. Instead of scolding, they would now be modern and sensible. They would distract the kid, and, if necessary, bribe him" (Leavitt and others 1973, p. 130).

Much research on organizational behavior seems to have been conducted by gathering data from workers in order to obtain understanding mainly for the benefit of management. This elitist bias in social science research is especially apparent in the Human Relations School. There is never really much doubt, when one reads the various books and other publications growing out of the Hawthorne studies, as to whom they are expected to benefit. The researchers seem to be rather firmly enlisted on the side of management, in a cozy partnership of Harvard University professors and Western Electric captains of industry. Of course the workers benefit also, if the executives really listen to the professors' research results about the importance of their needs and satisfaction, but management seems to definitely come first.[14]

THE CONTRIBUTION OF CHESTER BARNARD

In addition to the Hawthorne studies, the other main intellectual input to the Human Relations School was Chester Barnard's (1938) book *The Functions of the Executive.* Actually, Barnard was in close contact with Elton Mayo and his research group at Harvard University, and so it is not surprising that they agreed in putting forward a "social" worker in place of the "economic man" of the Scientific Management School. Instead of calling on empirical research studies, however, as did Professor Mayo and his group, Barnard depended upon his extensive and insightful experience as the top executive of the New Jersey Bell Telephone Company.

Barnard was not satisfied with the traditional definition of an organization. To him, the most essential characteristic of an organization was communication. He gave considerable attention to both the formal and the informal aspects of organizations. "Informal organizations," he wrote, "are necessary to the operations of formal organizations" (Barnard, 1938, p.

[14] This pro-management tilt on the part of organization researchers is paralleled by the source bias on the part of most past communication research. As a result, much research on communication in organizations is directed mainly toward the management of communication for the benefit of the organization's leaders. Too bad.

123): informal groups establish attitudes, norms, and individual codes of conduct within the formal system. Communication, cohesion, and protection of individual integrity are the main functions of informal organization. Barnard was one of the first organization theorists to give importance to human motivation as a crucial factor in production, and to recognize that economic motives were sometimes of minor significance.

"Though I early found out how to behave effectively in organizations, not until I had much later relegated economic theory and economic interests to a secondary—though indispensable—place did I begin to understand organizations or human behavior in them" (Barnard 1938, p. xxxi). Thus Barnard raised noneconomic motives to much greater attention than they had received at the hands of the Scientific Management School. Previously, most business managers thought that if they waved a fistful of green stuff in front of their workers' eyes, the latter would produce more. But Barnard's position flew in the face of this conception of economic man.

Barnard envisioned an essentially cooperative relationship between the individual and the organization. There are certain needs that any given individual cannot attain alone, hence he or she must cooperate with others in an organized way to achieve them. So the organization simply helps the individual do what he or she could not otherwise accomplish.

Publication of Barnard's book marked the beginning of the realization of the importance of communication in organizations. "The first executive function," he wrote, "is to develop and maintain a system of communication" (Barnard 1938, p. 226). Although communication was emphasized throughout his book, Barnard's conception of communication was a limited one, with the focus on its use by authority. To Barnard, communication was mainly what a source (usually a manager or executive) did *to* a receiver (a subordinate).

Barnard set forth a series of principles of communication in organizations, which today we would recognize as dealing mainly with formal, one-way communication. For example, he proposed (1938, pp. 175–181) that:

1. Communication channels should be clearly established through organization charts.
2. No "bypassing" of formal channels should be allowed.
3. Formal channels of communication must exist for everyone; each individual must report to someone and be subordinate to someone.

OTHER HUMAN RELATIONISTS: THE HUMAN RESOURCES SUBSCHOOL

While Barnard and Mayo–Roethlisberger–Dickson were the kingpins in the Human Relations School, several scholars, such as Professor Douglas McGregor of MIT, Rensis Likert of the University of Michigan, and Chris Argyris (formerly of Yale, and now at Harvard University), made important contributions in carrying on, expanding, and refining the main tenets of the Human Relations movement. These latter-day scholars are often labeled the "Human Resources" group, because they assumed that all segments of the organization (workers and managers) could benefit from more appropriate human relationships in the organization.

McGregor (1960) contrasted Theory X (based on the classical notion of a rational economic man) with Theory Y, a view of man as independent, responsible, and growth-oriented. Likert (1961, 1967) argued for a participatory style of organizational management, in which the workers are involved in decision-making processes. Argyris (1957, 1960) claimed that the employees' struggle for need satisfaction within an organizational structure often led to a conflict between the goals of the organization and those of the individual member.

The participatory management approach, promoted by Likert and other Human Relationists in the United States, may be culture-bound. Is a participatory leadership style appropriate, for example, in certain Asian nations where an authoritarian relationship between a boss and a subordinate has been institutionalized for centuries? If a superior in such a situation treated his employees as coequal participants in decisionmaking, he would probably be ridiculed by them.

However, the scarce evidence available to date suggests that a somewhat higher degree of participatory management may perhaps be related to organizational effectiveness, even in Asia. For example, one study shows that those family planning clinics in the Republic of Korea and in Singapore which were more participatory were somewhat higher in effectiveness.[15] Perhaps Likert-style participatory leadership is not so culture-bound after all.

In recent years, the "contingency" viewpoint that no one type of organizational structure or leadership style is most appropriate for all situations—has gained much credence. Such variables as the organization's objectives, its size, and the culture in which it operates must be considered in specifying its most effective organizational structure and communication behavior. In other words, what "works" in Keokuk may not work in Allahabad, and vice versa. Participatory management style may be appropriate in the General Motors plant in Flint, Michigan, but less so in the Singhania Textile Mills in Kanpur.

FROM S–M–C–R TO R–M–C–S

With the Hawthorne studies came the realization that informal group functioning was very much a part of the total organizational landscape.

---

[15] This investigation, whose results are not yet published, was coordinated by Dr. Hirofumi Ando of the Population Division of the United Nations ECAFE (Economic Commission for Asia and the Far East).

Attaining participation, strenghthening commitment to the organization, and maintaining group cohesion were seen as important functions of communication within informal work groups. Barnard perceived of communication as an essential characteristic of an organization: "In any exhaustive theory of organization, communication would occupy a central place" (1938, p. 8). Generally, *the Human Relationists saw communication as relatively more important than had the Taylorists. And they perceived of organizational communication, not just as a means of sources (that is, management) talking to workers, but of management listening to what the workers were saying.* The workers came first in the receiver-oriented approach to communication advocated by the Human Relations School.

In 1958, the American Management Association published "Ten Commandments for Successful Communication," an article addressed to business executives. An emphasis on communication, in the broadest sense of the term, was justified by the argument that efficient management depended on it. The ten principles of "good" communication dealt with planning, analysis, purpose, meaning and intent, receiver orientation, a long-range viewpoint, the consonance of actions with communication, and the virtues of being a good listener. The trend was toward a humanistic view of communication, in order to achieve "satisfied" workers. The informal communication system was understood and accepted. Focus was upon superior–subordinate interaction, and hence communication became almost synonymous with motivation and leadership in organizations. Participatory management became popular, and the Human Relationists believed that a high degree of interaction among individuals and groups, as exemplified by the Scanlon Plan, was needed for a truly "democratic" organization (Likert 1967).

"Many of the actually existing patterns of human interaction have no representation in the formal organization at all, and others are inadequately represented by the formal organization. . . . *Too often it is assumed that the organization of a company corresponds to . . . an organization chart.* Actually, it never does" (Roethlisberger and Dickson 1939, p. 559). This statement by the Hawthorne researchers illustrates their realization that communication in organizations was informal and interpersonal (actually, the Human Relationists may have overemphasized informal communication to the neglect of formal structure).

Because of their ubiquity in empirical investigations like the Hawthorne studies and the many researches that followed it, rumors [16] came in for heavy attention. Formal, vertical communication channels are often short-circuited or negated by the "grapevine"—as was shown in a noted study of rumoring conducted in the "Jason Company," a leather manufacturing

[16] A *rumor* is an unconfirmed message passed from person to person.

firm (Davis 1953a). The lesson for business managers, presumably, was to understand and use informal channels, rather than to ignore rumors and have their plans wrecked by them. Because rumors spread interpersonally and across hierarchical levels, the overwhelming importance ascribed to formal, vertical channels by the Scientific Management School came to be doubted by the Human Relationists. Their focus on the worker and on satisfying his or her needs as a means of achieving higher production led to their taking the worker's view of the organization, and of organizational communication as well. *The Human Relation School focused attention on informal communication among peers in an organization.*

"THE PLANT IS CLOSING, THE PLANT IS CLOSING"

In a spoof of the Human Relations approach, Etzioni (1964, p. 43) asks us to imagine a training movie in which we see "a happy factory in which the wheels hum steadily and the workers rhythmically serve the machine with smiles on their faces." But then a truck driver arrives and mysteriously unloads large crates containing new machines. "A dark type with long sideburns who sweeps the floor in the factory spreads a rumor that firing is imminent since the new machines will take over the work of many of the workers. The wheels turn slower, the workers are sad." That evening they carry their gloom home to their wives and families.

The next morning, however, the workers are reassured by the voice of their boss over the intercom system in the plant. "He tells them that the rumor is absolutely false; the machines are to be set up in the new wing and more workers will be hired since the factory is expanding its production. Everybody sighs in relief, smiles return, the machines hum speedily and steadily again." Only the floor sweeper is saddened, as nobody will listen to his rumors anymore.

The moral of this film is clear: had management adequately communicated its expansion plans to the workers, the near-crisis could have been averted. Or perhaps the workers should have been involved in making the decision to expand in the first place. In any event, a participatory-management would have considered the feelings and reactions of the workers.

The Human Relations ethic did transfer some degree of authority and power from the formal organizational structures to the peer group at the operational level. But management still wanted the game played according to the organization's rules, not just the workers'. The individual

was considered, and invited to participate in decision making, but with
the main objective of attaining greater work performance. Unfortunately,
there was an inauthentic quality to organizational communication as
viewed in this light: "A major effect [of the Human Relations movement]
was to reduce the honesty of communication; it led people to play games,
to delude one another, to talk at one level while communicating at another" (Leavitt and others, 1973, p. 42).

The Systems School

In the 1960s and 1970s a synthesis of the Scientific Management and
Human Relations schools began to emerge, as part of a gradual realization
that the assumptions of the first school best fit some types of organizations,
while the conceptions of the second school were more appropriate to
other structures. The Systems School that emerged represented a more
eclectic and encompassing viewpoint; in fact, the general systems theorists
claimed that their theoretical approach could be applied to any living
system (any biological or social system). That is, general systems theory
is a general theory of systems (Laszlo 1975). It conceptualizes an organization as a system of interrelated components, and stresses the orchestra-
tion of these parts as the key to maximizing performance.

The empirical scope of the Systems School was wider than that of the
Scientific Management and Human Relations schools. The latter had
focused mainly on factories in their empirical studies; only later was this
limited data base somewhat broadened. In contrast, a variety of types of
organizations were studied by the Systems researchers: prisons, schools,
armies, hospitals, and many kinds of business firms.

GENERAL SYSTEMS THEORY

Unlike its predecessors, which arose mainly from practical experience
and empirical research, the Systems School was grounded in a theoretical
perspective called "general systems theory." This intellectual viewpoint
has been the single most influential theory in contemporary scientific
thought, especially in the social sciences. Key figures in launching this
scientific revolution were the biologist and philosopher Ludwig van
Bertalanffy, the logician Anatol Rapoport, the philosopher–economist
Kenneth Boulding, and the sociologist Talcott Parsons.[17]

[17] They helped move the study of social systems from a *closed system* to an *open
system approach* (see below).

Theorists of this school conceived of a system as a set of interdependent parts (Bertalanffy 1956, 1962, 1968). One essential element of a system is communication, which links the parts or subsystems so. as to facilitate their interdependence. This focus on interaction as the lifeblood of a system was, of course, completely compatible with the view of organizations held by communication scientists. Hence general systems theory was welcomed by the field of communication in general, and has had a strong impact on the study of human communication. It also revolutionized organizational theory and has remained the dominant viewpoint in the field.

General systems theory had been defined as the "science of 'wholeness'" (Bertalanffy 1968, p. 37). It contends with wholes and how to deal with them, relationships between parts, interaction of wholes with the environment, the creation and elaboration of structures, adaptive evolution, goal seeking, and the control or self-regulation of direction (Buckley 1967, p. 2). The central credo of the systems viewpoint is the statement that the whole is more than the sum of its parts. The systems approach arose, and achieved a following in each of the social sciences, because it represented an alternative to the mechanistic atomism then common in most research on human behavior. The atomistic approach assumed that explanation is achieved by breaking down a phenomenon into its parts, and then understanding the parts. The whole was assumed to be just the sum of its parts. In contrast, systems theory is holistic. It assumes that the complex interactions among the parts of a given system are destroyed by the dissection of the system through atomistic research procedures. Instead, wholes have to be studied and understood as total units, as systems.

THE UNFULFILLED POTENTIAL OF SYSTEMS-ORIENTED RESEARCH IN ORGANIZATIONS

It was an easy and natural move foi organization theorists and communication scientists in the Systems School to apply the concepts and viewpoints of general systems theory to the study of organizations, and to the analysis of organizational communication. The systems approach to the study of organizations proceeds from the premise that an organization is a system, composed of a series of definite elements having limited goals. The organization's goal is to achieve optimal efficiency as a whole. Maximum efficiencies on the part of all of its elements are not so important, as the whole is more significant.

The new perspective in analyzing organizations provided by general systems theory, however, had little impact on the actual operations of research. Although social science systems theory provided a new and useful sensitizing orientation to the study of human behavior in organizations (in that it encouraged thinking in holistic terms), the needed research methods for studying behavior in a total-system context were not readily available.

The problem with the systems approach is precisely that it is difficult to effectuate in actual research operations. The vocabulary of systems theory ("structure," "feedback," "input–output," "open systems," "boundary maintenance") infected social scientific thinking in the mid-1960s, and provided a sensitizing function in the intellectual analysis of human behavioral problems (Buckley 1967, p. 7). But social scientists generally proceeded to use their previously existing research techniques within the new theoretical perspective of systems theory. For example, researchers would typically single out for research attention one or two variables that were easily measured, and ignore all other variables that might also be involved in the situation studied. The resulting research results fell far short of the promising potential of the systems approach.

Social science research has usually been concerned with trees rather than forests. Largely owing to influences from the physical sciences, the social sciences have generally studied specific parts of a system, in order to then proceed to understand the whole system. Or so they thought.

Most past communication research has been of this limited nature, and hence has been rather uninteresting from a systems perspective. Laboratory/experiment research methods in communication (and in other fields) have been relatively atomistic, while field studies have generally tended to be somewhat more holistic, but even they have been much less so than a true systems approach would demand.

We utilize a systems framework in this book to order and present our synthesis of what is currently known about organizational communication. Specifically, we follow an open system approach.

AN OPEN SYSTEM APPROACH

A *system* is a set of units that has some degree of structure, and that is differentiated from the environment by a boundary. The system's boundary is defined by communication flows; the units in the system have a greater degree of communication with each other than—across the boundary—with units in the external environment. But this does not mean that communication across the boundary is any less important for the system's maintenance than information exchanges within the system. In fact, any system that does not input matter, energy, and information *from* its environment and output messages *to* its environment will soon run down and eventually cease to exist.

The Systems School of organization theorists focused especially on *open* systems, because most organizations are relatively "open." What do we mean by open and closed systems?

A *closed* system is completely isolated from its environment. Its boundaries are closed to the exchange of information and energy with the environment.

By contrast, an *open system* continuously exchanges information with its environment. It imports information from its environment, transforms or processes this "raw material," and exports the finished product back into its environment.

A closed system does not admit matter–energy[18] from external sources, and therefore it is subject to "entropy" and the Second Law of Thermodynamics, which states that all (closed) systems move toward disorganization or death (Buckley 1968, p. xviii). *Entropy* is a measure of the degree of disorder in a system.

Open systems do not behave according to the Second Law of Thermodynamics, because they import matter–energy from their environments. If open systems became closed, they would eventually run down and die. "The open system does not run down, because it can import energy from the world around it. Thus the operation of entropy is counteracted by the importation of energy and the living system is characterized by negative rather than positive entropy" (Katz and Kahn 1966, p. 19).

An open system employs feedback mechanisms in order to provide a certain degree of self-regulation, so that deviations from equilibrium are constantly being corrected. Such mechanisms help the system achieve and maintain a *steady state*,[19] in which some aspect of the system remains constant in spite of its importing and exporting of information. Open systems tend toward increased specialization and differentiation. Open systems are capable of reaching the same end state despite different initial conditions (this quality is called *"equifinality"*).

Most *living systems* (that is, human or other types of biological systems, as opposed to physical systems) are thought to be open rather than closed. Certainly most communication systems, including organizations, are relatively open (Thayer 1972, p. 116; Katz and Kahn 1966). "Social organizations are flagrantly open systems in that the input of energies and the conversion of output into further energic input consist of transactions between the organization and its environment" (Katz and Kahn 1966, pp. 16–17).

The openness of open systems implies that a fast-changing environ-

---

[18] We use the concept of "matter–energy" because matter can be converted into energy, and vice versa. *Matter* is anything that has mass and occupies physical space; *energy* is the ability to do work (J. G. Miller 1971).

[19] A *steady state* occurs in a system when a slight disturbance in an equilibrium is counteracted so as to restore the previous state. So energy and activity are required to maintain a steady state.

ment causes appropriately rapid change in the organization. The open system approach pictures organizations as constantly changing—unlike the Human Relations School, which hardly allowed for change.

"Open system theory is not a theory at all" (Katz and Kahn 1966, p. 452), at least in the sense of providing a set of specific hypotheses that can be tested in empirical research. But the open system approach was certainly theoretical, in the sense that it provided an integrated body of concepts constituting a framework for the study of organizational communication. And the Systems School was thus distinctive in its foundations from the Scientific Management and Human Relations Schools, both of which arose inductively out of experience and empiricism.

LOOKING OUTWARD

So *the Systems School of organization theorists view an organization as an open system that inputs and outputs to the environment across its boundary* (Figure 2–2). Until the mid-1960s most organization scholars looked within the system for factors explaining the behavior of the organization and of its members. Their analyses usually stopped at the boundary. The organization was treated as an isolated entity; little attention was given to the environment, and to what went on in the environ-

FIGURE 2–2. Main Elements in an Open System Conceptualization of an Organization (*Note:*"Throughput" is the processing of information and materials by a system in which inputs are transformed into outputs).

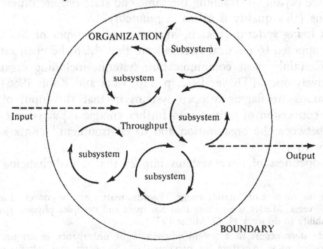

ment as an explanation of changes in the organization. The open system view implied the importance of the organization's environment, and led to intellectual attempts to classify environments.[20] *Openness,* the degree to which a system exchanges information with its environment, became an important variable in organization research.

An organization is a system composed of a set of subsystem components that each serve certain functions, and that are each in interaction with the other subsystems. An organization inputs information and matter–energy from its environment, and, after processing these elements, outputs them. Thus changes in the environment have a continuous impact on the organization, so that it is constantly adjusting to environmental change; contrariwise, the organization's internal changes have a continuous impact on its environment (Katz and Kahn 1966). The systems viewpoint, as we have seen, emphasized the interrelationships and exchanges betweeen an organization and its environment; the Scientific Management and Human Relations schools often studied an organization as an isolated entity, looking within the organization for explanations of organizational behavior. The Systems School also looked outside, to the organizational environment.

THE INTERNAL FUNCTION OF COMMUNICATION

The Systems School focuses upon the interdependency of the subsystem components of the system. Most organizations have, at the least, a production subsystem, a maintenance subsystem, and an adaptation or innovation subsystem. Each subsystem has certain goals, and each seeks to contribute to the system's overall objective, thus encouraging the interdependency of the subsystems. This interdependency depends on communication.

The units in a system do not all have an equal amount of communication with each other, and so it is useful to speak of subsystems within a system. A *subsystem* is a set composed of those units within a system that have more frequent communication with other units in their subsystem than with those units not in their subsystem. Thus subboundaries exist within the system's boundary that mark off the system's subsystems.

One problem is to specify exactly where a system's boundary is. This difficulty occurs because every system is part of a larger system, which is in turn a subsystem of a still larger system. The problem is to know where to stop. A similar problem occurs in specifying the subsystems within a system. Each of these subsystems, in turn, has subsystems.

The point here is that every organization is a nesting of systems,

[20] As, for example, to their degree of turbulence (Terreberry 1968).

composed of systems within systems. There are levels of systems, and the choice of what level to consider *the* system is somewhat arbitrary, depending in part on the purpose of the analyst. Often in research in organizations the system is specified by the identity of the organization.

DANIEL KATZ AND ROBERT KAHN

After general systems theory was begun by a small group of scientists at the University of Chicago, the University of Michigan became one of the academic centers of the general systems theorists. Professors Anatol Rapoport and Kenneth Boulding, for example, were faculty members, and it was natural that open systems thinking would be applied by their colleagues in Ann Arbor to the study of organizations. Professor James G. Miller at Michigan authored a series of influential articles in the mid-1960s and early 1970s on the theory of living systems; one of these dealt with organizations as living systems (Miller 1972). But probably the greatest boost to applying open system theory to organizations came from two University of Michigan professors, Daniel Katz and Robert Kahn, through publication of their book *The Social Psychology of Organizations* (Katz and Kahn 1966). This volume, based indirectly on the authors' extensive experience in investigating organizational behavior, set forth and illustrated the main credo of open system theory. Publication of the Katz and Kahn book marked the real beginning of the application of systems thinking to the study of organizations, and launched what we have called in this chapter the Systems School.

THE "TECHNOLOGY" SUBSCHOOL

During approximately the same period in which the open system theorists of organization were at work in the United States, especially at the University of Michigan, a related theoretical development in organizations theory was underway in England, centering around Joan Woodward and other researchers.[21] This approach focused on "technology" as the defining characteristic of organizations. "Technology" was used here not in the usual sense of machinery, but rather, more broadly, as referring to the tasks that organizations perform. Woodward (1958) classified technology as to whether an industrial production process was (1) unit or small-batch (like making custom suits), (2) mass or large-batch (like

---

[21] Other scholars whose work is somewhat related to Woodward's include: Perrow (1970a), Gouldner (1954), Burns and Stalker (1962), Lawrence and Lorsch (1967), Agarwala–Rogers (1973), and Hage and Aiken (1969).

automobile assembly lines), or (3) continuous flow process (as in chemical companies). In her sample of 100 English manufacturing firms, Woodward found that organizations in a similar category of technology had similar organizational structures. For example, supervision was more direct in the small-batch technology companies and less direct in the continuous-process firms, where the structure had more hierarchical layers. The higher degree of specialization in the continuous-process technology meant that a greater number of specialized work units, and hence more communication among them, was needed.

The technology approach to studying organizations is consistent with the general viewpoint of the Systems School, in that interdependence among subsystems is emphasized, but it differs in the heavy emphasis put upon the organization's task (its "technology'") as an independent variable explaining other aspects of the system's structure and its members' communication behavior. It is not yet known whether Woodward's approach is applicable to people-processing organizations, such as a government welfare agency, as well as to industrial firms.[22]

Out of these studies has come the realization that there is no one best structure for an organization, as an organization's structure should be suited to its "technology," environment, and goals (we previously termed this viewpoint the contingency approach to organizational theory). There are a great variety of organizations, and no one approach to organization theory will be useful in all of them. Scientific Management may still apply today to military organizations and assembly-line industries, and perhaps to hierarchical churches like the Roman Catholic. The Human Relations approach is more applicable to other types of organizations, especially those in which large numbers of professionals are employed at the lower operational levels, such as schools and universities and research and development firms. The Systems School provides a theoretical perspective that can be fruitful in understanding any organization.

THE SYSTEMS VIEW OF COMMUNICATION

As the Systems School recognizes the need to study interactions of the subsystems in an organization, it focuses on communication as the key to analyzing and understanding organizations as social systems. Consequently, communication and information theory were central in the development of systems theory (Wiener 1950—see Table 2–2).

[22] Yet another "subschool" of organization theory has many aspects of a systems approach, but tends to focus particularly on decision making as a means of understanding organizational behavior. Leading representatives of the decision-making subschool are Simon (1947, 1956) and Cyert and March (1963).

TABLE 2-2. Comparison of the Nature of Organizational Communication as Seen by the Three Schools of Organizational Behavior.

	SCIENTIFIC MANAGEMENT SCHOOL	HUMAN RELATIONS SCHOOL	SYSTEMS SCHOOL
1. *Importance of communication*	Relatively unimportant, and largely restricted to downward communication from management workers.	Relatively important, but mainly limited to peer communication; some attention to communication of needs from workers to management.	Very important; communication is considered the cement that holds the units in an organization together.
2. *Purpose of communication*	To relay orders and information about work tasks, and to achieve obedience and coordination in carrying out such work.	To satisfy workers' needs, to provide for lateral interaction among peers in work groups, and to facilitate the participation of members in organizational decision making. A high degree of receiver orientation in communication from management.	To control and coordinate, and to provide information to decision makers; and to adjust the organization to changes in its environment.
3. *Direction of communication flows*	Downward (vertical), from management to workers, in order to persuade or convince them to follow instructions.	Horizontal among peers who belong to informal work groups; vertical between workers and management (1) to assess worker needs, and (2) to make possible participatory decision making.	All directions within the system, including downward and upward across hierarchical levels, and across the organization's boundary with the environment.
4. *Main communication problems thought to exist*	Breakdowns in communication due to (1) bypassing a hierarchical level, and (2) a too-large span of control.	Rumors, which are communicated through the "grapevine"; a partially ineffective formal communication structure that is thus supplemented by informal communication.	Overload, distortion, and omission; unresponsiveness to negative feedback.*

* The concepts of overload, distortion, etc., are defined in Chapter 4.

56

Communication is the basic process facilitating the interdependence of the parts of the total system; it is the mechanism of coordination. The role of communication is to be a "harmonizer" of the organization, an orchestrator of its parts.

"Organizations draw their nourishment from information. They depend for their life on networks and systems of communication that make it possible for many people to work in concert. It is this flow of information that binds an organization together into a single, coherent unit" (Leavitt and others, 1973, p. 57). Information was seen by Systems theorists as "the glue that holds organizations together." In fact, *information processing came to be seen by the Systems School as the main function performed by all organizations; organizational systems were essentially communication systems.*

"The portals and orifices of the organization cannot be sealed off to ensure stability and predictability; instead, the environment must be allowed inside, to ensure adaptability" (Perrow 1970a, p. 179). As we pointed out previously, Systems theorists were paramount in recognizing the importance of external communication with the organization's environment; and they looked to the environment to find explanations for organizational behavior change. These matters are taken up in the next chapter.

Summary

There are three main "schools" identified in the study of organizational behavior: Scientific Management, Human Relations, and the Systems School. An understanding of these three theoretical positions is important in gaining an understanding of how organizations function, and of the role of communication in organizations. The three schools are examples of "invisible colleges" composed of scholars of similar outlook who are in close communication with each other.

The Scientific Management School, initiated by Frederick W. Taylor, contributed a set of principles to guide the actions of those who manage organizations. Taylorism viewed workers as human extensions of their machines, responsive to individual economic incentives. The Human Relations School was founded by Chester I. Barnard and Elton Mayo. The latter rediscovered the importance of informal work groups within the formal structure of the organization in the so-called Hawthorne studies; these researches paved the way for other empirical studies of organizational behavior. Unlike the Scientific Management School, the Human Relationists emphasized communication (especially that among peers) as a key to understanding organizational behavior. Along with the

Hawthorne studies, a main intellectual input to the Human Relations School was provided by Barnard's book *The Functions of the Executive*, based upon his personal experience as president of the New Jersey Bell Telephone Company.

The Systems School arose in the late 1930s though the writings of the general systems theorists such as Ludwig van Bertalanffy, who argued for a science of "wholeness"; they conceived of a system as a set of interdependent parts connected by communication flows. The scientific revolution caused by the systems paradigm led to a reorientation of organizational research. Unfortunately, the intellectual potential of systems theory had not yet been fully realized in the operations of organizational research, which are still mainly atomistic and mechanistic.

A *system* is a set of units that has some degree of structure, and that is differentiated from the environment by a boundary. An *open system* continuously exchanges information with its environment. The Scientific Management and Human Relations schools focused their main attention on the internal functioning of organizations, while the Systems School stressed the crucial role of external communication flows with the environment (in addition to analyzing internal communication).

The three schools of organizational behavior differ in their conceptions of communication. The Scientific Management School placed greater emphasis on vertical, downward flows; the Human Relations School stressed the crucial role of horizontal flows among peers; and the Systems School argues that all flows are important, some being more so for certain purposes or at certain times. Systems theorists give particular attention to communication with the environment and communication flows to link the subsystems within the organization.

So the Scientific Management School arose from an influential book about intuitively derived principles of management; the Human Relations School grew out of a classic empirical investigation; and the Systems School stemmed from a theory.

3. Open System Theory and Organizational Environments

"Men, like plants and animals, draw upon their environment for sustenance, and may be impoverished or enriched by it."
—Dean C. Barnlund

"Social organizations are flagrantly open systems in that the input of energies and the conversion of output into further energic input consist of transactions between the organization and its environment."
—Daniel Katz and Robert L. Kahn

An open system approach to understanding organizations necessitates important consideration of the organization's environment. In the present chapter, we explore in some detail the nature of communication in organizations when viewed from an open system viewpoint, placing special emphasis on the environment of the organization, and on how communication to and from this environment affects the organization.

As we have seen, an open system approach to studying organizations (1) elevated communication to high priority in the understanding of organizational behavior, (2) brought about a theoretical and methodological shift from individualistic to relational variables in analyzing organizational behavior, helping to put structure back in such research, and (3) influenced organization scholars to look outside of the organization's boundary at environmental variables for fuller explanations of organizational behavior.

Environment to the Fore

As we showed in Chapter 2, the Scientific Management and Human Relations Schools mainly looked within an organization's boundaries in order to find explanations for the behavior of its members. The internal structure was expected to provide the answers to such research questions as: "Why are some workers more productive than others?" "Why are some organizations more effective than others?" "What are the causes of change in an organization?"

The questions were pragmatically and theoretically important, but organizational scholars were looking in the wrong place for the answers. There are two main reasons why they looked within, rather than outside of, the organization: one reason was theoretical (they followed a closed system approach), and the other was logistical.

The theoretical reliance on closed system conceptions of organizations came about through an historical accident. Early social scientists took their lead mainly from the physical sciences, where closed system thinking was predominant, and largely appropriate. For the early social scientists, physical science was about "the only game in town." Physical science was much more mature than the social sciences, and the power of its methods was obvious. So since social scientists wanted to be "scientific," it was only natural that they copied their big brothers in physics and chemistry. The only problem was that the model mimicked was inappropriate for the nature of social systems.

Physical systems behave according to the Second Law of Thermodynamics: because they are closed systems, entropy causes them to run down in energy and eventually die. So should social systems, it was thought, at least until the "law of negative entropy" was proposed by general systems theorists: "Systems survive and maintain their characteristic internal order only so long as they import from the environment more energy than they expend in the process of transformation and exportation" (Katz and Kahn 1966, p. 28).

Gradually, social scientists became aware of the implications of open system theory for conceptualizing and analyzing human behavior. Katz and Kahn (1966), who pioneered in showing the utility of viewing organizations as open systems, argued that organization scholars should look outwardly across the boundary of the organization for explanations of what happens within it. The environment loomed large in open system thinking about organizations. Needed were ways of conceptualizing and measuring its relevant parts.

The second reason why the early organization scholars looked inward stemmed from the logistics of their research operations. One of the simplistic charms of studying human behavior in organizations, or so it was thought, was the neatness of the organization's boundary in specifying what should be empirically investigated, and what could be nicely ignored. Most early researches on organizational behavior were case studies of a single organization, usually a business firm or a factory. If the organization was too large for an individual researcher to observe or otherwise study alone, the researcher either employed additional research assistants or, more likely, simply concentrated the investigation within one sub-division of the organization. In either event, the formal structure of the organization specified a formal boundary, which dichotomized what was "inside" and what was "outside" the data-gathering operations. The re-searcher was forced to cut down the scope of the research to manageable size, and the boundary was a handy and seemingly logical point of de-marcation. The organization was to the industrial psychologist or or-ganizational sociologist what the peasant village was to the anthropologist: complex enough to be interesting, but small enough to be easily research-able.

The environment was not completely ignored by the two early schools of organizational behavior, but until open system theory came on the scene, there was no theoretical push in the direction of efforts to con-ceptualize and measure environmental variables.[1]

Increasingly in recent years, social scientists have come to think in terms of the *organization-in-an-environment* as their unit of study.

What Is Environment?

The *environment* is the totality of physical and social factors external to a system's boundary that are directly taken into consideration in the decision-making behavior of individuals in the system (Duncan 1972, p. 314; Zaltman and others, 1973, p. 114). This definition emphasizes the *relevant* portion of an organization's environment, and in this book we usually refer to this portion as the "relevant environment" or, more simply, as just the "environment." If we were to conceive of the environment as including *everything* other than what is within an organization's boundary, we would thereby define a limitless set of objects, individuals, and systems, one not very useful in understanding organizational behavior. From the viewpoint of comprehending what goes on in an organization, our main concern is with its relevant environment.

Where does an organization stop, and its environment begin? Every investigator of organizational behavior has to heuristically decide the boundary of the unit that he or she is studying.[2] Some scholars draw the

---

[1] The writings of the scholars associated with the Scientific Management and Human Relations Schools do not indicate the use of such concepts as "openness," "environ-ment," and "innovativeness." The Human Relations scholars "seldom actually deny the importance of the environment in organizational activity; rather, they simply set it aside to concentrate on informal problems and functions" (Mott 1972, p. 2).

[2] A safe and meaningful way is usually to establish the dependent variable (that which one wants to study or see changes and effects in), and then the boundary issue be-comes manageable and the contours of the relevant environmental dimensions will emerge.

line rather narrowly on the basis of including only those individuals who are part of a formal hierarchy: priests, but not parishioners; prison guards, but not inmates; nurses, but not patients (Etzioni 1961, p. 21). We think that these "lower"-level individuals should also be considered as participants in an organization, as they either feel involved in the organization or are subordinate to it in their behavior. Clearly the organizational boundary is not just a matter of formal membership or of a legal criterion of belonging. For instance, we would include the customers of a service agency as part of an organization for certain types of analysis, even though they are not within the formal boundary.

Exactly what is included within (1) an organization's boundary and (2) its relevant environment varies from organization to organization on the basis of the nature of the organization's goals, its internal structure, its relationships with other organizations, and many other factors (Figure 3–1), as we discussed in Chapter 2. So while we heuristically define here such concepts as "boundary" and "relevant environment," the exact operationalization and measurement of these concepts in any given organization must necessarily remain flexible. The specific location of an organization's boundary is admittedly often somewhat arbitrary, depending in part on the objectives of the researcher. In any event, the boundary as investigated does not always coincide with its official, formal specification; for instance, an organization may not consider its clients as within its boundary, but most analysts would feel it necessary to include the clientele in order to understand the functioning of the organization.

Research on Organizational Environments

One of the first organizational researches that took the environment into account was by the anthropologist W. Lloyd Warner, who studied how a change in the opportunities for acquiring social status in a community eventually led to a strike in the local factory (Warner and Low 1947). Warner had been involved relatively late in the Hawthorne studies, and his investigation of the factory strike helped the Human Relationists begin to look outside the organization for environmental influences on it.

But relatively little attention was given to the organization's environment until (1) the rise of open system theory as a dominant intellectual force in the field of organizational research, and (2) the publication of several influential books in the 1960s, each of which detailed empirical investigations of environment–organization interrelationships.

The more famous of these books was by Burns and Stalker (1961), who studied twenty English firms in electronics, rayon manufacturing,

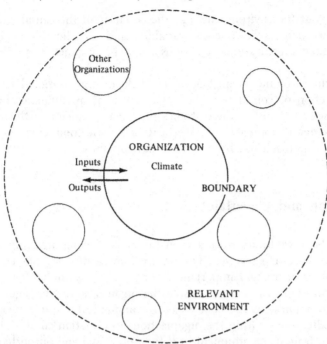

FIGURE 3-1. An organization's relevant environment consists of all factors outside of the system's boundary that are taken into consideration in the decision-making behavior of individuals in the system.

and engineering. They posited two types of management systems in these organizations: (1) "mechanistic," whose internal structures were appropriate in relatively stable environments, and (2) "organic," whose structures were suited to rapidly changing environments. Woodward (1958) surveyed a larger sample of 100 English manufacturing firms to show that particular management styles and organizational structures were needed in companies that used more complex, and less predictable, technologies of production. Their structure had to be able to cope with uncertainty from the external environment or from internal sources.

Finally, a monograph by Lawrence and Lorsch (1967) reported a study of ten American companies in plastics, food, and containers. The firms were selected to represent a range in the degree of diversity and uncertainty in their environments. The more effective organizations had an appropriate organizational structure for their environment; in particular, the more turbulent environments required a more differentiated and decentralized organizational structure. Lawrence and Lorsch (1967, p. 91) scored each organization's environment as to its degree of uncertainty for the firm's leaders, defined in terms of (1) the clarity of information they possessed about the environment, (2) the certainty of the causal relationships in the main environmental variables, and (3) how immediately feedback about organizational decisions could be obtained from the environment.

These three volumes helped move the field of organizational research in the direction of considering the environment as an influence on the system. However, none of these studies provided an adequate theoretical or methodological approach to investigating organization environments, and such an approach has been slow to develop since.

Information and Uncertainty

In this book we follow open system theory in viewing organizations as information-processing systems. This stance immediately implies that the environment is of primary importance. For often the stimulus for change in an organization comes from outside the organization: a change occurs in the organization's environment which is communicated to the members, leading to alterations within the organization. Information comes into the organization from its environment; it is then processed and outputted.

Organizations interact with their environments in order to cope with uncertainty, a lack of certain knowledge about future contingencies. We define *uncertainty* as the number of alternatives with respect to the occurrence of an event, together with the relative probabilities of these alternatives. Uncertainty implies a lack of order, of predictability, of stability.

Internally, structure gives an organization the capacity to cope with uncertainty. For instance, the hierarchy provides an expectation that an order will be carried out when it is passed from a superior to a subordinate. Of course, uncertainty can arise from within an organization as well as from external sources. For example, let's say that a chief decision maker leaves an organization and has to be replaced. This creates uncertainty among the organization members as to what to expect from the new boss. But the organizational structure helps cope with this internal uncertainty; it influences the new chief to follow policies similar to those of any predecessor. Most organizational uncertainty, however, probably arises externally in the environment, rather than internally.

Information is a change in the probability that some alternative will occur in a given situation. Information thus represents a reduction in uncertainty. An organization is constantly trying to gain information from its environment about the likelihood that some event might happen and thus reduce its uncertainty. For example, a business firm has a market research department to measure changes in its customers' likely buying behavior. An army unit has an intelligence section in order to learn as much as possible about the likely actions of the enemy. These boundary-spanning mechanisms allow the organization to gain information about certain alternatives, and thus reduce its uncertainty.

Inputs and Outputs

An organization is tied in to its environment through both its inputs and its outputs. *Inputs* to a system are the matter–energy and information absorbed by the system from its environment. These inputs may be raw materials, as an automobile manufacturer uses steel, rubber, plastics, fabrics, and human effort. The steel mill that supplies the auto company in turn inputs raw materials like iron ore, coal, electricity, and chemicals. The steel mill also inputs information, in the sense of orders placed by the auto company for certain types of steel. And the auto manufacturer subsequently inputs a variety of information: customer orders for new cars, governmental regulations specifying more stringent safety standards, and news of foreign imports. Inputs are equally important, although of a different nature, in a people-processing organization such as a hospital: supplies of drugs, food, and bed linens; sick and injured patients who come to be cured; and a staff of doctors, interns, nurses, and administrators.

Some systems theorists distinguish between two kinds of inputs to a system: (1) *maintenance inputs*, which energize the system and make it ready to function, and (2) *signal inputs*, which provide the system with information to be processed (Berrien 1968, pp. 26–27). Inputs consist of either matter–energy or information; most organizations take in both matter–energy and information from their environment, often at the same time. We usually just speak of "inputs." If the organization is mostly an information-processing system (like a newspaper or television station, for example), it is understood that the inputs are mainly of a signal nature. If the organization mainly processes materials (like a steel mill, for example), only some of the inputs are informational.

Outputs of a system are the information, matter–energy, and other products that the system discharges into its environment. These outputs may represent new cars, steel ingots, healthy people, or words, depending on the goal of the organization.

Obviously there must be a relationship between inputs and outputs. If the demand for the output of a system changes, information about this altered demand must reach the organization as an input, thus leading to an appropriate change in the rate or type of output. For example, in the late 1960s United States universities stopped growing so rapidly; as a consequence, government and foundation funds for graduate fellowships decreased and graduate schools cut down on their rate of producing new college professors (Zaltman and others, 1973).

We see from this illustration that feedback as a result of the output of an open system eventually returns as an informational input to the system. When the demand for new Ph.D.'s fell, feedback to the universities from their environment told them to slow down their rate of production. Such negative feedback from the environment acts as a self-regulating device to constantly correct and adjust the internal processes of an open system to the changes occurring in its environment.

Measuring Environmental Dimensions

Social systems like organizations usually lack the fixed physical structure of biological and other physical systems, and this is one reason why it may be difficult in the case of social systems to precisely specify the system boundary. Some organizations have more sharply defined boundaries than others; for example, a military unit or a mental hospital has very definite boundaries of membership.

In the earliest organizational studies, environments were conceived very broadly as the general social, economic, and political conditions in which a system operated. Thus environment was a residual category: it consisted of everything that was outside of the organization's boundary.

Obviously, this conception of environment had to be tightened up if it was to be measurable, and useful, in explaining organizational behavior. So the definition of environment was narrowed to comprise those individuals, groups, and other organizations with which an organization potentially interacts in making decisions (Emery and Trist 1965; Duncan 1972). A variety of terms have been given to this more restricted meaning, such as the "task environment" (Dill 1958) or the "interorganizational field" (Warren 1967). We prefer to use "relevant environment" (Duncan 1972; Zaltman and others 1973). In this narrower sense, the environment consists of those units relevant or potentially relevant to the organization's operations: for example, customers, suppliers, competitors, and regulations.

Environmental variables are usually measured in terms of either: (1) the *perceptions* of organizational members of the nature of their environment, or (2) the reported *communication relationships* of the organization with other units in its environment. The Lawrence and Lorsch (1967) study, mentioned previously, is an example of the perceptions approach; officials were asked whether they considered their organizational environment (1) simple or complex, on the basis of the number of factors they took into consideration in making decisions, and (2) static or dynamic, based on whether the environment remained the same or was in a continuous state of change. The degree of uncertainty faced by an organization seems to depend, in part, on these dimensions: *the greatest degree of uncertainty for an organization occurs when its environment is complex and rapidly changing.*

Another approach to measuring environments amounts to counting the number of communication relationships or other reciprocations with units in the organization's environment. For example, Aiken and Hage (1968) tabulated the number of joint programs (such as clients or personnel exchanged with other organizations, financial support from other agencies, and activities with other organizations) as a measure of an organization's dependence on its environment.

Both of these measures of environmental variables can be provided by the organization's leaders. Another means of measuring environmental variables is to perform a network analysis of the organization along with other organizations in the environment. Rogers (1974) obtained sociometric data from top administrators in 159 community development organizations in sixteen Iowa counties. He constructed indexes of centrality, cohesion, etc., for the network of 159 organizations, and measured the degree to which a given organization was connected to this larger network.

Boundary-Spanning Cosmopolites

While we often think of organizations as being relatively open or closed to their environment, this quality is in fact usually provided by certain *individuals* in the system. The individuals who provide an organization with openness are called "cosmopolites" or "boundary-spanners" (Thompson 1967). In most structures, cosmopolites are concentrated at the very top and at the bottom. At the top, executives travel widely and enjoy other types of contact with other organizations in the environment; they are in a position to obtain new ideas from sources external to their own organization. But most of their contact with the environment is at a relatively high level; they gather information about the "big picture" of changes in the environment without usually knowing the fine details.

In contrast, those individuals near the bottom of the organizational hierarchy also have a certain degree of "cosmopoliteness." For instance, in a product or service organization, lower-level workers deal most directly with customers and clients, with incoming materials and energy, and with other operational-level information. To the extent that these workers are able to transmit their knowledge of external conditions to top leaders through upward vertical flows, this knowledge can lead to appropriate organizational change.

Janowitz and Delany (1957) found that in three organizations in Detroit (a school, an unemployment compensation agency, and a retirement insurance agency), lower-level workers were superior to higher officials in functional knowledge about clients. The higher-level officials tended to outscore the workers, however, with respect to other types of knowledge that did not rest on contact with the environment of clients, such as substantive expertise.

"Most staff positions in an organization entail a high degree of contact with the environment: The personnel man recruits and discharges employers, the accountant records the intake and outflow of money, marketing predicts demand, and the R & D unit searches for technical developments that could lead to new products" (Perrow 1970a, p. 55). These are important contact points that organizations have in their transactions with their environments.

Thompson (1967) argues that organizations with complex environments tend to create specialized units to deal with inputs from their environment. The top executives and boundary-spanners act as buffers for the organization in protecting its "core technology" from environmental influences.

"Buffering" reduces the directness of environmental changes on an organization (Thompson 1967). For instance, when supplies of energy-producing materials threatened to be in short supply in the United States in 1974, many industrial plants stockpiled to maintain a steady input in the face of uncertain supplies; this strategy helped protect the system from perturbations in the environment.

Similarly, information may be stockpiled, in the person of boundary-spanners. Such a surveillance function is stressful for the individual, as it puts him in a marginal position between two or more systems.

Cosmopolites act as the open doors and windows of an organization, allowing for a cross-ventilation of new ideas. We discuss the cosmopolite role in more detail in Chapter 5.

COPING WITH THE ENVIRONMENT: THE TVA AND COOPTATION

The Tennessee Valley Authority (TVA) was created as part of the "New Deal" legislation of President Franklin Delano Roosevelt in the

Depression days of the 1930s. Its purpose was to provide electrical power, to prevent floods by constructing dams on rivers, to manufacture chemical fertilizer, and generally to bring about socioeconomic development in the Appalachian region of the United States. The TVA was essentially a government-financed but autonomous administrative agency.

Immediately after its creation, the TVA faced tremendous difficulties in simply surviving. Many political and business leaders perceived the TVA as representing a dangerous step toward socialistic planning. Federal agencies like the Soil Conservation Service and the land-grant universities and their agricultural extension services jealously viewed it as a rival that should be eradicated.

In the face of this threatening environment, the TVA had no choice but to join its enemies, which it could not "lick." This means of coping with an unfriendly environment was called "cooptation" by Philip Selznik (1949, p. 13), a sociologist who studied the TVA. *Cooptation* is the process of absorbing new elements into the leadership or policy-determining structure of an organization as a means of averting threats to its stability or existence. The TVA used many cooptation techniques, the most noted of which was its accommodation with the agricultural extension services in the Appalachian states. The TVA badly needed a channel for direct contact with farmers in the Tennessee Valley, in order to distribute the chemical fertilizers it manufactured and develop public support for its program. So the TVA made a contract with the extension services through which it contributed funds for the salaries of extension agents, who in turn promoted the diffusion of TVA fertilizer through demonstration farmers and its adoption throughout the Valley. Furthermore, representatives of the agricultural extension services and the land-grant universities were appointed to various policy-making boards and councils in the TVA. Many of the progressive ideals originally held by TVA officials had to be abandoned—or else they were subverted, in time, by the extension services. For example, early TVA policies called for concentrating the Authority's development assistance on smaller farmers, but accommodation with the extension services led to more contact with the relatively wealthier farmers.

A TVA official, quoted by Selznik (1949, p. 117), said: "In analyzing the relations between TVA and the extension service, the significant question for you to ask is whether the tail has not begun to wag the dog."

In concentrating on the mechanism of cooptation, Selznick was one of the first organizational theorists to realize the importance of an organization's relationship with its environment: "No organization subsists in a vacuum," he wrote (1949, p. 10). "Large or small, it must pay some heed to the consequences of its own activities (and even existence) for other groups and forces in the community."

The Environment and Organizational Innovation

"The interaction between the organization and its environment is crucial to the innovation process" (Zaltman and others, 1973, p. 120), and a number of researchers have investigated this relationship. In this section, we describe some main generalizations that have emerged from this research on the interaction between environment and organizational innovation (much further detail is provided in Chapter 6).

Many changes in an organization come about as a result of changes in the organization's environment. So for any organization to be innovative, it must have some degree of system *openness*, the exchange of information with its environment. New ideas often enter the organization across its boundaries, as does much of the information that creates the need for innovation, and so *openness to its environment facilitates an organization's innovativeness*.

Some organizations prefer not to be open, so as not to be innovative. For instance, a traditional mental hospital or a convent are rather completely insulated from their environment. They do not want to change. Many other organizations are selectively open to their environment, so as to intentionally pursue innovativeness.

An organization is more likely to innovate when its relevant environment is rapidly changing than when it is steady (Zaltman and others, 1973, p. 110). Rapid change in the environment leads to a need for rapid adjustment and change in the organization.

Organizations differ in the degree to which their decisions and actions are affected by the environment. This variable was termed "system connectedness" by Emery and Trist (1965), but we prefer to call the concept *external accountability*, the degree to which an organization is dependent on, or responsive to, its environment. An environment may be turbulent or placid, but this might not affect the organization's rate of innovation unless the organization is to some extent responsive to its environment. *Organizations which seek to control their environment rather than merely adjust to it, are more innovative.*

Performance gaps are discrepancies between an organization's expectations and its actual performance (Downs 1967, p. 169). This difference in how an organization's members perceive its performance in comparison to what they feel it should be can be a strong impetus for innovation.

One way in which system openness and environmental turbulence lead to innovation may be through the intervening variable of perceived performance gaps. "Performance gaps appear more frequently and expand faster in [organizations] dealing with rapidly changing external environments than in those dealing with relatively stable ones" (Downs 1967, p.

208). *Innovation in organizations is often motivated by performance gaps, which are more likely to occur in organizations with rapidly changing environments.*

PERCEIVED ENVIRONMENT AND
INNOVATION IN AGENCY A AND B

One of the authors recently was involved in conducting a comparative study of two organizations that differed widely in innovativeness. Both Agency A (a highly innovative system) and Agency B (an uninnovative organization) are located in small cities of similar size, both have about the same number of employees, and both reach about the same number of clients per year. The agencies are private organizations providing free family planning services to the public. Why is Agency A so much more innovative than Agency B? The answer lies in the agencies' relationships with their environments, as they perceive them.

Agency B is highly constrained by its environment: it perceives that its freedom to follow a course of action is limited by outside forces that are beyond its ability to manipulate. Its relationship to the environment is thus highly reactive, and its policies are shaped by anticipation of what the environment will do next to the organization, rather than by a sense of the power of the organization to shape its environment. We are describing the situation as it is perceived by Agency B, not necessarily as it in fact exists. Our investigation suggests that the organization is actually much less at the mercy of outside forces than it believes. Nevertheless, the environmental constraints are real to the organization. They may be grouped into three classes: funding, personnel, and the community.

Agency B appears to view its annual budget as a variety of divine gift, for which it should be duly thankful—and unquestioning. An enormous expansion of available funds occurred in 1969, when the federal government began supporting the agency, and a subsequent shrinkage of federal grants occurred in later years; both were treated as natural events over which Agency B had no control. The organization's efforts to raise money from the local community have been half-hearted at best; the successes are confined mainly to small grants from local foundations.

Each year's budget is approached with the attitude of "What activities can we support with the money that we have coming in?" rather than "Where can we get the money to carry out the program we want?" Even increases in funds reflect the organization's dependent relationship to its environment; a part of the original federal grant in 1969 had to be returned because of a perceived inability to utilize all the funds that were provided.

Just as this organization sees itself as limited by the funds which other systems make available to it, so it also sees itself as limited by the personnel available. The Board of Directors of Agency B is self-selecting, and it appears to seek elite individuals who are much like those already serving, instead of bringing in individuals who represent potential new areas of support or activity. The recent hiring of a new executive director consisted of reviewing applications that were received, rather than actively seeking candidates with certain needed qualities. In short, Agency B takes what it's offered in the way of personnel, and shapes its operations and structure to fit them.

Agency B is afraid of the community in which it is located, and sees itself as barely tolerated by a fundamentally conservative city. This perception makes the agency extremely defensive, apologetic, and reactive. It leads it to seek a low profile, to operate without publicity, and to limit its working relationships to only a few other service organizations. This perception constitutes a self-fulfilling prophecy in part: unless the organization moves outward into the community, it will remain marginal and vulnerable.

This apologetic attitude is further reflected in the agency's perception of its clientele. They are defined almost wholly in terms of who walks through the door of the agency's clinics. In the past four years, there has been a virtual explosion in the number of middle-class teenagers seeking contraceptive services, even though the only publicity about these services was through client word of mouth. This new clientele is regarded very gingerly by Agency B; there is a fear that some of the teenagers' parents might object and cause a public confrontation. Again, the low self-concept of Agency B leads to low performance in meeting a new need for its services.

In contrast to its counterpart, Agency A actively searches for new sources of funding, both in the state capital and in Washington, D. C. The executive director is an officer in a national federation of family planning agencies (which he helped found), and he uses this position to "sniff out" likely sources of federal funds; as a result, Agency A is usually one of the first to apply for new types of grants. This executive is an aggressive combatant with his environment, and he obviously enjoys playing the game of machinations involved in acquiring sufficient resources for his agency. He relished describing to research interviewers the way in which he selected his Board of Directors so as to avail the agency of their technical skills and political connections. The city in which Agency A is located is highly Catholic, and there is some religious opposition to family planning (actually somewhat more than in Agency B's city), but this does not seem to affect the activities of Agency A.

The staff of Agency A feel highly competent in their specialties, and are encouraged by the executive director to share their ideas for improving their jobs. Once each week, after the staff meeting, the executive director meets privately with each of the five department heads to discuss their problems individually. Much attention is given to innovation, and Agency A ranks as the most innovative of any family planning organization in its state. New contraceptive methods, additional client services (like infertility counseling and abortion), and new equipment have been added by Agency A in the past year.

The most important innovation was installation of a computerized client record system. When federal funds first became available in 1969, the agency found that the federal government required fifty-seven items of information on each client visit to the agency's clinics. With thousands of clients visiting the agency each month, two clerks were kept busy full-time just tabulating these data and mailing them to Washington. In 1972, the executive director convinced a local university professor on the Board of Directors of the agency, to design a computerized system that would not only fulfill the federal requirements but also allow analysis of the agency's operations by its staff so as to (1) obtain feedback and (2) decrease the uncertainty inherent in the agency's environment. For example, once the computerized system became operational, it was possible to immediately detect a shift in the agency's clientele from the poverty class (for which federal funds are provided) to middle-class teenagers (for which they are not). By knowing precisely the nature of this trend, the executive director was able to plan for its consequences before they occurred—such as by opening special "teen clinics." It was possible for Agency A to secure a special federal grant to cover the costs of installing the computer system—which were not all that much anyway, as the local university provided free computer time.

Thus we see that Agency A's greater degree of innovativeness is in part due to the control it exerts over its environment.

Organizational Climates

We have defined an organizational environment as lying entirely outside of the system's boundary. But there are physical and social factors somewhat akin to an environment which are located *within* the boundary of the organization; most scholars refer to these as the "climate" of the organization in order to avoid semantic confusion with the concept of "environment." A system's *climate* is the state of its internal nature, as perceived by its members.

We know from a number of studies that *an organization's climate exerts a strong influence on its members' behavior.* For example, the Hawthorne studies illustrated the importance of the climate of work groups.

Two small cliques were found in the Bank Wiring Room, one with a norm of high productivity and the other with an opposite norm (Homans 1950, pp. 54–72). In Chapter 5 we shall describe how these two differing climates had a *systems effect* (the influences of others in a system on the behavior of an individual member in the system) with regard to the workers' productivity in the Hawthorne plant.

Another illustration of the influence of organizational climates on individual behavior is provided by a study of the International Typographical Union (ITU) by Lipset and others (1956). This union is somewhat distinctive in the United States in that it has maintained a strong two-party system among its members. The research indicated a strong effect of the union local's political climate on the members' voting behavior. An individual with conservative political views might often vote for a liberal candidate if his close friends in the union, the members of his union shop, and the chairman of his local union favored the liberal candidate (Lipset and others, 1956, p. 383). Two different union locals might have widely different voting patterns: Local A votes 90 percent for the liberal candidate, while Local B votes only 20 percent. Each union local is associated with a different newspaper; for example, Local A may be the printers who work for the *New York Times*, while the members of Local B work for another newspaper. One might guess that the voting differences stem from the fact that the two newspapers employ somewhat different kinds of printers. Not so, find Lipset and others (1956, p. 386): "The *same kinds of men act differently* in the various shops, due to different atmospheres [climates] created by the most active and most ideologically sensitive men in the shop" (italics in original).

Presumably an organizational climate exerts its influence on members' behavior through interpersonal communication processes, a topic we explore in depth in Chapter 5 on network analysis.

Summary

We propose in this chapter that an open system framework is the most meaningful way presently available of looking at organizations in general and communication systems in particular. An open system approach to understanding organizations necessitates important consideration of the organization's environment. Accordingly, we place special emphasis on the environment of the organization, and on how communication to and from this environment affects the organization.

A *system* is a set of units that has some degree of structure, and that is differentiated from its environment by a boundary. An *open system* continuously exchanges information with its environment; it is this exchange which allows an open system to avoid running down through entropic processes. An open system has the following constituent elements: (1) inputs, (2) processes, (3) outputs, (4) feedback, (5) environment, and (6) communication.

The Scientific Management and Human Relations schools mainly looked *within* organizational boundaries to find explanations for the behavior of the system's members. The prevalant reference to the physical sciences as the model for studying organizations led to a closed system viewpoint in early social science studies. The book which revitalized the investigation of organizational behavior, by Daniel Katz and Robert L. Kahn (1966), established the "organization in an environment" as the main unit of study.

The *environment* is the totality of physical and social factors external to the system's boundary that are directly taken into consideration in the decision-making behavior of individuals in the system. Where does the organization stop and its environment begin? Every investigator of organizational behavior has to decide for himself the boundary of the unit under study. Hence the boundary, and with it the relevant environment of the organization, varies according to the purposes of the analyst.

Three main investigations have affected present thinking about organizations and their environments: (1) Burns and Stalker (1961); (2) Woodward (1958, 1965), who postulated a model of organization based on its "technological" environment; and (3) Lawrence and Lorsch (1967), who brought forward the "differentiated" and "integrated" environmental variables to the study of the "organization in an environment."

Information, a change in the probability that some alternative will occur in a given situation, reduces uncertainty in organizations as they interact with their environments. *Uncertainty* is the number of alternatives with respect to the likely occurrence of an event together with the relative probabilities of these alternatives.

An organization is tied to its environment through both its inputs and its outputs. The *inputs* to a system are the matter–energy and information absorbed by the system from its environment. The *outputs* of a system are the information, matter–energy, and other products that the system discharges into its environment.

Openness, the exchange of information by the system with its environment, facilitates an organization's innovativeness. When the environment is turbulent and rapidly changing, an organization is more likely to be innovative. *External accountability* is the degree to which an organization is dependent on, or responsible to, its environment. Organizations which try to control their environment rather than merely adjust to them, are more innovative. One impetus for innovation in organizations is provided by *performance gaps,* discrepancies between an organization's expectations and its actual performance. Performance gaps are more likely to be perceived by an organization when its environment is turbulent.

An organization's *climate* is the state of its internal nature, as perceived by its members. Researchers show that a system's climate can exert a strong influence on the members' behavior.

4. The Effect of Organizational Structure on Communication Behavior

"At the very highest level there is very little knowledge. They do not understand the opinion of the masses. . . . Their bureaucratic manner is immense. They beat their gongs to blaze the way. They·cause people to become afraid just by looking at them."

—Mao Tse-tung

"O it is excellent to have a giant's strength; but it is tyrannous to use it like a giant."

—William Shakespeare

In this chapter, we look at a variety of researches that deal with the relationship of organizational structure and communication behavior. Most of this work assumes that structure determines communication behavior, but in a later section of this chapter we also review research and experience bearing on the opposite relationship: viz., that communication determines organizational structure. This viewpoint of the reversed relationship is not very commonly espoused in the literature so far.

Our concern in this chapter is mostly with communication within organizations, as our previous chapter dealt with communication between the organization and its environment. Our first step is to probe the nature of structure.

What Is Structure?

Structure is the arrangement of the components and subsystems within a system. It refers to the patterns of relationships among the units in a social system, relationships which may be expressed in terms of power, status, or other variables. Structure can be understood in terms of its various dimensions, like the degree of formalization, centralization, delegation of authority, etc. Structure exists in a system to the extent that the units in the system are differentiated from each other. Organizational structure refers to the properties of an organization, not those of its members (Blau and Meyer 1971, p. 80). For example, hierarchy is a property of an organization, not of an individual in an organization (although the existence of a hierarchy may of course affect the individual's behavior).

The organization maximizes its effectiveness in achieving its goals by requiring its members to work with certain individuals and not with others, to take orders from some persons and not from others, and generally to behave according to the way which the organization's formal structure dictates. So the organization's structure acts as a constraint on the individual's behavior; or, in other words, it is structure that makes an individual's behavior distinctive in an organization. In this chapter we explore just how this is so.

THE ORGANIZATION CHART AND THE FORMAL STRUCTURE OF AN ORGANIZATION

An organization chart, sometimes also called an "organigram," is a description of the formal structure in an organization (Fig. 4-1). The lines connecting the boxes show the *authority*[1] and formal communication relationships among the position. "An organizational chart is like an x-ray of the hierarchical structure within an organization" (Argyris 1974, p. 1).

When we look at an organization chart, we can learn much about a system's operation and about its formal communication channels. Even though an organization chart fails to capture the total dynamics of human interaction, it nevertheless provides much information in a convenient way, partly because "the organization usually has come to consider relationships in terms of the dimensions of the chart" (Cyert and March 1963, p. 289). Thus the organigram not only expresses the expected patterns of formal communication, but also acts as a self-fulfilling prophecy to guide these patterns in the directions that it dictates.

The structure of a social system is not as visible (at least not in the same way) as in biological or mechanical systems. It often cannot be seen, but must be inferred from actual operations and/or from the organization chart. The formal structure consists of the patterns of formal relationships and duties, job descriptions, formal rules, operating policies,

---

[1] *Authority* is that ability to influence others that is sanctioned and viewed as legitimate by members of a system. For example, a company president is perceived by the company employees as having the authority to ask them to work overtime.

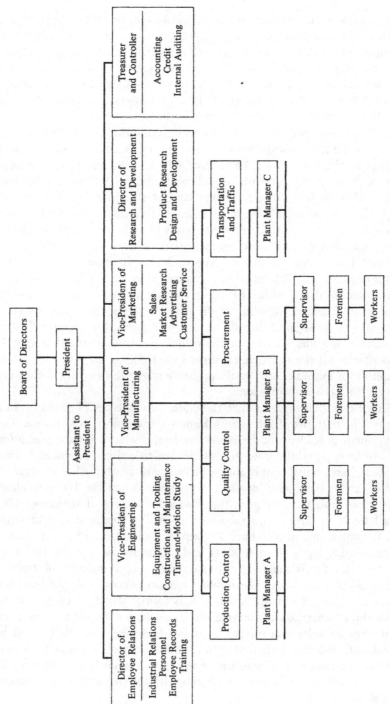

FIGURE 4-1.   Simplified Organization Chart of a Typical Manufacturing Company

work procedures, compensations and rewards, etc. In other words, organizational structure consists of those aspects of the patterns of behavior in the organization that are relatively stable and that change only slowly. In fact, *one purpose of structure is to provide stability, regularity, and predictability to the organization.* It is the presence of structure in an organization that makes human behavior in organizations somewhat different from that occurring in other contexts.

In one sense, structure is the lack of randomness and the presence of pattern in the relationships between units in a system. Let's say we bring together in the same place 100 individuals who are complete strangers. Perhaps they are army recruits, or college freshmen. Within a very short time, as they begin to interact, some kind of structure will begin to develop. Certain individuals begin to assume leadership roles, while others are influenced by them. Certain persons will talk more with particular others, and thus patterns of communication emerge. These patterns provide useful knowledge to anyone who understands them, as they lend a certain degree of predictability to the question of who will communicate with whom. So if one wishes to send a message from any given individual to someone else, understanding of the patterns or structure provides clues about how to do so most directly or most effectively. Or if one wished to introduce a new idea to any one individual, and have it spread as quickly as possible to all the other ninety-nine, knowledge of the structure would be useful; for example, one would probably start the new idea with a key leader who has many followers.

Our illustration suggests that there are various types of structure in a system. The patterns of interaction form a communication structure. The arrangement of leaders and followers constitutes what is often called a formal structure, especially if we give the leaders titles like "president," "vice-president," etc., which imply that a hierarchy of positions has emerged.

All systems have some degree of structure. When the 100 individuals initially assembled as strangers, they had a low degree of structure. After several hours or days of interaction, they had a greater degree of structure. Organizations usually have a relatively high degree of structure, and this patterning lends them stability and predictability. Usually the structure becomes formalized; for example, after several months of training and experience, certain of the military recruits become corporals and sergeants while others remain privates. This formal structure exists because it aids the organization in carrying out its goals; for instance, when a sergeant gives an order to a private, there is a high likelihood that it will be carried out. But the formal structure never completely explains or predicts the behavior of the members of the system, even in the most rigidly structured systems, as numerous communication researches in organizations show.

RUMORS AND THE INFORMAL COMMUNICATION STRUCTURE

In addition to the formal structure of hierarchical statuses and patterned communication flows, every system has an informal structure that is also very much present.[2] "Both formal and informal systems are necessary for group activity, just as two blades are essential to make a pair of scissors workable. Both formal and informal organizations comprise the social system of a work group" (Davis 1967, p. 212).

As discussed in the previous chapter, one of the surprising findings of the Hawthorne studies was the important role of informal communication relationships in determining worker productivity. Informal communication may be vertical—upward or downward—or horizontal—in or out of departments (Hage 1974, p. 156). The formal and informal communication channels in an organization are usually complementary and substitutable (Downs 1967, pp. 113–14). Sometimes a considerable overlap occurs between the formal organizational structure and the informal communication patterns (Allen and others 1971), but sometimes they are quite distinct.

This interrelationship is illustrated in Figure 4–2. As we show in our discussion of network analysis (Chapter 5), the degree to which the informal communication behavior corresponds to the formal structure is sometimes used as an indicator of the adequacy of the formal structure, and of formal communication within the organization.

Factors affecting the informal structure are proximity and mutual at-

FIGURE 4–2. The formal structure and the informal structure of an organization usually overlap and tend to complement each other.

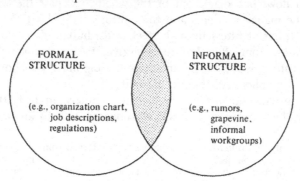

FORMAL STRUCTURE

(e.g., organization chart, job descriptions, regulations)

INFORMAL STRUCTURE

(e.g., rumors, grapevine, informal workgroups)

[2] By failing to perceive this informal structure, the Scientific Management school may have presented an overly rational picture of organizational behavior (Brewer 1971).

tractiveness of individuals who interact in work activities, and also their similarity of values and social characteristics such as social class, status, income, etc. In any organization, there is often a certain degree of discrepancy between the formal, official structure and the informal, unofficial behavior. Pointing out this discrepancy is "one of the true delights of the organizational experts" (Perrow 1972, p. 62). There are many reasons for such discrepancy: (1) the formal structure is always somewhat out-of-date; (2) it deals primarily with routine situations, and not as well with the nonroutine; and (3) it seldom makes the fine distinctions that are necessary in every specific event. In certain types of organizations, like prisons, informal communication networks are in open conflict with the formal structure (Tichy 1973). In the whole, the formal structure provides a limited perspective in understanding organizational behavior.

"I HEARD IT THROUGH THE GRAPEVINE": RUMORS

The informal structure is generally a breeding place for rumors. A *rumor* is an unconfirmed message transmitted along interpersonal channels.[3] Or, more technically, "rumor is grapevine information which is communicated without secure standards of evidence being present" (Davis 1967, p. 268). Managers may try to cultivate the grapevine themselves; they may as well, because the grapevine "cannot be abolished, rubbed out, hidden under a basket, chopped down, tied up, or stopped. It is as hard to kill as the mythical glass snake which when struck, broke into fragments and grew a new snake out of each piece," says Keith Davis,[4] a professor of management at Arizona State University, who has been studying rumors in organizations for twenty years. Professor Davis advises that wise organization leaders should "feed, water, and cultivate the grapevine." This amounts to telling the truth, and telling it early.

Rumors spread quickly. "With the rapidity of a burning powder train, information flows like magic out of the woodwork, past the water fountain, past the managers' doors and the janitor's mop closet. As elusive as a summer zephyr, it filters through steel walls, bulkheads or construction glass partitions, from office boy to executive."[5] Almost anyone can be a target: "[A rumor] will carve up and serve the big brass, the shop foreman, and the stenographer with fine impartiality."[6]

Rumors usually do not follow official channels; in fact, this is one reason why they spread so quickly. Anyone can talk to anyone about a

---

[3] We do not imply that *rumors* are synonymous with informal communication, as much informal communication deals with verifiable information. Only a small portion of the informal communication in an organization typically consists of rumors.

[4] In *Time* magazine, June 18, 1973.

[5] Taken from Joseph K. Shepard, *Indianapolis Star Magazine*, 1959.

[6] Ibid.

rumor. Indeed, rumors are almost entirely oral, and the fact that they are not written allows them to jump the formal channels of communication. Yet there is usually *some* degree of predictability to how a rumor will spread in a given organizational setting (Sutton and Porter 1968).

One might expect that a rumor would be a grossly unreliable source of information, but in fact most rumors that have actually been studied in organizations turn out to have been reasonably accurate (Pool 1973, p. 13) although, in many cases, somewhat distorted. Often it is the kernel of truth on which a rumor is based that gives it believability.

BUREAUCRACY

One means of understanding the nature of formal structure is to look at organizations that possess a very high degree of formalization: bureaucracies. The French root of "bureaucracy" implies that its meaning derives from governmental organizations (that is, government by bureaus), but today, in English, we use the word to mean any type of organization with a high degree of formal structure.

Max Weber (1946), the great German sociologist of seventy years ago, claimed that bureaucracy was man's greatest social invention: "The decisive reason for the advance of bureaucratic organization has always been its purely technical superiority over any other form of organization" (Weber 1948).

Large-scale organization is a wonderful form of social technology, without which most of the benefits of modern life could not have been obtained. Bureaucracy, especially in the capitalistic nations of the West, can more efficiently coordinate the work of large numbers of individuals than organizational forms based on kinship or personal loyalty. Given that society has a need for the performance of certain tasks, then, there is a certain inevitability to bureaucracy. "Bureaucracy is a form of organization superior to all others we know or can hope to afford in the near and middle future; the chances of doing away with it or changing it are probably nonexistent in the West in this century" (Perrow 1972, p. 7).[7]

ELEMENTS OF BUREAUCRATIC STRUCTURE

The main characteristics of a bureaucracy, as originally identified by Max Weber and specified by many other organization scholars since, are (1) rules and regulations, (2) a specialized division of tasks, and (3) a hierarchy of formal positions that contributes to rational efficiency in per-

[7] By no means do all organization theorists agree. For example, Gouldner (1961, p. 82) says: "Instead of telling men how bureaucracy might be mitigated, [some social scientists] insist that it is inevitable."

forming the organizational tasks. "Precision, speed, unambiguity, knowledge of the files, continuity, discretion, unity, strict subordination, reduction of friction and of material and personal costs—these are raised to the optimum point in the strictly bureaucratic administration" (Weber 1948).

Rules and Regulations

Every bureaucratic organization has rules, and in most cases these are written out in a codified form as regulations. The purpose of rules is to justify already decided on behavior or to enable the organization members to cope with variability and complexity in the information that they process. For instance, the grading rules of universities provide a means for professors to classify all types of student performance into a small number of categories: A, B, C, and so forth. Such standardization of evaluation procedures provides many advantages to the university as an organization. An "A" grade to a student in one course can be averaged with a "C" grade in another, along with his other grades, to provide an overall picture of the student's performance (assuming, that is, that the university's rules have effectively standardized the meaning of each of the letter grades to all professors).

But there are certain disadvantages to having such rules, or at least to following them too rigidly, such as applying a set of rule-prescribed categories to specific situations where they may not be fully applicable. Rules should be thought of as providing a general framework, not as an exact set of prescriptions to be applied to *all* situations. For instance, most universities do not approve of a professor giving an "A" grade to every student in one of his or her classes, even though the professor may feel that such an exception to the grading rules might be justified on a rare occasion.

There are informal as well as formal rules in most organizations. For example, most professors understand that a higher proportion of "A" and "B" grades, and few "Cs", should be assigned to graduate students as compared to undergraduates, although this "rule" is usually not official.

One means of reducing the number of written rules in a bureaucratic organization is to employ personnel who already have internalized the relevant rules; these employees are usually called "professionals" (Perrow 1972, p. 27). Owing to their lengthy formal education and training, such professionals as engineers, teachers, scientists, social workers, and accountants already know, without having to consult rules, what to do in a great many organizational situations. And this is one reason why most organizations hire large numbers of professionals, even though they are relatively expensive (Hall 1968). In short, professionals generally make excellent bureaucrats.[8]

---

[8] Except, of course, when their professional goals conflict with the organization's goals. This may happen, for example, when the organization requires an individual to perform some behavior that he or she has been taught in their professional training to regard as unethical ("unprofessional").

Specialization

Professionals also facilitate a high degree of specialization in the work of various units within the bureaucracy. This division of labor usually has advantages in attaining a high level of efficiency. For instance, assembly-line manufacture of automobiles allows each worker to perform only a single, very specialized task, such as bolting on a fender to each of the hundreds of car bodies that pass by him on the assembly line. If each worker were required to assemble all the thousands of parts that make up a modern automobile, the rate of production of the factory would be much less.

Adam Smith, writing in his *The Wealth of Nations*, illustrated the advantages of a division of labor for higher productivity. Smith found that a worker by himself could produce about 20 pins a day. But if the work was broken down into 18 different and specialized tasks, and each worker performed one of these tasks, output jumped to 4,800 pins per worker—240 times what the worker could produce alone!

Hierarchy

The principle of hierarchy simply states that every member of an organization has one individual in a position above him from whom he mainly receives directions. As this boss also has a boss, who in turn also has a boss, the organizational hierarchy is so structured as to form a kind of pyramid, with authority and power concentrated at the top.[9] Hierarchy is the most characteristic aspect of a bureaucratic organization, even more so than rules and impersonality (Perrow 1972, p. 32).

A bureaucratic hierarchy has a powerful effect on communication behavior. For one thing, it tends to channel communication, at least formal communication, in largely vertical directions. Commands and instructions come down the organization; reports and other information go up.

Organizational hierarchy commonly discourages certain types of messages from being communicated. The nature of hierarchical structure, and the related reward system, discourages subordinates from passing bad news to their bosses (Wilensky 1967, pp. 42–48). So bureaucracy, even though its main advantage is to rationalize human behavior in organizations, can also lead to irrationality and inefficiency.

"BUREAUCRACY" AS A DIRTY WORD

Max Weber realized that bureaucracies had a contradictory nature, that even though they were intended to achieve rational efficiency, they could also at times be dysfunctional. If he were alive today, Weber would undoubtedly be surprised that "bureaucracy" has become a hated epithet, usually connoting red tape and inefficiency. "Bureaucracy" is "a dirty word,

[9] A hierarchy does not necessarily indicate the locus of power; it only shows the positions of individuals and their authority. A lower-ranked individual may have more power to influence other members than an executive near the top of the organization.

both to the average person and to many specialists on organizations" (Perrow 1970a, p. 50). Why did it become so?

Actually, all organizations of any size are bureaucratized to at least some degree. They have rules and regulations, a specialized division of tasks, a hierarchy of positions, and a certain machinelike impersonality in handling interpersonal relationships. These characteristics make for a tremendous efficiency in handling large-scale administrative tasks. But such a structure is also dehumanizing to the people who work in the organization, or who seek to deal with it as clients. Bureaucracies have the built-in potential of turning human beings into robots. As Max Weber described bureaucracy, it has the potential for removing much of human emotion from the social relationships in an organization. Love and hate, attraction and dislike, are all eliminated or deemphasized in a bureaucracy, so that human relationships become like well-oiled ball bearings.

Many attempts have been made by social scientists and others to redesign organizations so that certain of their advantages of efficiency and standardization can still be achieved while their main disadvantage of dehumanized personal relationships is minimized. For instance, Rensis Likert (1961, 1967) and his colleagues in the Institute for Social Research at the University of Michigan pioneered in redesigning organizational management so that it was more participatory: the workers and other operational-level employees were involved in certain important decisions through a system of committees and other procedures.

THE BLACK HOLE OF CALCUTTA AS A COMMUNICATION BREAKDOWN IN A BUREAUCRACY

In 1756, the Nawab of Calcutta, Siraj-ud-Dowla, led his Indian troops in a surprising uprising against the British East India Company fort and trading post at Calcutta. The attack was successful, and the British surrendered. The Nawab ordered his lieutenants to put the 146 British captives in prison for the night. The only facility available was a small dungeon, about 20 feet by 20 feet with two small windows, which the British had used to lock up an occasional thief caught stealing company property. It was known locally as the "Black Hole."

The Nawab gave the order to lock up the prisoners and promptly went to sleep for the night. All 146 of the British men, women, and children were forced into the small space, ordinarily sufficient for only about 10 prisoners. But orders were orders, and the Nawab's lieutenants carried them out. The crowded prisoners immediately began to fight for air, as claustrophobia seized them in the hot night. Some were trampled. Others went insane. Appeals to the guards, who dared not awaken the Nawab, were not answered.

In the morning, only 23 of the prisoners came out alive.

The Black Hole of Calcutta became a shocking symbol of inhumanity to the British in India, and a rallying cry that led to the eventual defeat of the Nawab by Robert Clive in the battle of Plassey, an historical event that marked the beginning of India as an English colony.

What caused the many deaths in the Black Hole of Calcutta? Watney (1974, p. 96) comments that the tragedy began with a "not very intelligent subordinate who . . . obeyed [orders] in too literal a fashion. Later, no one . . . dared to take the responsibility of releasing the prisoners on their own initiative. Tragedies are often caused by such acts of bureaucratic inefficiency."

ALIENATION ON THE ASSEMBLY LINE

The dreary monotony of assembly-line work is a serious human problem. Social science investigations of assembly-line workers by Walker and Guest (1952) and Chinoy (1955) emphasized the seriousness of such monotony for automobile workers. A former worker on an automobile assembly line, for example, recalls: "I used to work on the chassis line. When I used to get home my hands would go like that. [His hands shook helplessly.] . . . When I worked on the line I felt so bad that when I came home I couldn't do anything" (Chinoy 1955, p. 71).

The speed of the assembly line is mechanically set; the cars move down the conveyor belt at a predetermined rhythm. Workers cannot vary their pace at their own discretion, and they complain about the feeling of powerlessness, or loss of control, that this causes (Blauner 1964, p. 115). They feel chained to their machine. Unsurprisingly, then, as one assembly-line worker commented: "The guys yell 'hurrah' whenever the line breaks down" (Walker and Guest 1952, pp. 51–52).

Automobile assembly-line workers feel isolated as well as alienated because their automated jobs allow few opportunities for interpersonal communication (Faunce 1968, p. 3). This lack of opportunity for interaction breeds worker dissatisfaction, and most employees on assembly lines report hoping that the line will break down, so they can get at least a short break from its grinding boredom and be able to talk with each other (Chinoy 1955, p. 71).

Job Enrichment as an Antidote

Because this monotony and alienation often lead to lower production, as well as to such associated problems as absenteeism and high employee turnover, a great deal of organization research has focused on these issues and how to deal with them. One approach used by many companies is called "work redesign" or "job enrichment."[10] Sometimes the assembly line is dismantled and replaced by the pre–Henry Ford approach of having a small group of workers assemble the whole car, or at least a major sub-assembly of it. One of the best-known cases is the Volvo automobile company of Sweden, where the assembly line has been almost entirely replaced in recent years. The workers perform rotating tasks in small groups of three or four, with the team members deciding among themselves who will work on what part.

In an Indian cotton weaving mill, Rice (1958) made the workers' tasks interchangeable and formed semiautonomous work groups. As a result, morale increased, the rate of waste decreased, and production rose. More recently, Walton (1972) incorporated in the design of a new plant such features as autonomous work groups, job enrichment, and participatory decision making. The result? Lower overhead, reduced costs including lower labor requirements, and higher production.

Despite this recent focus, most assembly lines are still intact in larger manufacturing firms, and, more generally, the problems of monotony and alienation continue to plague most large and highly bureaucratic organizations, whether their work is done on an assembly line or not.

MAO TSE-TUNG'S ANTIBUREAUCRACY IN CHINA

One country and its top leader stand almost alone in attempting to find alternatives to Western-type bureaucracy. That is the People's Republic of China and its Chairman, Mao Tse-tung. For some fifteen years after 1949, when the Communists came to full power in China, the government was patterned after Russian-style bureaucracy, consisting of a hierarchy of specialized positions to which individuals were appointed and promoted on the basis of their technical competence.

As early as 1933, when the Communists controlled only a tiny portion of the country, Mao had complained: "This great evil, bureaucracy, must be thrown into the cesspool." Then, during the Cultural Revolution from 1966 to 1969, Mao directed a massive attack on the growing bureaucratization of Chinese society. Officeholders were publicly criticized for selfishly seeking power and advancement on the basis of their formal education.

---

[10] *Job enrichment* or *job enlargement* seeks to improve work efficiency and enhance employee satisfaction by building into individuals' jobs a greater scope for personal achievement and recognition and more challenging and responsible work, with a concomitantly greater opportunity for advancement and growth (Paul and Robertson, 1970, p. 17).

Thousands in high positions were put out of office and replaced by individuals who might be less expert or less skilled but who were politically more pure, as evidenced by their class origins, their loyalty to the Party, and their political enthusiasm (Whyte 1973). Dress and other symbols of status were standardized; for instance, all ranks and insignia of rank in the army were eliminated. The hierarchy of offices was deemphasized, and all officials were required to work with their hands in farms and factories for about a month each year. The Maoists instituted a participatory style of leadership and decision making in which subordinates take part. Requiring obedience to a superior just because of his higher formal position is considered "dulling the initiative of the masses." The ideal relationship is comradeship, rather than formalistic impersonality.

Universities were closed down, and when they were reopened the criteria for admission were changed to give priority to individuals who were sons and daughters of peasants and factory workers, and who were politically zealous. After graduation from high school or college, young people were ordered to live in remote villages for the rest of their lives. If they served the people in a highly altruistic and devoted way, after some years they might be admitted to a university for further training.

Through these steps, the bureaucratic form of organization in China was replaced by a Maoist model for development. Until the Chinese experience, most observers had felt that Max Weber (1968, p. 225) had been essentially correct in concluding that formal bureaucratization would increase in socialist, as well as capitalist, countries as they became more developed. But as the Maoist critique of bureaucracy has become widely understood outside of China, many organization scholars have realized that bureaucratization is not an inevitable ingredient of socioeconomic development and may not be totally appropriate to all developing countries (Whyte 1973).

Structure's Effect on Communication [11]

Communication in an organization occurs in a highly structured context. How does this structure affect communication behavior? Generally, the organizational structure limits and guides communication flows. Just by knowing the formal structure of an organization (as from its organization chart), we can usually predict a great deal about the nature of the communication flows within it.

[11] Certain ideas in the following section originally appeared in Rogers and Agarwala–Rogers (1975a), and are used by permission.

RESTRICTED FLOWS AND INFORMATION OVERLOAD

There is a common misconception about communication problems in organizations: viz., that the main problem is restricted flows, and that the solution is to unclog blocked communication channels. "The discovery of the crucial role of communication led to an enthusiastic advocacy of increased information as the solution to many organizational problems. More and better communication (especially more) was the slogan" (Katz and Kahn 1966, pp. 224–25). But the probem, and hence the solution, is often just the opposite: the major communication problem is often *information overload* (Figure 4–3),[12] to which the solution is obviously less, not more, communication.

Similarly, Read (1962) cites what might be called the myth of freer communication in an organization: "There seems to be a widely held notion that for organizations to function effectively, information must flow freely and unrestricted upward, downward, and across. . . . Once a power hierarchy of virtually any kind comes into existence, information-exchange

FIGURE 4–3. Information overload occurs when communication inputs are too excessive to be processed, leading to breakdown.

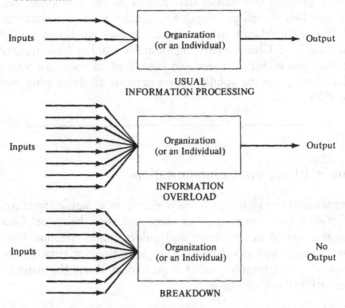

[12] *Information overload* is the state of an individual or a system in which excessive communication inputs cannot be processed and utilized, leading to breakdown.

is no longer free but restricted, shaped and controlled." We thus see that *one of the most important functions of organizational structure is to restrict communication flows, and thus decrease problems of information overload.*

Indeed, communication research has shown that freer or less restricted communication flows may cause problems more often than it solves them. The degree of information overload in his organization became so serious that the New York City Superintendent of Schools recently ordered a moratorium on all written reports, complaining that "the number of unnecessary—and often unread—reports is beyond belief."

An organization's structure must operate so as to condense information, or else its higher officials will drown in a sea of paper. Suppose, for example, that each official on the bottom rung of a seven-tier hierarchy generates one unit of information. If the average span of control is four, then 4,096 units of data are produced per time period at the bottom rung (Downs 1967, p. 117). At each of the six higher rungs, half of the data are usually screened out, so that only 1/64 of all data gets through to the top boss (and 98.4 percent has been screened out).

An individual who is overloaded not only is inefficient himself, but, as he is integrated into communication networks with other individuals in the organization, is the cause of inefficiency in others. "The overloaded individual is as likely to neglect obligations to other group members, thereby increasing their error, as he is to neglect his own control responsibilities" (Lanzetta and Roby 1957).

In fact, one consequence of information overload for one individual in an organization is to cause information overload for others in the organization. "Under pressure that greater amounts of required communication be handled at once, the individuals . . . probably neglected to forward some problem-relevant information and/or duplicate previously-forwarded information; this in turn gives rise to information-seeking questions. These questions, because answers are required, further increase the communication load" (Shelly and Gilchrist 1958, p. 43).

Unfortunately, "when channels prove to be reliable in their regularity, and when there seldom is omission or inaccuracy, these very channels will tend to be used more often. But this greater usage will increase the likelihood of the channel being overloaded, thereby making it less reliable and less accurate" (Guetzkow 1965, p. 561). We all know the expression: "If you want a job done right, give it to a busy man." The consequence: even greater overload for those who are already overloaded.

Organizations use a number of ways to cope with information overload, as Miller (1960 and 1962), Platt and Miller (1969), and Meier (1963) note. A typical response is for the organization to increase the input–output channels; for example, if an individual is overloaded, he is given an assistant. Or the overload may be handled by filtering out certain categories of input; an example would be an officeholder who simply ignores all third-class mail. Another way of coping with overload is queuing, the delaying of information processing during periods of peak load in the hope of catching up during lulls. This is what we do when we take work home, or with us on a vacation.

The ideal communication system is one in which flows are at least partially restricted,[13] and in which the structure is so designed that information reaches those locations at which it is most needed, and only those. Thus, in most organizations, direct communication with one's boss's boss is discouraged (Figure 4–4). The boss acts as a gatekeeper[14] in screening the messages that reach the higher official, thus preventing an overload of communication messages. Decreasing inputs to the overloaded unit is the best cure for information overload. Methods of coping with information overload amount to restricting communication flows, usually by restricting the accessibility of individuals to certain sources. We conclude that *organizational structure can restrict the accessibility of receivers to sources, and thus help to deal with the problem of information overload* (Rogers 1973, p. 333). Bureaucracies can deal with information overload more readily than other types of organizations.

FIGURE   4–4.   Organizational structure can restrict communication flows so as to prevent information overload.

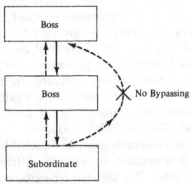

DISTORTION AT MY LAI

The echelons (or levels of responsibility) in a hierarchy especially act as points in an organizational structure at which distortion is likely to

[13] Although if the communication flows are too highly structured, it is possible that "information underload" might occur (Danowski 1975).

[14] A *gatekeeper* is an individual who is located in a communication structure so as to control the messages flowing through a communication channel.

occur, both in command messages flowing downward and in reports flowing upward (Miller 1972). Such distortion seems to have been responsible for the My Lai massacre of Vietnamese civilians by American troops in 1968.

Newspaper reporters in Vietnam at the time observed that Army orders tended to be interpreted quite broadly, and frequently with distortion, as they passed from echelon to echelon down the chain of command. For instance, a war correspondent was present when a hamlet was burned down by the United States Army's First Air Cavalry Division. Inquiry showed that the order from division headquarters to the brigade was: "On no occasion must hamlets be burned down."

The brigade radioed the battalion: "Do not burn down any hamlets unless you are absolutely convinced that the Vietcong are in them."

The battalion radioed the infantry company at the scene: "If you think there are any Vietcong in the hamlet, burn it down."

The company commander ordered his troops: "Burn down that hamlet."

DISTORTION AND OMISSION

Ironically, solutions to the problem of overload usually create other problems. *The solutions to problems of information overload in an organization which restrict communication flows, such as gatekeeping, filtering, and queuing, tend to cause problems of distortion and omission. Distortion* is the transformation of the meaning of a message by changing its content. *Omission* is the deletion of all or part of a message.

How do organizations typically deal with problems of omission and distortion?

1. *Redundancy* is the repeating of a message in different forms, over different channels, or over time. For instance, written messages are one means of providing redundancy over time, because such messages can be read and reread. If an official has reason to doubt the accuracy with which events are reported by those under his authority, he may establish two or more channels (sometimes competitively) to report the same event. "The classic antidote for monopoly is competition" (Downs 1967, p. 119).

2. *Verification* is insuring the accuracy of a previous message. When bias is suspected in a message, an individual often seeks to obtain a counterbias, so that differences in interpretation then can be isolated.

"The recipients of information at each level in the hierarchy are well aware that the data they get is distorted. Every general was once a lieutenant and remembers the type of distortion he used when he forwarded information to his own superiors" (Downs 1967, p. 121).

Awareness by officials of the possibility of distortion, then, helps them to cope with it. "Distortion of organizational records [that is, upward feedback] is a widespread phenomenon. Frequently, those receiving reports or records are as aware of discrepancies as those making the reports, and have practiced the same or similar deceptions themselves" (Thompson 1967, p. 125).

The organization's reward system may actually encourage distortion. "Each official tends to distort the information he passes upward to his superiors in the hierarchy. Specifically, all types of officials tend to exaggerate data that reflect favorably on themselves and to minimize those that reveal their own shortcomings" (Downs 1967, p. 77). The degree of distortion in upward-flowing messages, then, depends on the subordinate's (1) feeling of insecurity, and (2) desire for promotion (Read 1962; Athanassiades 1973).

3. *Bypassing* is elimination of intermediaries in a communication flow. Bypassing may be accomplished as follows:

1. By creating "flat" organizations with only a few hierarchical levels, so that vertical communication flows (from lower levels up to the top echelons) are more direct. The number of levels in an organizational structure can have an important effect on the amount of distortion and omission: "If verbal information in a policy issued by top management has to pass through five or six or more levels of management in getting to the employee, the chances are slim indeed that it will reach different plants and departments meaning exactly the same thing as when it left top management" (Baker 1948, pp. 55–57).

2. By having high officials directly inspect the operational level.

3. By using such devices as suggestion boxes and "ombudsmen."

Unfortunately, all of these methods of coping with distortion and omission depend upon creating a *larger* volume of messages, and thus a greater potential for overload (Figure 4–5). An event at the operational level is usually badly distorted by the time it reaches the top of a six-level hierarchy; but if bypassing is encouraged, the top executive receives duplicated and unprocessed messages and may be overloaded. Clearly, no communication structure is best for all purposes. Each must be tailored to particular information needs, such as whether an organization is more troubled by information overload or by distortion/omission problems.

OMBUDSPERSONS AS BYPASSING DEVICES

"Ombudsman" is a Swedish word meaning "one who represents someone." In Scandinavian countries, ombudsmen—state-appointed individuals who investigate citizens' complaints about their treatment by government

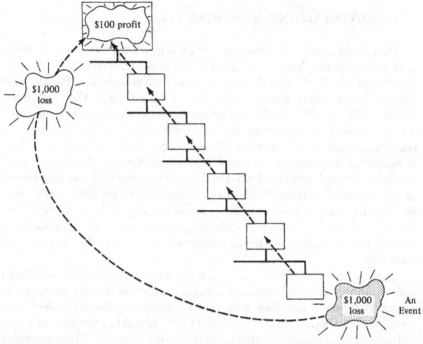

FIGURE 4-5. Solutions to omission and distortion problems include redundancy, verification, and bypassing, all of which unfortunately increase information overload.

agencies—have flourished since 1809, as an appeal mechanism for the complaints of citizens. Usually the ombudsman is a retired judge or lawyer, independent of the government but well versed in its operations. The idea of ombudsman has spread outside Scandinavia (Rowet 1965; Gellhorn 1966a) to such places as New Zealand and Mauritius, and has been recommended for widespread use in the United States (Gellhorn 1966b).

An ombudsperson, then, is a spokesman of the people, perhaps linking the customers or clients of an organization directly to higher levels. The ombudsperson hears complaints against governmental bureaucracies, hospitals, university administrations, etc., and has the power to act freely in order to solve problems. An ombudsperson can be a powerful agent of bottom–up social change, as seen by the experience of Tanzania, where President Julius Nyerere appointed a corps of officials to whom any citizen could make a complaint. Nyerere uses ombudspersons as a means to maintain more direct contact with his followers, and to give greater power to the people. In the United States, all hospitals over a certain size are required to have a "patient representative"; and some city councils and a number of universities now have ombudspersons.

HORIZONTAL AND VERTICAL FLOWS

Horizontal communication flows in an organization are more frequent than vertical flows. Why? One reason is that individuals communicate more openly and effectively with their equals than with superiors. "Men are more prone to speak freely and openly to their equals than to their superiors" (Downs 1967, p. 116). Horizontal exchanges between organizational equals are less subject to distortion, because peers share a common frame of reference. Furthermore, the content of messages carried by horizontal flows is mainly of a coordinating nature, whereas downward flows are mainly authoritative and upward flows chiefly provide feedback on operational performance; so vertical flows carry messages that are potentially more threatening. Finally, horizontal flows are more likely to be informal, rather than formal. And informal channels are generally more rapid and facile, as there is no verification mechanism (thus also increasing the possibility of distortion).

Organizational structures tend to discourage horizontal flows between individuals in different divisions. Messages are supposed to be passed up to a mutual superior and then back down. Naturally, this slows down the speed of these horizontal flows. Fayol (1949) advocated the idea of a special provision for cross-communication in an organization: "There are many operations where success depends on rapid execution; we must find some means of reconciling respect for the hierarchic channel with the need for quick action." Such a particular horizontal formal channel is called a "Fayol's Bridge" (see Figure 2–3).

Downward communication flows in an organization are more frequent than upward flows. Communication in an organization, like water, tends to run downhill; those at the top are more likely to initiate communication flows. When there is contact between individuals of different status, communication from the superior to the subordinate takes place more easily than communication from the subordinate to the superior (Simon and others, 1950, p. 235).

There is often relatively little upward communication in an organization. A study of assembly-line workers found that 70 percent initiated communication contact with a supervisor less often than once per month (Walker and Guest 1952). Initiation of communication was more frequent by individuals at higher levels in the organization, as Agarwala–Rogers (1974) found in an Indian manufacturing plant. Top executives initiated a high proportion of messages, but received a low proportion.

SCARCITY OF UPWARD NEGATIVE FEEDBACK

We have so far argued that vertical communication flows are less likely to occur in an organization than are horizontal flows, and that in the case of the former, upward communication is less frequent than downward. Additionally, we can note that in the case of upward communication, the content is more likely to be positive than negative. A superior tends to receive reports that tell him primarily what his subordinates want him to hear (Downs 1967, p. 118). Upwardly mobile bureaucrats are especially likely to send messages to their superiors that are aimed to please, rather than to accurately reflect negative feedback. When rewards for good performance are based on positive feedback, rather than on *accurate* feedback, negative feedback is discouraged (Thompson 1967, p. 125). In most organizations, annual or monthly reports of performance are widely acknowledged to be deceptively overstated. Bosses, of course, recognize this tendency, as they probably once practiced the same deception themselves.

"The upward flow of communication in organizations is not noted for spontaneous and full expression, despite attempts to institutionalize the process of feedback up the line" (Katz and Kahn 1964, p. 246). Employees tend to send sugar-coated messages from the operational level to higher officials. The net result is highly inaccurate feedback to the top about the actual accomplishments at the bottom of an organization. "A system tends to distort information in a direction to make it more likely to elicit rewards or less likely to elicit punishments" (Miller 1972).

"SOUND OFF" AT THE BANK

An example of the resistance to upward negative feedback in an organization is provided by the "Sound Off" program that was launched in February 1968 in one of the largest banks in the United States, headquartered in New York City (Berlo and others, 1970). An announcement was posted on all bulletin boards in the bank, recommending that workers take all problems to their supervisor. The announcement did not make clear (1) whether an employee could continue his complaint up the usual chain of command, or (2) whether an employee could bypass his direct boss and go to the central Personnel Office.

The bank's management failed to adequately publicize the existence of the "Sound Off" program; only about 25 percent of the workers were aware of it, and only 40 percent of the supervisors. The latter did not like the new system: 90 percent did not think that workers should use it, as they felt it was improper. As one supervisor told the communication researchers: "There have been several cases of people bypassing me. I don't feel mad about it, just hurt. They should follow the chain of command. I don't take any disciplinary action, but I don't like it."

Most supervisors were afraid of the consequences of their workers talking to higher-ups; they felt it was their job to keep problems *away* from their boss. So any contact between their subordinates and their boss was threatening. As one supervisor remarked, "If people go to my supervisor with problems, my evaluation goes down" (Berlo and others, 1970, p. 48).

The employees did not feel that it was improper to bypass their supervisor, but most thought it dangerous to do so. For example, one employee felt that there was racial discrimination in his department, and that it was encouraged by his supervisor. When asked why he did not go to his boss's boss or to Personnel, he said: "You bypass the supervisor once and get fired. There is nobody to appeal to, buddy. The supervisor ... he's it. If you go to Personnel, the first thing they do is get the supervisor on the phone and tell him everything. Next, you're in trouble."

Given these perceptions of the punishments accorded by the bank for expressing upward negative feedback, it should be no surprise to learn that very few of the bank's employees availed themselves of the "Sound Off" program.

In the late 1960s the Minister of Family Planning in Pakistan demanded a monthly report on the number of IUDs inserted in each district. The district family planning officials were each assigned a specific target, and if this was not met, the minister would call them to his office for a strong reprimand. This pressure from above caused widespread overreporting by district officials, especially when negative rumors about the IUD caused a plateau in actual rates of adoption in Pakistan. As the misreporting became more serious, the Minister of Family Planning grew increasingly out of touch with his program's actual performance (Rogers 1973).

Consider a factory producing delicate instruments. A small change occurs in the quality of the steel used to produce certain parts, and many of the assembled instruments have to be scrapped because they do not meet the inspectors' standards. A report should be sent immediately to the factory's purchasing department so that the mistake can be corrected and the proper quality of steel again be obtained. But this negative feedback is delayed. Meanwhile, of course, the scrap heap grows in size and production falters. In this case, an original change in the factory's environment (the lower quality steel shipment) demanded a speedy reaction from the organization's operational levels.

The larger the system and the greater the number of hierarchical levels, the greater the difficulties in communicating accurate feedback messages. As organizations become larger and more complex, "the men at the top . . . depend less and less on firsthand experience, more and more on heavily 'processed' data. Before reaching them, the raw data—what actually goes on 'out there'—have been sampled, screened, condensed, compiled, coded, expressed in statistical form, spun into generalizations and crystallized into recommendations" (Gardner 1964, pp. 78–79).

Top executives, then, receive only "filtered experience" from the operational level. "The picture of reality that sifts to the top of . . . organizations . . . is sometimes a dangerous mismatch with the real world" (Gardner, 1964, pp. 78–79).

Accordingly, a central problem for every large organization is to obtain adequate and accurate negative feedback from the operational level. We have shown that such flows are extremely rare in most organizations, because these messages are subject to a great deal of intentional distortion by subordinates who are hesitant to inform their superiors of bad results. Negative feedback is suppressed or intentionally misinterpreted; the result is that those at the top of any organization have a very distorted picture of the actual conditions at the operational level. Yet these executives are expected to make decisions as if they possessed full knowledge of grass-roots problems. A study by Janowitz and Delany (1957) of officials in public agencies in the United States showed that the higher executives had a more limited grasp of operational details than did officials at lower levels.

"When managers die and go to heaven, they may find themselves in charge of organizations in which subordinates invariably, cheerfully, and fully do as they are bid. Not here on earth" (Kaufman 1973, p. 2). This is why they need feedback from the operational level about how their subordinates are carrying out their decisions. On the other hand, a research in nine federal government agencies showed that high officials had adequate means of feedback from the operational level, but did not make very full use of them (Kaufman 1973, p. 63). Perhaps the officials did not *want* to know fully about their subordinates' noncompliance.

If upward negative feedback from the lower levels is so important for change in an organization, how can it be facilitated? Obviously, it should be rewarded instead of punished. Special channels for such feedback, such as employee suggestion boxes (one large automobile company annually spends over 5 million dollars on such a system), need to be provided. An ombudsman offers a communication channel that bypasses intervening echelons to directly reach top management. These approaches provide "a special communication channel for such fragile things as innovative ideas" (Guetzkow 1965).

Information that can be easily expressed in words and numbers is more likely to get through to the top of an organization. But many important ideas cannot be so easily expressed. "Language is well developed for describing and communicating about concrete objects. . . . On the other hand, it is extremely difficult to communicate about intangible objects and non-standardized objects" (March and Simon 1958, p. 164). Top leaders can escape the limitations of such abstraction by directly visiting the operational level—executives should regularly take an "unflinching look at unreconstructed reality" (Gardner 1964). Mao Tse-tung has insisted on a policy in China that every official must "go down" to the operational level for one month each year, to work as a peasant or a factory worker.

RED HAMMERS IN PEKING

The message was clear when workers at the Peking machinery plant presented hammers to the seventeen newly elected members of the plant's Communist Party committee. "Physically not alienated from labor," said an inscription in red paint on the handle of each of the hammers, and "mentally not alienated from the masses." In other words: "Don't sit in the office all the time. Get out and get your hands dirty."

But that was back in 1971, and memories of the message had faded. That is, they had faded until the party comrades were reminded again recently in an abrupt manner.

"Where are the party members' hammers?" demanded a wall poster put up by workers at the plant. The poster took the Committee members to task for sitting on their "backsides" and not participating in manual labor each year in accordance with instructions from Party Chairman Mao Tse-tung.

"Do you still remember the hammers presented to you by the 2,800 workers of the factory when you were first elected?" the poster asked pointedly. "Where has each hammer gone? What you have lost is not just a hammer. It represents the trust of the 2,800 workers of the factory."

FORMAL AND INFORMAL COMMUNICATION FLOWS

One evidence that the formal structure of an organization does not completely predict communication behavior is the existence of informal communication flows in organizations. One of the surprising findings of the classic Hawthorne studies was the great importance of informal peer relationships in determining worker productivity. "The vast majority of all communication in large organizations [is informal]" (Downs 1967, p. 269). Such informal communication springs up whenever an official feels a need to communicate with some individual with whom no formal channel exists (Downs 1967, p. 113).

"When one enters a concrete organization in order to observe closely the behavior of its members, it becomes extremely difficult to distinguish what is formal and what is informal in their actions" (Mouzelis 1967, p. 70). Nevertheless, many communication researchers have found this categorization to be useful, and have been able to determine whether communication is formal or informal. *Formal communication* transmits messages explicitly recognized as official by the organization. They are more likely to be in written form, and to be vertical in direction.

The formal and informal communication channels in an organization are complementary and substitutable. "Prevalence of [informal] channels means that formal networks do not fully describe the important communication channels in a bureau. . . . The more stringently restricted the formal channels, the richer will be the flowering of subformal ones. . . . Within every organization there is a straining toward completeness in the overall communication system" (Downs 1967, p. 114). But Allen and Cohen (1969) observed considerable overlap between the formal organizational structure and informal communication patterns in two research and development laboratories.

Informal communication often contributes toward an organization's effectiveness in reaching its goal. This functionalness of informal communication is true even though (1) it springs up spontaneously within the organization; (2) it is not controlled by top executives, who often cannot even influence it; and (3) it is largely motivated by individual self-interest.

Both formal and informal communication links enable the members of an organization to process information, and these two types of channels are substitutable. For instance, informal channels may take up a need for communication not filled by the formal channels. However, this complementarity may not always occur, as other investigations indicate. "Even if there is effective formal communication in an organization, there is usually also an active grapevine" (Miller 1972). The conclusion that can be drawn from these studies is that *informal communication is always of some importance in an organization, whether or not the formal channels are functioning adequately.*

INFORMAL COMMUNICATION ROLES

A further type of evidence about the relationship between organizational structure and communication behavior is the existence of informal communication roles within the formal structure. One such specialized role is that of *liaison*, an individual who interpersonally connects two or more cliques within a system, without himself belonging to either clique.

Another kind of specialized communication role in an organization is that of the *gatekeeper*, mentioned previously. A *gatekeeper* is an individual who is located in a communication structure so as to control the messages flowing through a given communication channel.

Neither liaison nor gatekeeper roles are usually acknowledged formally in organization charts (Chapter 5). However, the existence of these communication roles provides evidence that the *formal structure does not completely determine communication behavior and that an informal communication structure also exists.*

Communication Behavior as a Determinant of Organizational Structure

We have just discussed communication as a consequence of organizational structure; however, communication may, under certain conditions, be a determinant of structure.[15] An example of the latter phenomenon is *bürolandschaft*, a highly controversial and unconventional approach begun in Germany and Sweden, and then introduced in the United States in 1966 as "office landscaping" or "nonterritorial offices." The term "office landscaping" derives from the low planters that were used as flexible barriers between work groups.

Usually, the physical structure (walls, corridors, and floors) of an organization is established according to the organizational structure, and the physical structure in turn largely determines the communication flows. For example, Allen (1966) found in research and development laboratories that "the two people who are on the same floor, if separated by more than 25 yards, will rarely have any significant communication."[16]

Physical proximity plays an especially important role in who interacts with whom at the early stages of social acquaintance (Barnlund and Harland 1963). As the acquaintance process proceeds, the individual is likely to communicate with others on the basis of their technical competence, personal attraction, and other qualities, and the relative importance of physical location declines.

Thus we usually find that organizational structure determines physical structure, which determines communication behavior. The assumption of office landscaping is that by keeping the physical structure more flexible (such as by removing walls and other immovable barriers), communication flows will affect the physical structure, and in turn the organizational structure. For example, in the nonterritorial office, employees are allowed to move their desks into a physical arrangement that best suits their functional needs to interact with one another. Who-to-whom communication network sociograms (see Chapter 5) may be constructed as a step toward evolving an optimum physical environment, which may in turn bring about organizational changes (Pile 1967). As work functions shift over a period

---

[15] This particular viewpoint is a fairly new one, and there is only sparse research evidence to back it up.

[16] Such studies on nonterritorial offices as Allen and Gerstberger (1971) are subject to certain reservations before their conclusions can be considered as definitive. For instance, in these before–after experimental approaches, only very small samples have been investigated (Lin 1973, p. 15), and this may be one reason why the respondents' work performance did not increase when placed in a nonterritorial office.

of time, the employees' desks can be rearranged to accommodate to the new communication networks that emerge.

There is a parallel to the landscaped office in the so-called "open school." Great flexibility is offered to students and teachers in their physical and social arrangements. Because the open school is located on a flat plane with movable equipment, the students may work individually or in small or large groups. Such flexibility of arrangements encourages team teaching and the use of teacher aides. Again the physical structure and the organizational design are allowed to follow the communication structure that emerges out of the working or teaching situation.

BÜROLANDSCHAFT: *OFFICES WITHOUT WALLS*

Success has come to Mr. Big in climbing the corporate ladder. His choice corner office has a magnificient view. His desk is dark mahagony, and his carpet is thick. He has a key to the executive washroom, and an attractive secretary on guard outside his office. Such status symbols shout to the world that Mr. Big has arrived.

Such signs of executive success are less evident in the business world today, however, than previously. For today Mr. Big is sitting right out there among his employees in plain sight—because in his division, there are no walls. Everything—except the building itself—is portable. And one of the main advantages of *bürolandschaft* is the flexibility thus afforded; if an individual is working more closely with work group B than with work group A (to which he was originally assigned), he simply shifts his desk a few feet toward his new colleagues in group B. The formal organization chart can catch up later.

Another advantage of office landscaping is the increased visibility thus afforded. No need to telephone Mr. Small to see if he is available for a quick conference; one can tell at a glance. Supervision of office employees is enhanced by removing the walls, as is the employees' interaction with each other in solving group problems. Perhaps it is significant that reporters' desks in a newspaper newsroom have been arranged in *bürolandschaft* style for years, presumably because of the high degree of collaboration necessary in meeting a daily deadline.

The demand for privacy on the part of many organization executives may simply be a cover for a desire for symbolic status. The accoutrements of status can still be provided in a landscaped office, although the exact symbols may be different than in a walled office. In Figure 4–6, Mr. Big still has his corner office and a private secretary to guard his "doorway." But every employee now has thick carpets, as well as access to the splendid corner-office view (in the lower left-hand corner of the Krupp headquarters office shown in Figure 4–6).

Some degree of privacy is also needed for certain office functions (such as personnel matters), however, and so private offices and small meeting rooms may be provided. Meditation areas provide harried employees with a place to unwind alone; in the Chicago headquarters of the MacDonald Corporation, which is completely office landscaped, a mammoth waterbed is available as a "think tank." Another approach is to provide movable partitions at eye level between the desks of each work group. In some open schools, an "isolation tent" is available for children to crawl into when they want to avoid the fishbowl nature of the unwalled classroom.

A serious problem with office landscaping often occurs in connection with how it is introduced to employees. A considerable change in work style, and especially in communication behavior, is required from employees when they move into an open office. A small "test office" is often created to work out the bugs in office landscaping procedures, and to gradually acclimate employees to the new arrangement. For example, before the some 6,000 employees of Standard Oil of Indiana moved into their new open offices in Chicago, the 53 members of the marketing staff were placed in an open office for two years.

Employee resistance to *bürolandschaft* is partly due to the fact that at first glance it looks bad—messy, untidy, and chaotic (Pile 1968). The usual geometric arrangement of desks and aisles is no longer necessitated by square walls. The neat visual arrangement of straight rows of desks usually evident in walled offices is replaced by a seemingly random scattering of furniture with the location of desks only a temporary arrangement dictated by who needs to work with whom.

Another problem with the landscaped office is noise. Typewriters. Telephones ringing. Accordingly in the *bürolandschaft* approach, floors are carpeted and ceilings treated acoustically to bring down the noise level. Where the ambient noise level is too low, "white" or "gray" noise may be added through the air conditioning system or a wired sound system (like Musak) to create an optimum level of hum.

Office landscaping can lead to greater organizational effectiveness. At the Chicago headquarters of the MacDonald Corporation, staff efficiency improved 35 percent after *bürolandschaft* was introduced. The rate of turnover among the secretarial force, which had averaged 100 percent every two years in the old offices, decreased to 25 to 30 percent.

By no means is office landscaping a cure-all for most communication problems in organizations, nor is it appropriate for all organizations. But increasing numbers of offices, schools, banks, and factories are being constructed without walls. *Bürolandschaft* illustrates dramatically that we need not always assume that communication structure must follow a physical structure planned to reflect the formal organization chart. Communication

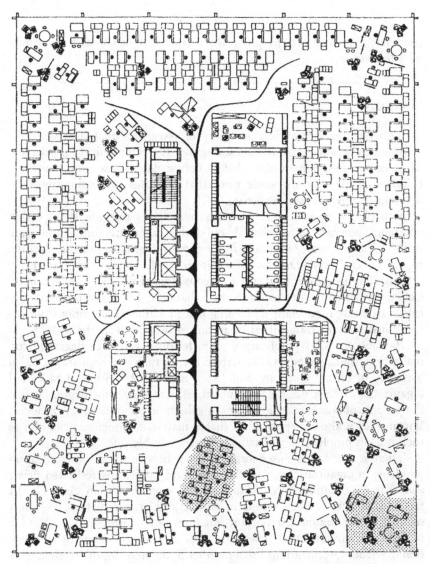

FIGURE 4–6. The Landscaped Office of the Headquarters of Krupp at Reinhausen, Germany (*Note:* This building provides a wide-open space without any walls and unencumbered by columns. Facilities like bathrooms, large meeting rooms, central files, copy machines, and a library are provided in the central core. There are no private offices, although areas of greater privacy are provided for executives—an example is the shaded area in the lower right-hand corner, showing an executive, his small conference area, and his secretary. A work group of eight individuals is depicted in the shaded area in the lower center; the location of their desks facilitates their interaction. Other work groups of various sizes can be identified from the spatial clustering of the desks. In the lower left-hand corner is a small lunch and coffee-break area, where the view is enjoyed by all.)

can come first, with the the physical structure designed so as to maximize its effectiveness.

Summary

This chapter summarizes a variety of researches that deal with the relationship between organizational structure and communication behavior. Most of this research implies that structure determines communication behavior; we also review some work that indicates that communication determines organizational structure.

Structure is the arrangement of the components and subsystems within a system. The *organization chart* describes the formal structure of an organization. *One purpose of structure in an organization is to provide stability, regularity, and predictability.* In addition to its formal structure, every organization has an informal structure consisting of interpersonal communication flows that do not follow formal channels. The informal communication structure is generally a breeding place for rumors. A *rumor* is an unconfirmed message transmitted by means of interpersonal channels.

Bureaucracy is a type of organization having a very high degree of formalization. Bureaucracy is characterized by (1) rules and regulations, (2) a hierarchy of formal positions, and (3) a specialized division of tasks. All organizations of any size are bureaucratized to at least some degree. While the purpose of bureaucracy is to achieve a high degree of rational efficiency, bureaucracy is also a dirty word in that it may lead to inefficiencies and to such human problems as alienation on the assembly line.

There is a common misconception about how to solve communication problems in organizations: viz., that the main problem is restricted flows, and that the solution is to unclog blocked communication channels. In fact, this freeing of flows results in an overload of information. We thus see that *one of the most important functions of organizational structure is to restrict communication flows, and thus decrease problems of information overload.* Organizations use a number of different means to cope with information overload; a general approach is to *restrict the accessibility of sources to receivers by means of organizational structure.*

Ironically, attempts to cope with information overload result in other problems. *The solutions to problems of information overload in an organization that restrict communication flows, such as gatekeeping, filtering, and queuing, tend to cause problems of distortion and omission.* Organizations cope with omission/distortion problems by redundancy, verifying, and bypassing.

Individuals tend to communicate more openly and effectively with their peers than with their superiors. Hence, *horizontal communication flows in an organization are more frequent than vertical flows.* When there is contact between individuals of different status, communication from a superior to a subordinate takes place more easily than in the reverse direction. Thus, *downward communication flows in an organization are more frequent than upward flows.*

Upward negative feedback is often very scarce in an organization. The content of the message going upwards from subordinates to superiors tends to be positive, rather than realistic. Hence, inaccurate feedback is sent to the top. As a result, *officials near the top of an organizational structure may possess less operational information than do individuals nearer the operational level.*

One evidence that the formal structure of an organization does not completely predict communication behavior is the existence of informal communication flows in organizations. The existence of specialized communication roles, such as liaisons and gatekeepers, indicates that the formal structure does not completely determine communication behavior; an informal communication structure also exists. Informal communication is always of some importance in an organization, whether or not the formal channels are functioning adequately.

Under certain conditions, communication may determine organizational structure. *"Bürolandschaft"* or *"office landscaping"* allows flexibility in the physical structure of an organization, so that communication behavior determines the physical structure which in turn determines organizational structure, instead of the reverse.

5. Communication Networks in Organizations

> "Large organizations are not solid large units but more like patch-works of more or less loosely-connected little units. . . ."
>
> —Harold J. Leavitt

> "Acts of communication can be described as the thread that holds any social organization together, if not the skeleton that determines its structure."
>
> —Ithiel de Sola Pool

> "Throughout all this (survey research) one fact remained. . . . The individual remained the unit of analysis. . . . As a result, the kinds of substantive problems on which such research focused tended to be problems of 'aggregate psychology,' that is, within-individual problems, and never problems concerned with relations between people."
>
> —James S. Coleman

The purpose of this chapter is to describe what is known about communication networks in organizations. A network is a grouping intermediate in size between the individual and the organization. It also is intermediate in the degree of structure that is present. Our previous chapter looked at how organizational structure affects communication flows, and vice versa; in that analysis, the individual was the unit of analysis. Here, our work is relational in nature, and our data are generally sociometric. Here, our units of analysis are the communication relationships between individuals, rather than individuals themselves. After some preliminary discussion of communication networks, we review the results from two main types of network research: (1) laboratory experiments on artificial, small-group networks, and (2) sociometric surveys of communication flows in organizations, which are usually analyzed in order to identify cliques and such individual communication roles as liaisons and, more generally, in order to determine the degree of overlap between the formal and informal communication structures. We will find that the laboratory studies are of much less utility than the sociometric communication researches in studying organizational communication.

Why Are Networks Important?

As we showed in Chapter 4, with our illustration of the 100 college freshmen who came together for the first time, communication patterns soon develop as message flows become regularized. Among a large number of individuals, where each person cannot talk easily and equally with every other person, communication networks soon develop. There is a natural tendency for these subsystems to form, so that the individuals within them interact more with each other than with individuals outside of the subsystem. Needless to say, in a large organization composed of thousands of individuals, many, many networks exist. In fact, one way to think about communication in an organization is to see it as consisting of a great number of small communication networks, overlapping somewhat and interconnected so as to form a network of networks (Mears 1974). So our present discussion of networks is essential to an adequate understanding of communication in organizations. Network analysis is a type of micro-study that contributes to understanding the macro nature of organizational communication.

In most network analysis, the usual concern of communication research with the individual-level effects of a source–receiver communication event is replaced by a research approach in which no sharp distinction is (or can be) made between source and receiver. Communication flows occur among "transceivers" in the network, who are both transmitters and receivers (Pool 1973, p. 9). Communication, in this research conception, is truly a mutual interchange.

The term "network" is the communication analogue to the sociological concept of group; but "network" is distinct from "group" in that it refers to a number of individuals (or other units) who persistently interact with one another in accordance with established patterns. Networks can be measured sociometrically, but they are otherwise not visually obvious. Nevertheless, they are quite real. "The numerous case studies [of communication] show undoubtedly that sociometric patterns [that is, networks] are real" (Nehnevasja 1960, p. 751).[1]

---

[1] The best evidence for the validity of sociometric measures of communication flows comes from researches in which a multimeasurement approach is used. For example, a triangulation of measurements (perhaps including observation and tracer analysis along with sociometric questions) might be utilized in studying the same respondents in an organization. We agree with Webb and others (1966, p. 1): "No research

A *network* consists of interconnected individuals who are linked by patterned communication flows. When we talk about networks, then, we imply a concern with the regularized informal groupings of individuals within a formal system. Each network is a small pocket of people who communicate a great deal with each other, or a multitude of such pockets that are linked by communication flows.

The basis of association that holds a network together may be a mutual concern with a common work task (in which case the group is often called a "work group"), a common liking for or attraction to each other, of a mutuality of interest in some topic. Whatever the basis for the patterned interaction, the existence of regularized flows of interpersonal communication lends predictability to informal communication.

FORMAL STRUCTURE AND COMMUNICATION NETWORKS

In the previous chapter, we noted that one of the differences between formal and informal communication is the greater stability and predictability of formal communication, stability lent by the organizational structure. Now we see that certain of the informal communication behavior also has pattern and predictability, deriving not from the formal organization structure but rather from the regularized patterning of interpersonal communication flows. The fact that such networks exist leads us to speak of an "informal communication structure." We shall probe its nature in this chapter.

Still, communication networks are relatively much less structured than formal communication. Networks occur more or less spontaneously; they spring up out of the day-by-day communication behavior of individuals in an organization. Communication networks are constantly changing over time, and this is one main reason why they are not as predictive of human behavior as is the formal structure. So while the formal structure lends stability to communication relationships over time, the network flows energize the organization's daily activities.

One of the "true delights" of the organizational expert, says Professor Charles Perrow (1972, p. 42), is to find a wide discrepancy between the formal and the informal structure of an organization. The organization chart is simply a diagram of the expected or ideal communication rela-

---

method is without bias. Interviews and questionnaires must be supplemented by methods testing the same social science variables, but having different methodological weaknesses." Multi-measurement implies that "each method can be strengthened by appealing to the unique qualities of the other methods" (Sieber 1973). The general argument for a multi-measurement approach was posed by Campbell and Fiske (1959), and illustrated in the case of organization research by Pennings (1973).

tionships in an organization. What actually happens is usually quite different, as many organizational researches clearly show. And communication network analysis is one of the best available ways to find out the extent and nature of the difference.

We conclude that *while the formal communication system (like the organization chart) is to some extent forced on the members of an organization, the informal communication networks emerge spontaneously. Also, compared to the formal communication system in an organization, the informal communication networks are less structured, and hence less predictable.*

SYSTEM EFFECTS

In one of the first empirical studies of organizational behavior, the Hawthorne studies, cliques were found among the fourteen workers in the Bank Wiring Observation Room. Of the two main cliques (there were also three isolates), one had a much higher rate of performance than the other; this was partly cause and partly effect, as the higher-producing workers tended to be drawn into membership in this clique (Homans 1950, pp. 54–72), and once they were in it, the clique's norms of high production tended to raise the workers' output even more. Similarly, workers in the low-producing clique were restrained by peer pressures from producing "too much." So if one wished to thoroughly understand why some workers produced more than others, the communication networks could not be ignored.

Network analysis techniques were used to identify the cliques among the students in an English high school (Alexander 1964). Generally, the cliques were uniform in their members' drinking behavior: most cliques were composed of either all abstainers or all drinkers. The students who were deviant from clique norms (like a drinker in a nondrinking clique, or an abstainer in an imbibing clique) were less integrated into the clique, having fewer communication relationships with their peers.

Networks provide an understanding of their members' behavior. The characteristics of an individual's friends (those with whom interaction is most frequent) are important in explaining certain aspects of the individual's behavior. This is true not only in organizations, but also in a wide variety of other contexts. *System effects* are the influences of others in a system on the behavior of an individual member of the system (Rogers with Shoemaker 1971, p. 29).[2] Certainly there are usually strong network effects on the behavior of the network's individual members in

---

[2] Other authors have referred to system effects as "compositional effects," "contextual effects," or "structural effects."

an organization.[3] In fact, the norms and climate of the system exert their influence on the individual through his communication network relationships with others in the system.

Generally, we conclude that *the importance of networks in affecting behavior of individual members of an organization is suggested by system effects.*

"IT'S A SMALL WORLD"

In addition to sociometric measurement of communication networks, some researchers use a technique perfected by Professor Stanley Milgram that is called the "small world" approach (Milgram 1967, 1969; Korte and Milgram 1970; Travers and Milgram 1969; White 1970). Who has not been asked by a stranger, "Do you know so-and-so?" only to discover mutual friends? We usually exclaim in surprise, "My, what a small world!"

Milgram asks his respondents to advance a message from a randomly selected starter to an assigned target person by sending it to any personal acquaintance the respondent thinks is more likely than himself to know the target person. Amazingly, Milgram (1969, p. 112) finds that an average of only about 5.5 intermediaries are needed to transmit a message from starters in Nebraska to targets in Massachusetts. Most of the dyadic transmissions are highly homophilous; for instance, Milgram (1969, p. 114) finds that about 80 percent of the transfers are between sources and receivers of the same sex. Black starters are able to get a message through to a black target in somewhat fewer steps than to a white target, and white starters are similarly found to be less distant from white targets than black targets.

Actually, Pool (1973, p. 17) argues, Milgram's small world findings are not so surprising when one examines the probabilities involved. Pool finds that the average individual has from 500 to 2,000 close acquaintances (this is the size of the individual's total "personal communication network"). If each individual averages about 1,000 persons, then one's friends' friends would number about 1,000,000 if there were not much overlap (there is, of course, due to interlocking personal networks). A list of friends of friends of friends would number 1 billion, a staggering number. One can thus understand how a randomly selected starter in Nebraska, can reach a randomly assigned target person in Massachusetts in only 5.5 steps.

Pool (1973, p. 16) estimates that the longest possible chain in the United States would have about six intermediaries. What is the longest

---

[3] Although Shoemaker (1971) found only little system effects (from their school) on teacher's innovativeness among a sample of 585 teachers in 28 Thai high schools.

possible chain? Perhaps the "small world" linking two hermits on opposite coasts. But each presumably knows a storekeeper. Each storekeeper, in his or her list of acquaintances, has at least one individual who knows his or her congressperson. And there we are with another "small world"—with only a couple of more links, we could carry it to a peasant in India.

Small world studies have not yet been utilized very much in organizations,[4] although they are a special type of tracer study (described in Chapter 6) that could tell us much about how messages flow in an organizational structure. One of the few such studies in an organization is Shotland's (1969, 1970) research among students, professors, and administrators at Michigan State University.

Many student activists in the 1960s claimed that deans and presidents were too socially distant from them, and hence that the only message from students that could "get through" was an act of violence. Shotland's research was designed to determine the social distance between students, faculty, and administrators at a megauniversity of about 50,000 individuals. He found that the average number of intermediaries between randomly selected starters and targets was about five, a figure approaching Milgram's for the entire United States. Students had the longest interpersonal communication channels, and administrators the shortest. The widest social distance at the university was, indeed, from students to administrators.

PERSONAL NETWORKS: RADIAL AND INTERLOCKING

The term "network" is actually used by communication scientists to refer to three different concepts:

1. *Total system network*—comprising the communication patterns among all of the individuals in a system, such as an organization. This network may consist of thousands of individuals if the organization is a large one. In the present book, we usually use "network" in this context.

2. *Clique*—defined as a subsystem whose elements interact with each other relatively more frequently than with other members of the communication system. Most cliques consist of from five to twenty-five members, with some much larger than this. Cliques are thus one of the main components of a communication network in an organization (along with isolates, liaisons, etc.). We prefer to use the term "clique" for the type of subnetwork defined above, but some other authors also call this unit a "network," or a "group."

3. *Personal network*—defined as those interconnected individuals who

---

[4] Examples are the study of diffusion of a "planted" message in a boys' camp, by Larsen and Hill (1958); and an investigation of the communication of planted messages among teachers in St. Louis high schools, by Wager (1962).

are linked by patterned communication flows to any given individual (Laumann 1973, p. 7). For the purposes of our present analysis, we occasionally find it convenient to anchor a network on an individual, rather than on a clique or the entire system (Mitchell 1969, p. 14). Each individual carries around with him a personal network of other individuals with whom he consistently interacts about a given topic. Thus each individual possesses his or her own small communication environment. This personal network partly explains the individual's behavior. In this book, we refer to this individualized type of communication network as a "personal" network, to distinguish it from our broader use of the term "network."

We illustrate a personal communication network in Figure 5–1. Obviously, if we want to understand the communication behavior of Individual #7, we should look first at the five other individuals in his personal communication network (shown in Figure 5–1 as connected by solid lines). We also may want to look further, at the larger network which includes the personal networks of the five others in #7's personal network, and at the degree to which these five individuals are interconnected with each other (shown as dotted lines in Figure 5–1).

We find it convenient to distinguish two types of personal networks:

FIGURE 5–1. Personal Communication Network for Individual #7 in the ARC Company (Shown by the Solid Lines)

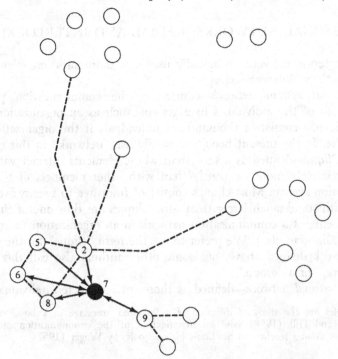

interlocking and radial. A *radial personal network* is one in which an individual interacts directly with friends who do not interact with each other. An *interlocking personal network* is one in which an individual's friends interact with each other (Laumann 1973, p. 113; Rogers 1973). Generally, interlocking personal networks are more numerous than radial networks, as an individual's friends are usually friends of each other (we are using "friend" in this context to mean an individual with whom one interacts frequently). But most personal networks are somewhat radial and somewhat interlocking; for example, Individual #7 in Figure 5–1 has some friends who interact, and some who do not.

THE STRENGTH OF WEAK TIES

The ingrown communication patterns in an interlocking personal network facilitate effective communication, but they also act as a barrier to prevent new ideas from entering the network. One's closest friends seldom know anything that one does not already know. Friends tend to tell other friends what they know more or less immediately. There is not much new information coming into an interlocking personal network; it needs some nonmutual communication flows to give it more openness. Otherwise, a pooling of ignorance may occur. For example, a study of the search for an abortionist by American women (conducted prior to 1973, when abortions were illegal) showed that most women went first to their best friends (Lee 1969). Unfortunately, these friends were members of interlocking personal networks with the respondent, so they were seldom able to provide any information about abortionists that the respondent did not already possess. One woman sought the name of an abortionist from several of her best friends, her mother, and a family doctor. All provided the name of the same abortionist (one, in fact, who was no longer performing abortions).

Human communication typically entails a balance between novelty and similarity. Communication research on personal networks has dealt with an issue that has come to be called "the strength of weak ties" (Liu and Duff 1972; Granovetter 1973; Rogers 1973). This research is summarized in the statement that *the information strength of dyadic communication relationships is inversely related to the degree of homophily (and the strength of the attraction) between the source and the receiver.* Or, in other words, a new idea is communicated to a larger number of individuals, and traverses a greater social distance, when passed through weak sociometric ties (in radial personal networks) rather than strong ones (in interlocking personal networks). There is little informational strength, then, in interlocking personal networks (Fig. 5–2). "Weak ties" enable innovations to flow from clique to clique via liaisons and bridges.

Network analysis of the diffusion of a family planning method (the IUD or intrauterine device) in the Philippines demonstrated the strength

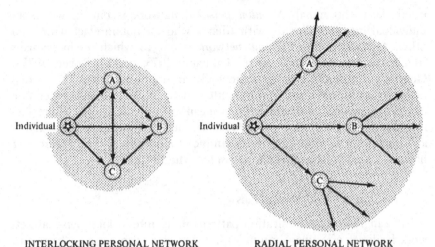

INTERLOCKING PERSONAL NETWORK   RADIAL PERSONAL NETWORK

FIGURE 5–2. Radial personal networks are more open than interlocking personal networks and thus are more effective in obtaining new information.

of weak ties. The innovation spread most easily within interlocking cliques, among housewives of very similar social status (Liu and Duff 1972). But heterophilous flows were necessary to link these cliques; usually these "weak ties" connected two women who were not very close friends, and allowed the contraceptive idea to travel from a higher-status to a somewhat lower-status housewife. So at least occasional heterophilous dyadic communication in a network was a structural prerequisite for rapid diffusion of the innovation.

Putting Structure Back into Organizational Communication

Open system theory influenced organization researchers to focus on a new set of within-organization variables, and especially to move from an atomistic research focus on individuals as units of analysis to dyadic or other relational units of analysis in which communication relationships were a priority focus, and to more systems-level concerns, in which communication network analysis was often utilized.

Prior to the rise of open system theory, organization scholars like Elton Mayo and Fritz Roethlisberger in the Hawthorne plant approached their respondents as individuals in a structure. That is, data were gathered mainly by means of observation of and personal interviews with individual workers. The workers might be queried about their communication (and other relationships) with their peers or their supervisor, but the main unit of analysis was the individual worker. Data about productivity were computed for each worker,[5] and other variables like job satisfaction and morale were measured in order to explain why some workers had higher production than others. Ample evidence was found in the Hawthorne plant, of course, for the importance of the informal peer group in affecting productivity, but this research finding did not have much effect on how later researches in the Human Relations School were conducted. The individual, not the work group or the clique or the communication network or even the dyad, remained the predominant unit of analysis. One disadvantage of this monadic approach is that the effects of organizational structure on individuals and their informal groupings could not be brought into the data analysis very directly. All that could be measured via this approach was the individual worker's *perceptions* of structural and relational variables (for example, the style of leadership he or she thought the supervisor provided). The relationships between the individual and informal groups, and between formal and informal structures, were ignored.

Even though organizational behavior is distinctive in part because it is affected by the organizational structure, the Human Relations researchers were never very successful in incorporating structural variables in their research operations. They couldn't, as long as they mainly used the individual as the unit of analysis. They could only explain his behavior as a product of individual-level independent variables.

Katz and Kahn (1966, p. 1) castigate these organization researchers, and psychologists in general, for their "inability to deal with the facts of social structure and social organization" in their studies, and for implicitly assuming that individuals exist in a social vacuum. Certainly this assumption is inexcusable when one is investigating behavior in an organizational structure. But most researchers prior to the advent of open system theory (and many still today) proceeded to gather data from individual members of organizations, and to treat their data as if the individuals' behavior was not affected by relational and structural variables. This procedure amounted, again, to artificially destructuring organizational behavior.

This situation was actually being corrected somewhat even before the rise of open system theory. Some investigators (for example, Jacobson and Seashore 1951) had begun in the early fifties to use sociometric questions to query their respondents about their communication patterns with others in the organization. In this approach to network sociometry, investi-

---

[5] In the Hawthorne research study conducted with the fourteen workers in the Bank Wiring Observation Room, the production of each worker was recorded by punched holes on a continuous strip of slowly moving paper tape; as each worker completed a finished product, he placed it in a hole in his work table, where it tripped a hinged door, which in turn punched a record of this output on the paper tape. The apparent ingenuity of this Rube Goldberg production counter does not disguise the fact that this dependent variable, and most of the independent variables used to explain it, were measured monadically.

gators could identify the interpersonal communication cliques within the formal organization structure and the liaisons linking these cliques, and thus compare the informal with the formal communication structure (more detail on this approach to communication network analysis is provided later in this chapter). These investigations, and a few others like them that focused on communication network relationships in organizations, represented a conceptual and methodological break from the previous "individual-in-a-structure" approach.

So progress in the direction of putting structure back into organizational research was underway. But the advent of open system theory gave it a tremendous intellectual boost. This theoretical perspective stressed communication as the vital ingredient in organizations (Chapter 2), and communication, as we saw in Chapter 1, is by nature relational. The systems approach encouraged social scientists to look at organizations as systems, rather than at the atomistic minutae of individual behavior. Systems theory was the "science of wholes." It was concerned with problems of relationships, of structure, and of interdependence, rather than just with the functioning and characteristics of individuals in organizations (Katz and Kahn 1966, p. 18).

We feel that *open system theory shifted the nature of organizational communication research from an atomistic research focus on individuals as units of analysis (1) to dyadic or other relational units in which communication relationships constitute the main research emphasis, and (2) to more system-level concerns, often involving communication network analysis.*

Acceptance of the systems viewpoint implied a concern with studying wholes, rather than mechanistically investigating the relationships among variables measuring some component of the individual or the organization. Furthermore, if one accepts the notion that all of the elements in a total system are in interdependent relationship with each other, the search for cause-and-effect relationships is futile. As we pointed out in Chapter 2, the potential of open system theory in affecting the actual research operations of communication investigations in organizations has not yet been fulfilled, because appropriate research techniques for studying "wholes" are not yet available. Perhaps communication network analysis offers the greatest opportunity in this direction.

We shall see exactly how in the remaining sections of this chapter.

Laboratory Experiments on Small Group Networks

In this section we shall review and criticize the body of communication research obtained from laboratory experiments with small group networks, from the perspective of what useful knowledge such research provides about networks in organizations. These experiments entail creating small communication networks in the laboratory, with different types of miniaturized organizational structure, so that the effects of such varied structure can be determined as it affects communication behavior.

Laboratory small groups studies have attempted a unique contribution toward understanding communication behavior in organizations, but they lack the reality of an ongoing, "live" organization. They have focused on the nature of the task, motivation of members, group size, and emerging patterns of interaction.

BACKGROUND OF THE SMALL GROUPS STUDIES

The studies we are concerned with are commonly known as "small group" research. About thirty years ago, most writings about small group behavior were only philosophical, intuitive, and theoretical. It was not until the mid-1940s that the small group became a focus of social scientific inquiry.

Laboratory experiments on small group communication sprang from three main origins:

1. the work of the social psychologist Kurt Lewin and his protegés: one of Lewin's researches (1958) dealt with the introduction of the idea of eating "sweetbreads" (undesirable cuts of meat) to small groups of housewives in Iowa City;
2. the sociometric studies of Jacob Moreno and his students, who investigated the patterns of social relationships among the members of communities, classrooms, and other real-life groups (Moreno 1953; Moreno and Jennings 1960); and
3. the Hawthorne studies (discussed in Chapter 2), which indicated the importance of small work groups in the factory in determining workers' performance.

Communication network research with laboratory groups became a standard experimental approach in the 1950s and 1960s. What effect does the structure of the group have upon the efficiency of its communication behavior? What effect does an individual's position in the group structure have on his or her morale and job satisfaction? Three experiments, conducted by Bavelas (1950), Leavitt (1951), and Shaw (1954, 1964), are summarized herein, as they are perhaps most representative of laboratory research on small group networks.

CIRCLE, WHEEL, AND CHAIN

Professor Alex Bavelas (1950) developed the technique of arranging small groups of individuals in cubicles, interconnected by means of slots in the cubicle walls through which the group members were asked to communicate by written messages. Various communication structures, such as the circle, wheel, and chain, were imposed upon the group members by closing certain of the cubicles' wall slots (Fig. 5–3). Each of the members was given certain information, which had to be shared in order to complete the assigned task. Generally, all network members organized themselves into a pattern by which peripheral individuals sent messages to the central members, who solved the problem and communicated the solution back to the peripheral members. (All members had to know the solution in order for the assigned task to be scored as successfully completed.) The dependent variables were the amount of time required to achieve the correct solution, the number of messages exchanged, the number of errors committed, sociometric leadership nominations, and perceived satisfaction with the job on the part of the group members.

Bavelas concluded that (1) highly centralized communication networks like the "wheel" are superior for routine tasks, where errors are acceptable; while (2) a decentralized network like the "circle" is better suited for less routine tasks, where adaptation and innovative thinking are required. When only centralized communication (as in the "wheel") was allowed, the task was seldom completed successfully; performance improved when decentralized communication (the "circle") was allowed. However, a completely interlocking communication network (the "all-channel") was no more effective than the restricted communication network (the "wheel").

Professor Harold Leavitt (1951) examined the relationship between different communication networks and task performance by asking his subjects to identify the one correct symbol which had been given to them on a card depicting six different symbols. Information was exchanged until all five

FIGURE 5–3. Some of the Five-Person Group Structures in Laboratory Experiments on Small-Group Network Communication

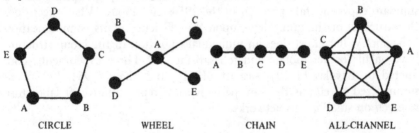

CIRCLE   WHEEL   CHAIN   ALL-CHANNEL

participants constituting a group knew the correct answer. Each small group of five subjects was given a total of fifteen consecutive trials in attempting this task. Group members were allowed to transmit and receive messages according to a structure predetermined by the experimenters (and similar to Bavelas's).

In the "wheel," peripheral individuals funneled information to the center, where a decision was made and then disseminated to the other four individuals. The "circle," however, showed no consistent organizational pattern, as all available links were used at some point during a given trial.

Work performance was measured in terms of (1) the speed in arriving at a correct solution, and (2) the proportion of errors committed by the group. Leavitt (1951) found that the "wheel" was considerably faster than the "circle" in solving the assigned problems. However, the "circle" groups made more errors than those in the "wheel." Whereas the individual occupying position "A" in the "wheel" is alone able to recode the information and detect errors, all five individuals in the "circle" can recode and hence check a particular solution to the problem.

Building on Leavitt's work, Shaw (1954) studied the concept of independence—the degree of freedom with which an individual could function in a group. Independence was greater in decentralized networks like the circle or all-channel, regardless of the type of task, and was positively related to individual satisfaction. A second concept that Shaw elucidated was "saturation," rather similar to our concept of information overload, which was the information input and output requirements for the individual. It was highest for Individual "A" in the "wheel" network. Saturation (overload) was negatively related to efficiency in solving group tasks.

The small groups experiments led to the following conclusions.

1. *Network centralization (such as possessed by the "wheel") contributes to rapid performance (especially of simple tasks), but the error rate is high, presumably because two-way communication and feedback is discouraged.* The more interconnected a network is, the more likely it is to solve a problem requiring the pooling of information held by the network members.

2. *Low centralization or high independence (as in the "circle") is associated with member satisfaction.*

3. *The network structure served to elevate certain individuals into leadership positions.* For example, Leavitt (1951) did not designate a formal leader in a laboratory network, but Individual "A" in the "wheel" always emerged as the sociometric leader named by the participants. In the "circle," the participants were less likely to feel that a leader emerged during the experiment, and if they did select a leader, their choice was distributed among all the positions in the circle.

4. *Being in a key position in a network, however, also led to information overload for the leader, through whom all the messages had to pass.*

CRITICISMS OF THE SMALL GROUPS STUDIES

One communication scholar claims that since most work in organizations is done in small groups of five or six persons, a large organization can be conceptualized as merely a collection of small groups (Mears 1974). If one accepts this argument, perhaps the findings from laboratory experiments on communication networks might be useful in providing an understanding of the networks that are embedded in organizations. We have some serious doubts.

After reviewing the laboratory network literature, Collins and Raven (1969, p. 146) concluded: "It is almost impossible to make a simple generalization about any variable without finding at least one study to contradict the generalization."

Findings from laboratory experiments on communication networks in small groups (like the wheel, circle, and chain) can be applied to organizational settings only with great caution. Student subjects in artificial, nonorganizational settings undoubtedly do not act in ways that help us understand the complexities of communication networks that are embedded in organizational structures. For this reason, Professor Howard Becker (1954) refers to the small groups research as "cage" studies, in a biting criticism of their unreality.

In retrospect, the paramount blunder committed by small groups researchers undoubtedly was the lack of a systems framework, as Starbuck (1965) points out. The individual-oriented psychological myopia of communication research in the 1950s and 1960s is well illustrated by these small groups researches.

Individuals were brought into experimental settings, as virtually total strangers, to perform tasks of a completely unreal nature. The experimental conditions did not reflect the real-life situations of large organizations. The integration of group networks within an organization through communication patterns was overlooked. So the lack of a systems approach was a serious oversight.

One of the most damaging criticisms of these studies is the limited variety of independent variables used in most of them. The major independent variables were size, network structure, and the complexity or simplicity of the task; Shaw (1964) suggested that other variables like organizational opportunity, personality variables, and noise and distortion should also have been studied. The main dependent variables were communication effects: speed of problem solving, accuracy, morale, and satisfaction.

Even though the size of the groups was a major focus of these studies, they overlooked the spatial arrangements of the members as an independent variable (Sommer 1967). The researchers apparently "treated space somewhat as we treat sex; it is there but we don't talk about it" (Hall 1959).

Perhaps the main contribution of the small groups studies was that they provided information about structural effects in communication networks. But the precise nature of the relationships among the variables involved still remained largely unclear. As Professor Donald Campbell (1969, p. 377) noted, experiments cannot prove theories, only probe them. And network analysis undoubtedly has benefited from the prior probing of conceptual issues in the small groups experiments.

Network Analysis

Network analysis is a method of research for identifying the communication structure in a system, in which sociometric data about communication flows or patterns are analyzed by utilizing interpersonal relationships as the units of analysis. Most past communication research, as well as organization behavior studies, has largely ignored the effects of structure on communication behavior. Network analysis is a tool that promises to capitalize on the unique ability of communication inquiry in ongoing organizations to reconstruct specific message flows in a system and to overlay the social structure of the organization on these flows. Communication inquiry in organizations makes manifest otherwise static structural variables; network analysis permits an understanding of the dynamics of organizational structure as it determines the flows of messages between units and across hierarchical positions. About the only example to date of communication research in which network analysis has been used to restore social structure to the communication process is that of several investigations of organizational communication centered in the Department of Communication at Michigan State University.

In the preceding section of this chapter, we reviewed the laboratory experiments on small group networks and expressed considerable reservations about the usefulness of this research in understanding the complex reality of communication in organizations. It was natural and logical for communication scholars to drop these laboratory experiments (few such studies are being conducted today) and move from the artificial and controlled setting of the laboratory to the reality of actual organizations, where real-life communication networks abound. This shift in the research setting being investigated also entailed a change in experimental design from one in which the structure could be manipulated by the experimenter (as in the "circle," "wheel," and "chain") to survey sociometry, in which the structural arrangements of real-life networks and cliques could be determined by network analysis but usually could not be manipulated as an independent variable.

BACKGROUND ON NETWORK ANALYSIS IN ORGANIZATIONS

Network analysis of organizational communication dates from a classic investigation of communication patterns among officials in the United States Office of Naval Research by researchers at the University of Michigan's Institute for Social Research in the early 1950s (Jacobson and Seashore 1951; Weiss and Jacobson 1955; Weiss 1956). This research caused little scholarly excitement at the time, and its impact went relatively unnoticed for almost two decades. But in retrospect, viewed from the vantage point of present-day approaches to research on organizational communication, the Jacobson–Seashore–Weiss research represents an important turning point in the study of communication in organizations.

In the early 1950s, the University of Michigan researchers were fully aware of the Hawthorne studies' earlier focus on "work groups" as communication subsystems within an organizational setting, and they were certainly alerted to look at informal communication patterns. But unlike all the Human Relationists of the day, who were largely ignoring communication networks, Jacobson, Seashore, and Weiss utilized survey sociometric techniques to gather data from naval personnel about their communication behavior. Each respondent in the organization studied was asked to indicate how frequently he talked with each other member of his organization. These sociometric data were then analyzed by using a modification of the matrix analysis procedures previously described by Forsyth and Katz (1946).

This technique arranged all of the organization's members down one side of a matrix (the "who," or "seeker," dimension), and all of the same individuals on the other side (the "whom," or "sought" dimension).[6] This who-to-whom matrix of interpersonal communication patterns was then rearranged so that individuals who interacted more frequently with each other were placed closer together on the dimensions of the matrix. The subgroupings or cliques that gradually emerged within the matrix were considered the building blocks of the informal structure. The "cement" that held these blocks together was the liaisons and bridges, who provided interpersonal connections among the subsystems. This focus on liaisons led to the realization, only very gradually in future years, that the integration of the informal subsystems within an organization was an important function of communication in organizations.

The Jacobson–Seashore–Weiss study was significant in that the methodology of network analysis represented a shift from the usual monadic analysis (focusing on individuals) toward a relational type of analysis,

---

[6] Such a who-to-whom matrix is sometimes called a "communimatrix"; it is a method for graphically displaying relational data about communication patterns among the members of a system.

which more appropriately fits our transactional definition of the communication process, and is more consistent with a systems approach to studying organizations.

For almost twenty years, no other communication researcher took up this type of network analysis, until Schwartz's (1968) study of 142 faculty members in the College of Education at Michigan State University. Soon thereafter, MacDonald (1970) used network analysis to investigate the cliques, liaisons, etc., among the 185 members of a federal agency located in the Pentagon. The studies by Schwartz and MacDonald were soon followed by several doctoral dissertations using network analysis in the Department of Communication at Michigan State University. The invisible subcollege was forming.

NETWORK ANALYSIS PROCEDURES

Network analysis of communication in organizations is usually carried out in order to determine the nature of interpersonal communication flows and how the formal and informal structures are related. This analysis is done by:

1. identifying cliques within the total system, and determining how these structural subgroupings affect communication behavior in the organization;
2. identifying certain specialized communication roles such as liaisons, bridges, and isolates (thus allowing communication research to proceed far beyond the relatively simpler issue of opinion leadership); and
3. measuring various structural indexes (like communication integration[7] or connectedness, and system openness) for individuals, cliques, or entire systems.

We describe these procedures in detail later in this section.

Network analysis necessitated a new kind of sampling, as well as a shift to relational units of analysis. Instead of random samples of scattered individuals in a large population, network studies depended on gathering data from *all* of the eligible respondents in an organization or subsystem, or in a sample of organizations or subsystems (Table 5–1).[8] As a result, the ability to generalize the research results is traded off for a greater focus on understanding the effects of structure on communication flows. For if these effects were to be understood, intact structures (like organizations), or at least the relevant parts of them, had to be studied.

---

[7] *Communication integration* is the degree to which the units in a system are interconnected by interpersonal communication.

[8] A high rate of nonresponse can leave gaps in the data matrix, so network analysts typically try to achieve a nearly 100 percent response.

TABLE 5–1. Comparison of Monadic and Relational Analysis in Communication Research

Characteristic of the Research Approach	Type of Communication Research Approach	
	MONADIC ANALYSIS	RELATIONAL ANALYSIS
1. Unit of analysis	The individual	The communication relationship between two (or more) individuals
2. Most frequent sample design	Random samples of scattered individuals in a large sample (in order to maximize the generalizability of the research results)	Complete census of all eligible respondents in a system (like an organization), or in a sample of such intact systems
3. Types of data utilized	Personal and social characteristics of individuals, and their communication behavior	Same as for monadic analysis, plus sociometric data about communication relationships
4. Main data analysis methods	Correlational analysis of cross-sectional survey data	Various types of network analysis of cross-sectional survey data
5. Main purpose of the research	To determine the independent variables (usually characteristics of individuals) related to a dependent variable (usually a communication effect)	To determine how structural variables affect communication flows in a system

Several difficulties are involved in communication network analysis. For one thing, perhaps the dynamic process of communication relationships among the members of a system is so fleeting that networks cannot be accurately charted, and the plotting of sociometric communication relationships within a formal structure is but an evasive illusion. Imagine trying to capture, in quantified terms of "arrows" and numbers, the total human interaction that occurs in even a small organization in one day! Impossible, you say. True. Sociometric data actually reflect only the grossest of communication behavior, the main lines of communication that are most frequently and heavily used. The "weak ties" that occur in organizations, the lightly used flows, seldom are reported by respondents in organizational researches, and hence are rarely analyzed in network studies; Granovetter (1973) argues that this problem is especially serious because these "weak ties" are different in nature from the "strong ties" or regularized communication patterns that are usually reported by respondents and investigated in network analyses. For example, as we showed previously, weak ties are more likely to be informationally rich.

Communication networks are the "threads" that hold a system together; they are important but difficult to study, as they are so numerous. The threads can easily become a tangled ball to the investigator. One of the practical problems of communication network analysis is the immensity of the task. In a system of 100 members, each of the 100 individuals can talk to the 99 others, so that 9,900 communication relationships are possible. In a 200-member system, 39,800 communication dyads are possible, and in a system with 5,000 members, nearly 25 million, which exceeds the processing capacity of most modern computers (Lindsey 1974, pp. 1–3). One solution, of course, is to break the total communication system down into subsystems, or cliques; this technique makes the complexity of interpersonal communication more manageable.

A further problem is that there is not just a single set of communication networks. A given individual may have a different set of communication partners for each of a myriad of topics; each of these personal networks may be somewhat overlapping and can be superimposed on the others. For example Berlo and others (1971) found somewhat different communication networks for the members of a federal government agency when the sociometric questions dealt with work-related matters, with innovations, and with maintenance. (We return later to a discussion of single-stranded versus multistranded network relationships.)

A common approach to network analysis of organizational communication consists of the following sequence of research steps:

1. Sociometric data about work-related (or other) interpersonal communication flows are gathered from each member in the organization, or from a subdivision or specific department of the organization. The sociometric data may be obtained via questionnaires or personal interviews, by observation, or by other means.

2. Cliques are identified among the members of the system on the basis of which individuals communicate most with each other. Such identification may be accomplished by visually representing the patterns of communication in a sociogram and rearranging together those individuals who interact most with each other. Or a computer program can be utilized to identify cliques as is more often done when many individuals are involved.

3. These cliques are then superimposed on the formal organization chart to determine the degree to which the two correspond. Presumably the organization chart represents the formally expected patterns of communication, while the sociometric data constitute the day-to-day reality of actual communication flows.

4. This assessment of the adequacy of the formal organizational structure from a communication point of view may lead to recommended changes in the organization chart through reorganization, or to the reassignment of certain individuals in the organization. For example, the network analysis may show that the organization contains isolates who do not

communicate with anyone else in their organization (or in their unit or department). Or it may show that the cliques are not adequately linked by liaisons or bridges, and these roles may need to be created.

AN ILLUSTRATION OF COMMUNICATION NETWORK ANALYSIS IN AN ORGANIZATION [9]

The present example comes from the ARC Company (an industrial company in India), studied by one of the authors (Agarwala–Rogers 1973).

Figure 5–4 presents a formal organization chart showing the hierarchical positions occupied by twenty-two individuals in the ARC Company's three largest divisions. The numbers within the blocks represent individuals in the company. Person #1 at the top is the president of the entire organization. The three persons immediately below him are the managers of the three divisions: Sales, Production, and Administration. The remaining individuals are employees in each division.

The main steps in our communication network analysis are:

1. To obtain sociometric data about work-related interpersonal communication contacts from the sample of twenty-two individuals. Each was given a questionnaire which listed all twenty-two names, and they were

FIGURE 5–4. Formal Organization Chart of the ARC Company, Showing Twenty-Two Individuals in Three Divisions

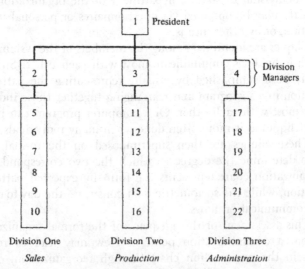

[9] Our illustration is similar to the hypothetical data provided in the description of H and M network analysis by Monge and Lindsey (1974).

asked how frequently they communicated with each of the other twenty-one individuals about work matters.

A sociogram of these responses is then constructed (Figure 5–5); for example, we see that Individual #1 says he frequently contacts Individuals #2, #3, and #4, the division managers, but his communication contacts with other lower-level members are less frequent or nonexistent.

2. To identify cliques in the communication network of twenty-two members on the basis of whom each individual communicates with. The lines indicate regular or patterned communication contacts. Some contacts are two-way, or reciprocal, and some are one-way. Two-way arrows connect Individuals #1 and #4, #1 and #2, etc., while nonreciprocal relationships exist between Individuals #2 and #3, #4 and #17, etc. The one-way arrows are nonreciprocal communication contacts (in actuality, most communication contacts that are *reported* as one-way probably also entail

FIGURE 5–5. Sociogram of Four Communication Cliques in the ARC Company, Showing Liaison and Isolate Individuals

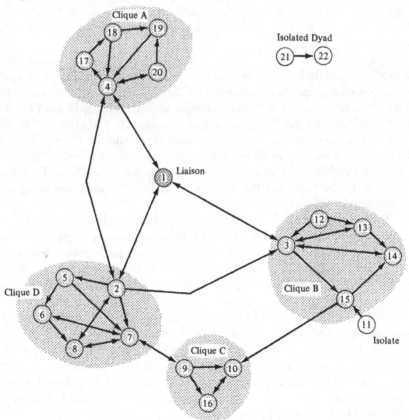

a good deal of reciprocal exchange, so we do not make as much of a distinction between reciprocal and nonreciprocal communication as do some other authors).

Most network analysis seeks to categorize individuals into cliques by arranging people together who interact more with each other than with other individuals (outside of the clique). However, the Richards (1971) approach to network analysis uses a different criterion for grouping individuals into cliques: viz., whether or not the individuals share a common set of other persons with whom they communicate. For example, Individuals #5 and #8 in Figure 5–5 both communicate with Individuals #2, #6, and #7, even though they do not communicate directly with each other. So the Richards-type network analysis puts Individuals #5 and #8 together in Clique D (Figure 5–5).

There are four cliques in the ARC Company: A, B, C, and D (again, a *clique* is a subsystem whose elements interact with each other relatively more frequently than with other members of the communication system). Clique A is composed of Individuals #4, #17, #18, #19, and #20; Clique B of Individuals #3, #12, #13, #14, and #15; and so on. *Most clique members are relatively close to each other in the formal hierarchy of the organization, suggesting the similarity of the formal and informal communication systems.*

Individual #7 is a *bridge,* a person who is a member of one communication clique and links it, via a communication dyad, with another clique. Thus, Individual #7 is a member of Clique D and communicates with Individual #9, who is a member of Clique C. Individual #11 is an *isolate,* an individual who has few communication contacts with the rest of the system. Individual #1 is a *liaison,* an individual who interpersonally connects two or more cliques within a system without himself belonging to any clique. Individual #1 connects Clique A, Clique B, and Clique D. If this liaison were removed from the network, it would be a much less integrated or interconnected one.

3. To superimpose the informal communication cliques on the formal organization chart (Fig. 5–6) in order to determine the degree to which the two correspond. Clique A is composed of five individuals (#4, #17, #18, #19, #20), all of whom are members of Division Three. What about Individuals #21 and #22? They are also in Division Three, but are an isolated dyad. So in Division Three, two members are not communicating with the others in their division. Here the formal structure does not correspond to the informal communication structure.

Clique C has members in both Division One (Sales) and Division Two (Production). This clique does not correspond with the formal organization chart. Are their communication relationships dysfunctional to the formal organization? Or does their cross-division coordination perform an important task in the company?

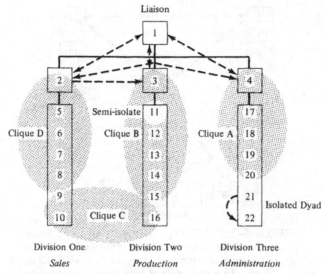

FIGURE 5–6. Interpersonal Communication Structure Superimposed on the Formal Hierarchy of the ARC Company (*Note*: Dotted lines, showing interpersonal communication flows, are not shown within cliques in this diagram for the sake of simplicity).

Clique D is closest to the formal structure; all members belong to the same division.

In addition to *H* (for "holistic") network analysis, which was just demonstrated (Richards 1974a, 1974b, 1974c, 1974d, 1974e), we can also perform an *M* (for "mechanistic") network analysis (Lindsey 1974) in order to determine the degree of similarity between the formal and informal communication structures.

The *M* technique is basically similar to the previous type of *H* network analysis, except that instead of identifying cliques on the basis of interaction patterns, the *M* technique begins with those groupings that are dictated by the organizational structure as constituting the departments or bureaus or divisions within the organization. It then proceeds to determine the communication flows within, and between, these formally determined groupings. *M* analysis thus assumes that the formal organizational structure is adequate, and communication flows are evaluated in terms of this structure. Thus, the *H* technique identifies individuals who actually *are* liaisons linking cliques, while the *M* technique shows which individuals *should be* liaisons between formal groupings. Naturally, both types of network analysis can be used with communication data from the same system in order to compare the results obtained from these two approaches.

Figure 5–7 presents an *M*-type network analysis for the data from the

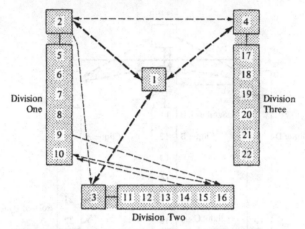

Division One

Division Three

Division Two

FIGURE 5–7. "M"-Type Network Analysis, Showing the Relative Overlap of the Informal with the Formal Communication Structure in the ARC Company (*Note:* The dark dotted lines represent communication patterns consistent with the formal structure of the organization, while the light dotted lines represent communication patterns that are not consistent with the formal structure. Within-division communication patterns are not shown in this diagram for the sake of simplicity.)

ARC Company; we see a relatively high degree of overlapping of the informal and formal communication structures. Most of the interpersonal communication is within the formal structures (the divisions); along with the top executive (Individual #1), it links the three divisions.

4. To recommend changes in the organization chart, or different assignments for certain individuals in the organization.[10] For instance, Clique C includes individuals in two divisions (Sales and Production); they act informally as a work group or Fayol's Bridge to develop new product lines for the company. Perhaps this clique might be formalized on the official organization chart if its functions are to continue, and if they need recognition.

Individual Communication Roles in Organizations

The individual members of an organization are not equivalent in their communication behavior. Certain individuals "keep the organization's

[10] Obviously it is crucial for the communication network analyst to know the organization thoroughly if he is to meaningfully interpret the highly quantitative results of the analysis; this knowledge of the "territory" is especially important when formulating recommendations.

gate" on message flows; they are gatekeepers. Others are located in a crucial position so as to connect the canvas of cliques; they are liaisons. Some are dominantly influential in an informal way; they are opinion leaders. "Boundary spanners" or cosmopolites are the organization's "windows to the world," in that they relate the system to its environment. Figure 5–8 graphically depicts these four types of individual roles.

GATEKEEPERS

A *gatekeeper* is an individual who is so located in a communication structure as to control the messages flowing through a communication channel.

FIGURE 5–8.   Individual Communication Roles in Organizations

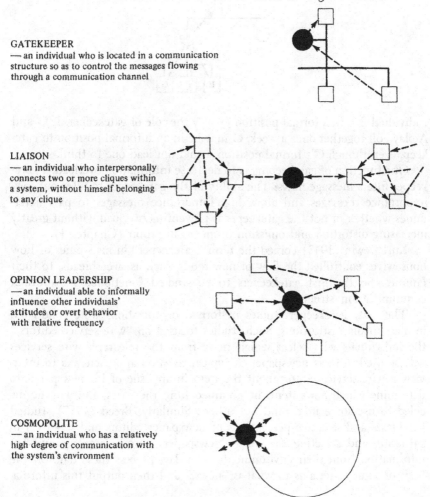

GATEKEEPER
— an individual who is located in a communication
structure so as to control the messages flowing
through a communication channel

LIAISON
— an individual who interpersonally
connects two or more cliques within
a system, without himself belonging
to any clique

OPINION LEADERSHIP
—an individual able to informally
influence other individuals'
attitudes or overt behavior
with relative frequency

COSMOPOLITE
— an individual who has a relatively
high degree of communication with
the system's environment

Thus a gatekeeper is similar to a valve in a waterpipe. If you have ever tried to get a rush memo into your boss, and his secretary told you he was "in conference," you know what a gatekeeper is. Secretaries are only one type of gatekeeper, of course. Any individual in *any* communication network, formal or informal, that approaches a chain is a gatekeeper. For example, in the chain network:

➛ ➛ A ➛ B ➛ C ➛ ➛

Individual B plays the role of gatekeeper. Likewise, any individual in a position in an organizational hierarchy through which messages must pass is to some extent a gatekeeper. For example, in the following three-level organization:

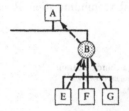

Individual B is in a formal position to play the role of gatekeeper. If G and A play golf together once a week, G may be in an informal position to gatekeep, even though G's formal position would not lead one to think so.

One function of gatekeeping is to decrease information overload; a gatekeeper filters message flows. The ability of the gatekeeper to filter out low-importance messages and allow high-importance messages to pass determines whether or not the gatekeeper is preventing overload without greatly increasing distortion and omission in an organization (Chapter 4).

Kurt Lewin (1943) coined the term "gatekeeper" in his studies of how housewives controlled the flow of new foods, such as sweetbreads, to their families. So the first gatekeepers to be studied functioned in informal communication structures.

The early gatekeeper studies in formal organizations were conducted in mass media institutions. Such studies focused on "wire service editors," the individuals who select which news from the telegraph wire services will be used in their newspaper. A typical research approach was to interview a wire service editor about the item in an issue of his newspaper to determine which news items he obtained from the wires, and why he decided to use some items and not others. Similarly, Breed (1955) studied the biases and selective perceptions of newspaper editors and reporters in gathering and selecting the news. Newspapers absorb large amounts of information from their environments each day, process these data on the basis of some criteria as to what is "news," and then output this information to the public on the printed page. So newspapers, and other mass media institutions, are classic examples of gatekeeping organizations (Dimmick 1974).

The process of gatekeeping occurs within a total systems framework; an organization is made up of a series of cliques whose primary function is the control of information flows.

Professor Thomas J. Allen and his associates at the Sloan School of Management at MIT have conducted a comprehensive series of studies of scientific gatekeepers in research-and-development laboratories (Allen 1966; Allen and Cohen 1969). T. J. Allen (1970) sociometrically determined the communication flows among the research-and-development scientists. Individuals called "technological gatekeepers" by Allen controlled the flow of technical and scientific knowledge among scientists. They typically made contact with many other scientists both outside and inside their laboratory. "Such men are able to operate in one system, [receive] messages . . , reprocess the information, and pass it on to their colleagues in a recorded form which they can use" (Allen 1969). In a study of An Foras Taluntals, the Irish Agricultural Institute, Allen and others (1971) found that technological gatekeepers played an important role in communication across international boundaries. They attended international meetings, received foreign degrees, and while on sabbatical leaves from AFT, worked in foreign countries.

More research needs to be done on gatekeepers in organizational communication; to date the surface has scarcely been scratched. Which positions in a clique do the most gatekeeping, and why? To what degree do formal and informal gatekeeping roles overlap? How effective are gatekeepers in controlling information flows so as to decrease overload without causing distortion and omission? What criteria are used by a gatekeeper in regulating the message flows through a channel?

LIAISONS

A *liaison* (sometimes called a "linker" or "linking pin" in the research literature) is an individual who interpersonally connects two or more cliques within a system, without himself belonging to any clique. (Certain individuals play a quasi-liaison role but are themselves members of a clique; they are called "bridges.") Thus liaisons are positioned at the crossroads of information flows in an organization. Liaisons have been called the "cement" that holds the structural "bricks" of an organization together; when the liaisons are removed, a system tends to fall apart into isolated cliques (Fig. 5–9).

Liaisons are important in getting communication messages from one subsystem to another within an organization. "The liaison is crucial, be-

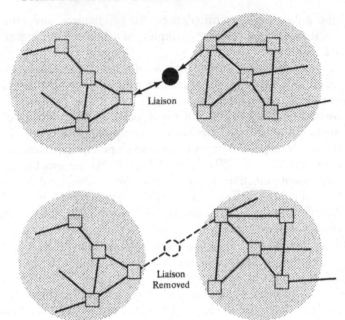

FIGURE 5–9. The interconnectedness of two cliques breaks down when the liaison is removed.

cause his loss destroys the connected unity of the organization. From the dynamic view, his non-substitutability in paths influences the flow functions of an organization. . . . If a liaison person is a bottleneck, the organization suffers badly, while if he is efficient, he tends to expedite the flow of the entire organization" (Ross and Harary 1955).

Because of their great importance in within-organizational communication, liaisons have been the subject of much communication research of a network analysis sort. Organizational communication research first focused on liaisons in a study by Jacobson and Seashore (1951), described in the previous section. They noted that "some individuals appear to function as liaison persons between groups [cliques], and characteristically have many, frequent, reciprocated, and important contacts which cut across the contact group structure. The [liaisons] . . . participate widely in the communication system but are not identifiable in any simple way with a single sub-group [clique]."

Actually, Jacobson and Seashore (1951) were not looking for liaisons when they found them for the first time; the objective of their research was to formulate and construct sociometric measures of clique membership. But once they identified the cliques within the Naval Research Laboratory, they could see that liaisons linking these cliques existed in the total network. If the liaisons were removed from the network, it decomposed into separate, unconnected cliques (Fig. 5–9).

The research on liaisons conducted since this pioneering study has concentrated on such questions as: How many liaisons typically exist within a communication network in an organization? How stable are liaisons across time, and across different message topics? What are the personal and communication characteristics of liaisons?

Not long after Jacobson and Seashore's investigation, the role of liaisons in the "Jason" Company was studied by Davis (1953a), who reported that only 10 percent of the 67 company executives were liaisons. Professor Davis did not specifically define what he meant by "liaison," nor did he relate exact criteria for identifying liaisons, so the seemingly small number of liaisons that he found may simply be an arbitrary artifact of his research procedures. Nevertheless, one might expect that most company executives would play a liaison role to at least some extent. (In fact, a common research finding in network analyses of organizations is that many individuals in higher management tend to be liaisons; this tendency is illustrated by Individual #1 in the ARC Company, shown in Figure 5–6.)

In the Schwartz (1968) study of 142 professors in the College of Education at Michigan State University, 22 liaisons (15 percent of the total faculty) were identified. They linked 29 work groups (cliques) of varying size. Thirty-two liaisons linked the 27 cliques and 501 individuals in a federal government agency (Berlo and others, 1972). Most network analyses find that from 5 to 20 percent of an organization's members are liaisons. But the exact number (and percentage) of liaisons identified in a network depends upon such factors as the exact sociometric question asked (for example, compare "Whom in this system do you talk with about work-related matters?" with "How often do you talk with each of the following individuals who work here in your system?") and the nature of the organizational task (for example, whether interdependence or independence is necessary among the workers).

One recent development in research on liaisons may have put to rest the issue of how many liaisons exist in an organization. Amend (1971) argued that instead of thinking of individuals as liaisons or nonliaisons, it is more fruitful to conceive of *every* individual in a system as playing a liaison role to some extent. So Amend measured the "liaisonness" of each of the agricultural extension service specialists in his sample, and correlated this variable with various others. The liaisonness scale gives points to a respondent for providing connectedness to the total communication network of an organization.

The issue of the stability of networks over time and across different message topics has remained relatively unexplored. In the original study of liaisons, Jacobson and Seashore (1951) assumed that the communication network of an organization remains relatively stable regardless of personnel changes. But this assumption could not be tested, nor has it been since, as data about sociometric communication patterns have not been gathered at more than one point in time.

Considerable attention has been focused on the stability of liaisons and other aspects of network structure across various topics of discussion, but the research results have been somewhat mixed. In network analysis research in organizations, of course, the usual procedure has been to query respondents about their work-related communication. Often this topic has been further broken down in terms of whom the respondent talks to about production matters, about maintenance activities, and about innovations.

In essence, respondents are asked whether their personal communication networks are "unistranded" (or "uniplex") or "multistranded"— that is, whether they name the same or different individuals as communication partners with respect to different subjects. Individuals in multistranded personal networks are presumably less able to withdraw from one another than those in unistranded networks, so the degree of control of the clique over the individual is greater in the former (Laumann 1973; Mitchell 1969).

The research results on the characteristics of liaisons are more clearcut. They generally have personal attributes that are little different from those of other members of the system. *The distinctiveness of liaisons stems not from their personal lifestyle (an individual characteristic), but from their unique communication-bridging function in the organization's network.*

Indeed, liaisons have been found to possess exactly those qualities that one would expect of individuals marginal to two or more cliques. For example, Yadav (1967) found that liaison farmers in two Punjabi villages in India possessed a degree of agricultural innovativeness intermediate between the norms of the cliques that they linked. Thus, a liaison who linked an innovative and an uninnovative clique was typically characterized by a degree of innovativeness somewhat less than that of the progressive clique and somewhat more than that of the backward clique. In general, liaisons characteristically have one foot in each of two or more different "worlds."

The liaison role has important practical implications for organizational communication, as liaisons are undoubtedly crucial for the effective operation of an organization's interpersonal network. Liaisons occupy strategic positions within organizations; they can be either expediters of information flow or bottlenecks in communication channels. Liaison roles may have to be formally created in an organization if they do not exist informally.

OPINION LEADERS

Opinion leadership is the ability to informally influence other individual's attitudes or behavior in a desired way with relative frequency. So opinion leaders are informal, rather than formal, leaders. The concept of opinion leadership was originally coined by Lazarsfeld and others (1948) as part of the two-step flow model, which hypothesized that communication messages flow from a source, via mass media channels, to opinion leaders, who in turn pass them on to followers in the public audience.

Leaders obtain their position of influence by rendering valuable and rare services to their system. Leader conformity to norms is a valuable service to the system in that the leader thus provides a living model of the norms for his followers. "A man of high status [that is, leadership] will conform to the most valued norms of his group as a minimum condition of maintaining his status" (Homans 1961, p. 339).

Opinion leadership has been studied in a wide variety of communication situations, ranging from peasant villages to medical doctors in Illinois cities (Rogers with Shoemaker 1973, Chapter 6), but seldom has it been studied within formal organizations like industrial plants, civil bureaucracies, or hospitals. Generally, opinion leaders tend to have greater access to external and expert sources of information, and their function is "to bring the group into touch with this relevant part of its environment" (Katz 1957).

The general picture of opinion leaders that emerges from their study in a variety of contexts is that, in comparison with their followers, they are characterized by (1) a wider range of exposure to external and technically competent sources of information, (2) greater accessibility to their followers, and (3) higher conformity to the norms of the group they lead.

Like gatekeepers and perhaps liaisons, opinion leaders may or may not be differentiated by topic. In an interview with the chief of a Turkish village, Professor Daniel Lerner of MIT asked a village chief about his influence on his villagers. The chief replied: "About all that you or I could imagine, even their [the villagers'] wives and how to handle them, and how to cure their sick cow" (Lerner 1958, p. 26). The degree to which opinion leaders are influential across various topics in a system varies from situation to situation.

In most organizations, opinion leadership is not possessed solely by higher executives. For example, in Figure 5-5, we see that Individual #1, the ARC Company president, has less opinion leadership than Individuals #3 or #4 (five sociometric choices) or Individual #7 (four choices). The Hawthorne studies clearly showed that informal leadership patterns operated to affect the performance of members in a work group, wherein the workers were equivalent in hierarchical position but certain workers were undeniably opinion leaders.

COSMOPOLITES

A *cosmopolite* (or "cosmopolitan") is an individual who has a relatively high degree of communication with the system's environment. To the extent that an organization has *openness*,[11] it must have at least some members who are cosmopolites. In most systems, cosmopolites are concentrated at the very top and at the bottom (Chapter 3). At the top, executives travel widely and enjoy other types of contact with other organizations; they are in a position to obtain new ideas from sources external to their own organization. Most of their contact with the environment is at a macro level, as they gather information about changes in the environment without usually knowing the fine details.

In contrast, individuals near the bottom of the organizational hierarchy also have a certain degree of cosmopoliteness, as they deal with the operational aspects of environmental change. Thus, the organization's lower-level workers deal directly with customers, with incoming materials and energy, and with other operational-level information. Their cosmopoliteness is at the grass-roots level.

In one sense, cosmopolites are a special type of gatekeeper as they control the communication flows by which new ideas enter the system. The cosmopoliteness of individuals is indexed by their wide travel, readership of nonlocal publications, national and international group affiliations, and membership in professional occupations with a high rate of migration, such as college professor, salesman, or minister.[12]

The cosmopoliteness of certain individuals in an organization is a resource to the system, in that such individuals enable the organization to cope with its environment. The ability to predict future changes in the environment is important for the survival of any system. Certain formal positions in organizations, such as market research analyst, ombudsperson, public relations officer, research and development scientist, and sales manager, provide opportunities for wider contact with the environment. As a result, these individuals are more likely than others to be cosmopolites.

The four communication roles that we have described here each represent a special function that needs to be played in a communication network:

COMMUNICATION ROLE	FUNCTION IN THE NETWORK
1. *Gatekeeper*	Prevents information overload by filtering and screening messages
2. *Liaison*	Integrates and interconnects the parts (cliques) of the network
3. *Opinion leader*	Facilitates informal decision making in the network
4. *Cosmopolite*	Relates the system to its environment by providing openness

[11] *Openness* is the degree to which a system exchanges information with its environment.

[12] The usual measure of organizational cosmopoliteness is in terms of the individual's loyalty to the organization. A typical question that has been asked to index cosmopoliteness is: "In the long run, would you rather be known and respected (1)

Communication Structural Variables

As we pointed out in Chapter 1, almost all communication research to date uses the individual respondent as the unit of data analysis, and concentrates on determining the effects of communication. In this book we have argued for the advantage of operationalizing communication *relationships* between two or more individuals, usually utilizing some types of sociometric measurement. Several types of relational analysis of communication behavior can then be utilized to probe the nature of the communication relationships at the level of: (1) the individual's personal communication network, (2) the clique, and (3) the system. At each level, various indexes can be constructed to operationalize the type of communication structure that is present.

PERSONAL COMMUNICATION NETWORKS

At the lowest level, an important structural characteristic is the degree to which a person is integrated with the individuals in his personal communication network. *Personal communication network integration* is defined as the degree to which communication links exist among the members of an individual's personal communication network. The greater the number of these links, the greater the degree of integration of a particular individual's communication network. As we showed previously (Fig. 5–2), an interlocking personal network has a high degree of integration, while a radial personal network has a low degree of integration. In the latter case, one's friends are not friends of each other; this type of unintegrated network is more open to its environment, and we expect that an individual who has this type of network will receive a particular message that is circulating in his or her system relatively earlier than one with an interlocking network. So more highly integrated personal networks are informationally weaker.

Liaisons in a network of agricultural extension specialists at a state university were found to have a higher degree of personal network integration than nonliaisons (Amend 1971, p. 46). The liaisons communicated about work-related matters with peers who were not linked with each other. Such a diversity in personal networks is exactly what we would expect to characterize liaisons, who are by definition in a marginal position between two or more cliques in their system. We also might expect opinion leaders in an organization to have less integrated (and informationally stronger) personal networks.

---

throughout the institution where you work, or (2) among specialists in your field in different institutions?"

Personal network integration is greater for some topics of communication, like sensitive or taboo[13] issues, than for others.[14] Laumann (1973, p. 125) found that urban men in Detroit discussed such issues as voting and what kind of a new car to buy with less integrated personal networks (that is, in more radial networks), but the same respondents communicated about more sensitive topics, like a serious medical problem, with more integrated (that is, interlocking, or closed) personal networks.

So the degree of integration in personal communication networks has been related to (1) special communication roles in a system, like liaisons, and (2) different topics of conversation.

CLIQUE-LEVEL ANALYSIS

At the clique level of analysis, we can consider a variety of structural variables that can be measured: (1) clique connectedness, (2) clique dominance, (3) clique openness, and (4) clique integration into the larger system.

1. *Clique connectedness* is the degree to which the members of a clique are linked with each other by communication flows. The actual degree of connectedness among the individuals in a clique (measured by the number of interpersonal communication flows) can be compared to the total possible degree of connectedness that could potentially exist (Fig. 5–10). Such an index of communication connectedness can be computed for each clique, and the clique then becomes the unit of analysis. This index allows us to investigate the relationship between the degree of connectedness in a clique and various other clique-level variables, like the relative speed of diffusion of a new idea in one clique as compared with others.

For example, Berlo and others (1972, p. 14) found that the degree of clique connectedness among twenty-seven cliques in a federal agency in the Pentagon ranged from 85 percent (this clique was centered in the agency director's office) down to 11 percent (for a clique in the planning office, where presumably the need for clique members to work in close connection was much less). As might be expected, larger-sized cliques had less connectedness; it is more difficult for everyone in a larger clique to communicate with everyone else. The highest degree of connectedness was for work groups of about seven to ten members. The planning office clique, with only 11 percent connectedness, had seventeen members. An implication for reorganization of this agency might be to formally divide

---

[13] *Taboo* communication is that category of message transfer in which the messages are perceived as extremely private and personal in nature because they deal with proscribed behavior.

[14] Kincaid (1973) found that the degree of personal network integration among slum dwellers in Mexico City, measured in an approach similar to Laumann's, was related to the adoption of family planning methods.

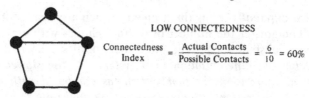

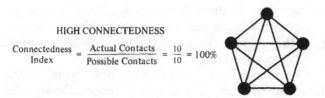

FIGURE 5–10. An Illustration of Low and High Communication Connectedness in a Small System

this unit into two subgroups if a higher degree of connectedness were desired.

2. *Clique dominance* is the degree to which the patterns of communication relationship among clique members deviate from equality. The "wheel" network shown in Figure 5–3 has a high degree of dominance, in that all communication flows must pass through one individual. Such centralization causes information overload and tends to limit openness. Berlo and others (1972) measured clique dominance in a federal government agency and found it to be highly related (negatively) to clique connectedness.

3. *Clique openness* is the degree to which the members of a clique exchange information with the clique's external environment. Where new ideas must enter a clique from external sources, as is often the case, those cliques with greater openness are expected to be more innovative.

4. A final structural index at the clique level of analysis is *clique integration* into the larger network. This measure is analagous to the integration index for personal communication networks discussed previously, but here we are measuring the degree to which a single clique is linked with others in the system. Such integration rests on the number of liaisons and their location in the total communication network for the organization.

To date few researches have been conducted using clique openness or clique integration indexes.

SYSTEM-LEVEL ANALYSIS

Once we have isolated, measured, and analyzed communication structural variables at the personal network and clique levels of analysis, we can also compute structural indices for entire systems, like organizations.

System differentiation is the degree to which a system contains distinct cliques. The greater the number of distinct cliques within a social system (at a given constant size),[15] the more that social system is differentiated. *The greater the differentiation in a system, (1) the slower the rate of diffusion of innovations in that system (as compared with others), and (2) the lower the system's productivity in accomplishing tasks that require collaboration by the total system.*

System connectedness is the degree to which the cliques in a system are linked to each other by communication flows. This index enables us to represent mathematically the relative degree of clique interlinkage within a particular social system.

Betty's (1974) investigation of forty-one family planning clinics in the Philippines illustrates use of the system connectedness index. His dependent variable was the productivity of each clinic, as measured by the number of adopters of family planning methods secured by the clinic staff each month. Independent variables, such as the degree to which its staff were dependent on each other for information, were communication indexes for each clinic. The connectedness of the clinic staff members was tested to determine its importance in intervening between the independent variables and the dependent variable of clinic productivity. In diagramatic form:

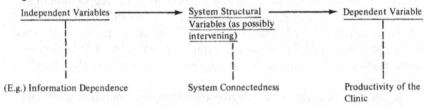

Although Betty's empirical results did not provide much support for his theoretical design, his paradigm is provocative in terms of further investigation. Significantly, it utilizes the organization (in this case, the clinic) as the unit of analysis.

Another research using system connectedness was conducted by Allen (1970) in two innovative and two noninnovative high schools in Michigan. The innovative systems had a higher degree of connectedness among the teaching staff; the noninnovative schools had more isolates, and the cliques among teachers there were interlinked less closely by interpersonal communication patterns. Generally, we expect that the degree of connectedness in a communication network is positively related to the rate of diffusion of innovations.

System dominance is the degree to which the patterns of communication relationships among cliques in a social system deviate from equality.

---

[15] We can remove the effects of the number of individuals in a system by making the measure relative to the size of the system.

Thus it is a measure of the degree of centralization governing interclique communication. The greater the control by a single clique over the communication flows within the entire set of cliques, the higher the system dominance. A system with high dominance should be able to make decisions quickly, but its openness to the environment should be less and hence information should be less likely to penetrate the boundary of the system. R. K. Allen (1970) found only weak support for this proposition, however, in his investigation of both innovative and noninnovative high schools in Michigan.

System openness is the degree to which a system exchanges information with its environment. As we argued in Chapter 3, systems with greater openness are likely to be more innovative.

We summarize the various indexes of communication structure in Table 5–2. The possibility of using these measures to probe their relationships with organizational innovation and productivity has been appreciated only in recent years, and so much of our preceding discussion of communication structural variables has necessarily been hypothetical, rather than a synthesis of completed research. These communication structural variables can help point the way toward new types of network analysis communication research in organization.

Summary

The purpose of this chapter was to describe what is known about communication networks in organizations. A *network* consists of interconnected individuals who are linked by patterned communication flows. Networks depict the "micro" aspects of communication in the "macro" settings of organizations. The importance of networks is suggested by the existence of *system effects*, the influences of others in a system on the behavior of an individual member of the system; such effects are exerted on the individual through his communication network relationships. The formal communication system of an organization may be forced on its members, but *the informal communication networks emerge spontaneously and are less structured and hence less predictable.*

Personal networks consist of interconnected individuals who are linked by patterned communication flows to any given individual. Personal networks are either (1) *radial,* in which an individual interacts with friends who do not interact with each other, or (2) *interlocking,* in which an individual's friends interact with each other. *The informational strength of dyadic communication relationships is inversely related to the degree of homophily (and the strength of the attraction) between the source and the receiver.*

TABLE 5-2. Summary of Communication Structural Indexes at the Personal Network, Clique, and System Levels

Communication Structural Index	Level of Analysis		
	PERSONAL NETWORK	CLIQUE	SYSTEM
1. *The degree of integration of the unit with a higher-level unit*	*Personal network integration:* the degree to which communication links exist among the members of an individual's personal communication network	*Clique integration:* The degree to which communication links exist between a particular clique and all other cliques in the system	*System connectedness:* the degree to which the cliques in a system are linked to each other by communication flows
2. *The degree of interconnectedness among units in a higher-level unit*		*Clique connectedness:* the degree to which the members of a clique are linked with each other by communication flows.	*System dominance:* the degree to which the patterns of communication relationships among the cliques in a system deviate from equality
3. *The degree to which the communication relationships among units in a higher-level unit deviate from equality:* dominance		*Clique dominance:* the degree to which the patterns of communication relationships among clique members deviate from equality.	
4. *The degree to which a unit exchanges information with its environment:* openness		*Clique openness:* the degree to which the members of a clique exchange information with the clique's external environment	*System openness:* the degree to which a system exchanges information with its environment
5. *The degree to which a higher-level unit is composed of distinct subunits:* differentiation			*System differentiation:* the degree to which a system contains distinct cliques

Open system theory influenced organization communication researches to focus on new within-organization variables, and especially to move from atomistic reseach utilizing individuals as units of analysis (1) to dyadic or other relational units in which communication relationships constitute the main research emphasis, and (2) to more systems-level concerns, in which communication network analysis is often utilized. Open system theory stressed communication as the vital ingredient in organizations; communication is by nature relational. One important type of communication research using relationships between individuals as units of analysis is network analysis.

The laboratory small groups studies attempted a unique contribution toward understanding communication behavior in organizations, but they lacked the reality of an ongoing, "live" organization. Communication network research on laboratory groups became a standard experimental approach in the 1950s and the 1960s. *These researches provided information about the structural effects in communication networks, but the precise nature of the relationships among the variables involved remained largely unclear.*

Network analysis is a method of research for identifying the communication structure in a system in which sociometric data about communication flows or patterns are analyzed by utilizing interpersonal relationships as the units of analysis. Communication inquiry in organizations generally makes manifest the otherwise static nature of structural variables; network analysis permits understanding the dynamics of organizational structural variables as they determine communication flows between units and across hierarchical positions.

Most clique members in a network are usually relatively close to each other in the formal hierarchy of the organization. Three main communication roles have emerged in network analysis: *isolates*, *bridges*, and *liaisons*. An *isolate* is a person who has few communication contacts with the rest of the system. A *bridge* is a member of one communication clique who links it with a member of another clique. A *liaison* is an individual who connects two or more cliques within a system without himself belonging to any clique.

Three other special communication roles that individuals play in organizations are: (1) a *gatekeeper*, an individual who is located in a communication structure so as to control the messages flowing through a given communication channel, (2) an *opinion leader*, who has the ability to informally influence other individuals' attitudes or behavior in a desired way with relative frequency, and (3) a *cosmopolite*, an individual who has a relatively high degree of communication with the system's environment. Each of these communication roles represents a special function that needs to be played in a communication network. The gatekeeper prevents information overload by filtering and screening messages; a liaison integrates and interconnects the parts (cliques) of the network; an opinion leader facilitates informal decision making in the network; and a cosmopolite relates the system to its environment by providing openness.

Although almost all communication research to date has used the individual as the unit of analysis, we propose that the *relationship* between individuals ought to be the unit of analysis, using some type of sociometric measurement. Three relational levels at which communication relationships can be studied are: (1) personal communication networks, (2) cliques, and (3) systems.

6. Innovation in Organizations[1]

"An innovative organization is one which is continuously learning, adapting to, as well as initiating, changes within itself and its environment."

—Bjarne Ruby

Kurt Lewin once said that if someone wants to thoroughly understand how something works, he should try to change it. The process of innovation and change illuminates much about the nature of the object that is changing.

In the present chapter we investigate innovation in organizations in order to better understand the nature of organizational structure and how it affects one particular type of communication, that which is involved in innovation. Communication is a necessary ingredient at every step in the innovation process, as we shall see in later sections of this chapter.

Bureaucracies are created to handle routine tasks and to lend stability to human relationships. Their efficiency as a means of organizing is in part due to this stability, which stems from the relatively high degree of structure that is imposed on communication patterns. This advantage is best realized when the rate of change is slow. When the environment changes rapidly, causing a need for correspondingly rapid change in the organization, the organizational structure becomes so temporary that the efficiencies of bureaucracy cannot be achieved (Perrow 1972, p. 5).

One might think that innovation would be a very rare occurrence in organizations. In fact, though, innovation is going on all the time in almost every organization, and most organization scholars consider the innovation process as one of the main functions in organizations, along with production (activities concerned with getting the work done), and

[1] This chapter is coauthored by John D. Eveland of the University of Michigan. We are greatly indebted to Professor Lawrence B. Mohr of the University of Michigan for his valuable discussions of, and insight into, the innovation process in organizations. Parts of the present chapter were originally written for the Office of National R&D Assessment of the National Science Foundation.

maintenance (Katz and Kahn 1966, p. 39). We are often more aware of what is stable about an organization than of what is changing, and so we usually underestimate the rate of innovation in an organization. This is not to imply that all organizations are appropriately receptive to innovation. For example, many recent college graduates who go to work in large organizations are filled with creative ideas that might be useful to their organization, but which they cannot get adopted owing to their low position in the organizational hierachy. With a more adequate understanding of the innovation process, these new professionals might be more effective in securing adoption of their innovations.

Innovation and Innovativeness

An innovation is usually defined as "an idea, practice, or object perceived as new by the individual" (Rogers with Shoemaker 1971, p. 19), and this meaning is sufficient for most purposes. But when we are discussing innovation in organizations, we need to broaden the definition from "by the individual" to "by the relevant unit of adoption," whether it is an individual or an organization (Zaltman and others, 1973, p. 10). So we define an *innovation* as an idea, practice, or object perceived as new by the relevant unit of adoption.

In considering organizational innovations, we distinguish two general types of innovations, which are characterized by very different dynamics in respect of the innovation process. "Innovations *of* the organization" are those innovations adopted as a result of an organizational decision which do not require most members to behave differently as individuals (for example, the addition of a new product line by a manufacturing firm). The organization as a whole changes, but not most of the people within it. "Innovations *in* the organization" are those innovations which require changes in individual behavior (for example, installation of the Scanlon Plan).

The first investigation of the diffusion of an innovation was a study by Bryce Ryan and Neal C. Gross (1943) of hybrid seed corn in Iowa. The adopters of this innovation were individual farmers. A great many of the some 2,700 publications about the diffusion of innovations published in the thirty-three years since the Ryan and Gross study have investigated individuals—farmers, consumers, medical doctors, and school teachers— as the units of analysis. Often this focus on the individual as the unit of adoption of the innovation was appropriate. In many other cases, it was not.

Certainly many innovations are adopted by organizations rather than by individuals. In recent years this fact has become more clearly recognized, and a number of publications on innovation in organizations appeared in the late 1960s and early 1970s. Unfortunately, this literature generally features "treatments of innovations vis-á-vis organizations [that] tend to follow the individual-oriented approaches" (Zaltman and others, 1973, pp. 10–11).

In the present chapter we shall review and synthesize this research literature on innovation in organizations. It consists mostly of studies in which the organization is the unit of analysis, and in which sample survey data are gathered via questionnaires sent only to the chief executive of the organization (such as a school superintendent or factory manager). As a result of this methodological approach, we have gained considerable knowledge about how innovations spread *from* organization to organization,[2] such as from hospital to hospital, but we lack an understanding of how communication and decision-making processes are involved in the adoption of innovations *within* organizations. Intraorganizational innovative behavior cannot be properly understood if it is viewed only through the eyes at the top.

In this chapter we propose a model of the innovation process in organizations. As relatively little research has been completed on this topic, our approach must necessarily be somewhat hypothetical and suggestive.

A central problem in studying innovation in organizations is that the development of models of innovation has not kept pace with interest in the topic. Usually, in the development of a social science research area, the research stages are as outlined in Table 6–1. The study of innovation has not followed this pattern. Virtually all research attention to date has been concentrated at stage #3 in the process: the standard pattern has been to concentrate on the relationships of various organizational variables to "organizational innovativeness." To a large degree, the variables studied have been derived from other social science research rather than from a consideration of innovation as an organizational process in its own right.[3]

We believe that additional work is needed at stage #2 of the process —the identification and testing of new variables. This chapter outlines a model of the innovation process which introduces concepts and variables not usually studied: performance gaps, slack resources, and external accountability.

In the remainder of this chapter we speak frequently of two concepts which sound alike but which mean rather different (although related) things. *Innovation*, as we have noted above, is the process of adopting new ideas. *Innovativeness*, on the other hand, is a property of the adopting

[2] To be more specific, we understand something about certain characteristics of organizations that are related to their "innovativeness," but we do not yet have the type of studies which would enable us to understand the innovation process in organizational settings.

[3] We pointed out in Chapter 1 that invisible colleges emerge among scholars which influence the thinking, writing, and research done in a given area. The invisible college sets the agenda of what is going to be studied.

TABLE 6–1. A Classification of Stages in Social Science Research

RESEARCH STAGE	RESEARCH PURPOSE	RESEARCH METHOD
1. *Problem delineation*	To define what we are looking for, and the extent to which it constitutes a social problem	Qualitative analysis, such as observation, case studies, unstructured interviews, and literature review
2. *Variable identification*	To identify variables which might be linked to the problem, and to describe possible relationships among these variables	Exploratory case studies, and other qualitative methods that are low on their degree of structure
3. *Determination of relationships among the variables*	To determine the clusters of relevant variables required for prediction, and to analyze their patterns of relationships.	Cross-sectional, correlational analysis of quantitative survey data
4. *Establishment of causality among the variables*	To determine which factors are critical in promoting or inhibiting the problem	Longitudinal studies, and small-scale experiments with (1) over-time data, (2) in which at least one variable changes prior to the others, so that we can determine time order
5. *Manipulation of causal variables for policy formation purposes*	To determine the correspondence between a theoretical problem solution and the manipulatable factors	Field experiments
6. *Evaluation of alternative policies and programs*	To assess the expected, as well as the unanticipated, consequences of various programs and policies before and after they are applied on a large scale, and to determine the effectiveness of such programs in overall problem solution	Controlled field comparisons, such as the interrupted time series field experiment

NOTE: Based on Gordon and others (1974a).

unit: viz., the degree to which a given unit is earlier than other units in adopting innovations. Innovativeness is measured in two different ways, depending on the specific type of problem being studied. In studies of a single innovation, it is usually indexed in terms of the "earliness of adoption" of the new idea. In studies of multiple innovations, it is usually measured as the "total number of innovations adopted at any point in time." In either case, it is primarily a measure of the proclivity of the organization to reach outside itself for solutions to its perceived problems.

In the process terms we use in this chapter, innovativeness is not the ultimate dependent variable, but more of an intervening variable that is predictive of the organization's effectiveness.

INNOVATION AND CHANGE

A distinction is sometimes made between innovation and change in an organization. Whereas innovation implies adoption of an idea perceived as new, change may also involve the replacement of an already existing idea by another idea. The idea being adopted may be perceived as new (and thus be an innovation), or it may be a familiar, accustomed idea. So some changes are innovations, but not all.

Most people, however, use the terms "innovation" and "change" almost interchangeably. We, too, do not find it fruitful to make much of the distinction. The communication patterns for change and innovation in organizations are rather similar.

There are several ways to bring about change in an organization, in addition to innovation. One way is to terminate or destroy the organization. What emerges out of the surviving fragments will be different from the previous organization, so destruction is one means of changing a system. This extreme approach is sometimes advocated by radical revolutionaries as a means for changing society. It is a costly strategy in terms of the disruption it wreaks in the lives of the system's members and in the disturbance created in the functions performed by the organization that is destroyed. But it usually does bring about large-scale change.

Another type of change in a system occurs when the communication structure is altered, such as by installing an automated information system using computers. In this case, not only may there be greater cost effectiveness in performing certain information-handling tasks, but there may also be an impetus for many other innovations by the organization. The new technology opens up new communication channels and brings new information to bear on decisions.

Another effect of introducing computers into an organization, however, is to decrease human interaction. Insurance clerks whose work was computerized spent more of their time working alone and less in communication with their peers (Whisler 1970). An Air Force officer remarked on the consequences of a computer system after it was introduced in a military command center: "One of the queerest observations that I have made concerns this mass of engineers, technicians, machine operators, and operations people milling around and working almost unaware that anyone else exists" (Whisler 1970, p. 76).

Another route to changing organizations is to reorganize their subunits. This type of reorganization amounts to maintenance of the overall organization along with destruction of some or all of its subsystems. The reorganization approach to organizational change is frequent in federal, state, and city governments. Often it is done to give the appearance of change without really effectuating much real change. Boxes in the organizational chart are shuffled and often renamed, but the same individuals are usually retained in the organization, and the organization still fulfills about the same functions and in approximately the same way as before the reorganization. Reorganization does serve to highlight functions in a different way, and the reaction of the public to the reorganized structure (in the case of a governmental organization) is likely to be different. By thus changing public expectations (an environmental variable), reorganization can bring about more organizational change over time then was either foreseen or desired, by those who originally carried it out.

Yet another change strategy in organizations is to change the individual members within the existing structure. One set of individuals may be discharged and a different set of individuals hired, perhaps with different qualifications or attitudes than those they are replacing. Or the same individuals may stay in the organization but be trained or retrained so that they gain a new point of view or improved competencies. In either event the structure is not directly altered, and so the effect of the new training or employees is usually dampened by the unchanging structure. A common experience with employees who are retrained is that when they return to their old positions in the organization, the effect of the training is short-lived, and they soon revert to their old ways. The net result: little real change.

On the other hand, changing the personnel in an organization *may* lead to innovation if a policy of recruiting innovative individuals is followed for some time. Davis (1965) found evidence supporting this strategy in his analysis of one innovative and one traditionally oriented liberal arts college. The hiring policies of the two institutions proved to be the single most important differentiating factor. The innovative college selected faculty members on the basis of their experience with teaching innovations, and eventually this policy created a norm favoring constant change.[4]

The Human Relations School of organizational theory has virtually preempted the study of organizational change. Most books whose titles

[4] However, the rapid turnover of faculty may prevent the continuing *implementation* of innovations. Mitchell (1970) found that the continuity of individuals involved with an organizational innovation improved the chances that the innovation would continue to be used. When the top executives in the university he studied resigned or were fired, the innovation they had promoted throughout the university disappeared with them.

indicate that they deal with organizational change, such as Bennis's *Changing Organizations* (1966), are actually more concerned with changing individuals within organizations. Of 109 articles in sociological journals about organizational change, 84 were actually about changing individual attitudes or work behavior within organizations, not about changing the organizations themselves (Baldridge and Burnham 1973, p. 3).

Why have most studies of "organizational change" taken this individualistic bent? For one thing, many of the researchers were psychologists or social psychologists, trained to focus primarily on the individual. Also, many of these research studies were conducted in order to provide utilizable results, and it was assumed that individual attitudes and behavior were more manipulatable than organizational structure. Again we see an example of individual-blame, as opposed to system-blame, assumptions in defining a social problem, and of how this perception influences the approach to research that is followed by the invisible college of scientists in a field.

We feel it is intellectually more fruitful to focus on the innovation process in organizations than to adopt any of the previous approaches to change in organizations.

The Process of Innovation in Organizations

Oddly enough, it is only relatively recently that students of organization have begun to consider the *process* nature of innovation. The notion that innovation takes place over time, and that there are defined stages in the process, has been late in emerging.

One explanation for past inattention to the innovation process in organizations lies in the attraction of the alternative of studying innovativeness as a dependent variable. Innovativeness is relatively easy to identify, measure, and correlate with other phenomena. Studying any process over time, by comparison, is complex and difficult. However, the potential value of a process model of innovation warrants future research in this direction, rather than on organizational innovativeness. Only if we can in some sense approximate the actual behavior of organizations as they make and implement decisions to innovate can we hope to make them more effective in this regard.

In this section we shall present a model of the innovation process which assumes that (1) innovation is one of a number of possible responses by the organization to a confluence of external forces acting on it; (2) innovation proceeds through a number of stages, representing increasing commitment by the organization; (3) the process is not unidirectional but interactive, subject to backtracking and change; and (4) one of the best measures of the effects of innovation is change in the overall effectiveness of the organization. Our approach requires explicit consideration of the time dimension—a methodologically difficult procedure, but the only one which promises an opportunity to directly relate innovation to the observable activities of the organization.

Only a process model can adequately incorporate communication variables into an analytical approach to innovation. We have noted in Chapter 2 the importance of the time element in communication behavior, a factor extremely difficult to deal with in cross-sectional research.[5]

INNOVATION AS A STEPWISE PROCESS

The notion that the innovation process consists of a series of defined stages has been current for a number of years. One distinction that is frequently made is between two main stages in the innovation process: (1) *initiation*, the process by which an organization becomes aware of an innovation and decides to adopt it; and (2) *implementation*, the process by which an organization puts the innovation into practice, and eventually institutionalizes it into its ongoing operations.

Sapolsky (1967) argues that *those structural characteristics of an organization (such as high complexity, low formalization, and low centralization) that facilitate initiation of the innovation process by opening the organization to its environment make it difficult for the organization to implement the innovation* (Table 6–2).

This paradox of organizational structural variables in the innovation process might be solved if an organization could create a subsystem (like a research and development unit) that is complex, informal, and decentralized to initiate innovations, while the remainder of the organization remained low in complexity, formalized, and centralized in order to facilitate the implementation of innovations (Duncan 1974). Or a new product group in a manufacturing organization might be so organized as to emphasize complexity, informality, and decentralization while they are initiating an innovation, and then reorganized so as to emphasize the opposite type of organizational structure when implementing the innovation (that is, producing the new product). Such a dual structure, however, may be impractical or impossible for most organizations.

The idea that different structural characteristics of an organization may have different effects on the innovation process at different times is a useful one. We feel, however, that a more subtle model than this two-

---

[5] A more appropriate research technique for investigating the over-time process aspects of innovation in organizations is the so-called "tracer" approach, in which the stepwise stages in the innovation process are reconstructed from various sources, including official records and interviews with the participants.

T A B L E 6–2. Organizational Structural Variables Play Different Roles at Different Stages in the Innovation Process in Organizations.

Organizational Structural Variable	*Effect on the Innovation Process*	
	INITIATION STAGE	IMPLEMENTATION STAGE
1. *Complexity* (the number of occupational specialties and their professionalization)	+	−
Complexity encourages members to conceive and propose innovations, but makes it difficult to achieve consensus about which innovations to implement.		
2. *Formalization* (emphasis on following rules and procedures in role performance)	−	+
Formalization inhibits consideration of innovations by organization members, but encourages implementation of innovations.		
3. *Centralization* (concentration of power in an organization)	−	+
Centralization inhibits generation of innovations, but facilitates their implementation.		

stage approach will better describe the course of innovation events in most organizations. In the present section we outline such a model, along with the assumptions about organizations on which it is based.

In the innovation literature, it is common to treat innovation as in some sense an "inevitable" phenomenon. This view of innovation as always "good" has hampered our understanding of the innovation process. In fact, innovation is a highly contingent process, and the decisions surrounding it are by no means unidirectional.

PERFORMANCE GAPS AND PROBLEM DEFINITION

Problem definition is the process by which an organization defines and specifies its *performance gaps*, perceptions of discrepancies between the organization's expectations and its actualities. Performance gaps may be defined by the organization (or parts of it) with widely varying degrees of specificity, from the most general statements of concern to the most operationally precise instructions for needed action.

The measurement of performance gaps is one of the most difficult problems in organizational studies. The key to the existence of a performance gap is a difference between an expectation and a reality; gaps can thus be created or removed by changes in either dimension. For measurement purposes, therefore, it is necessary to obtain parallel measures of perceived expectations and perceived realities in related problem performance.

This assessment might consist of a set of scales to quantify the degree to which respondents perceive particular problems to be relevant to the organization. Another approach is to ask respondents to define their principal expectations for the organization and their assessment of the degree to which those expectations are being met. These two approaches could, when combined, identify the areas in which expectation and reality differ.

PERCEIVING A PERFORMANCE GAP

Within three months after the Surgeon General's report was published in 1964, cigarette consumption in the United States dropped 11 percent. Many consumers soon recovered from the scare and took up smoking again. But the tobacco companies had learned a lesson, and they began (1) to devote increased research to creating a safe cigarette, and (2) to diversifying their product line by purchasing dog-food and pineapple companies (Hage and Aiken 1970, pp. 78–79). Tobacco companies engaged in a frantic search for new alternatives in the face of a suddenly altered environment and a dramatic performance gap, illuminated by the difference between their pre-scare and post-scare sales. The companies' search behavior was a means of coping with environmental change, and led to the adoption of innovations.

Another illustration of the difference between an objective, and a perceived, performance gap is provided by Hirschman's (1973, p. 45) analysis of the Nigerian railways, which gave poor service and were faced with strong competition from truck transportation, yet failed to change. Many customers switched to truck transportation (what Hirschman calls "exit"), but the railway officials were unconcerned, because the loss of revenues was not important to the government-managed firm. "Voice" (that is, feedback from dissatisfied customers) was also ineffective in motivating innovation on the part of the officials; they simply did not perceive a performance gap. In a situation in which the services provided by an organization are declining, continued loyalty by the organization's customers or clients may simply delay the realization by the organization's leaders of a performance gap (Hirschman 1973). If customers would switch to a competitor, or complain loudly about the inferior service being provided, they would actually be helping the organization more than by their loyalty.

On some occasions, there may a lengthy period before an organization recognizes a performance gap and takes action to do something about it. Often the realization of a performance gap occurs because the system compares itself, and its relative effectiveness, with another system. Hence, interorganizational relationships with other systems in the relevant environment may be important in facilitating perception of a performance gap and thus stimulating innovation. For example, the launching of Sputnik by Russia in 1958 was interpreted by United States officials as indicating a performance gap in technological prowess. They immediately adopted a number of innovative programs to try to close the performance gap, and eventually did close it in 1969.

In these examples, *a performance gap creates a search for innovations (among other possible alternatives)* in order to close the gap. On the other hand, when an organization becomes aware of the possibility of better performance if it were using an innovation, the innovation *creates* a perceived performance gap.

Four main classes of factors affect the nature and direction of the innovation process: (1) *knowledge of innovations*, (2) *external accountability*, (3) *slack resources*, and (4) *organizational structure*.

KNOWLEDGE OF INNOVATIONS AND REINVENTION

The likelihood of an organization's bringing an innovation "through its boundary" (Chapter 3) and incorporating it into its structure is influenced by the number of innovations of which the organization is aware, and its perception of their salient characteristics. This knowledge factor is influenced partly by characteristics of the personnel in the organization (such as their cosmopoliteness and professionalism) and partly by the existence of defined search processes. The manner in which a problem and a suggested innovation are defined by the organization determines whether the innovation will be adopted. The innovation must be perceived as potentially closing the performance gap in order for its adoption to occur.

Past research on innovation in organizations has assumed that a new technological idea enters the system from external sources and is then adopted (with relatively little change or adaptation) and implemented as part of the organization's ongoing operations. In actuality, however, *many innovations go through extensive revision, essentially amounting to "reinvention," in the process of their adoption and implementation within the organization.* For example, Charters and Pelligrin (1973) found that in public schools, the innovation of "differentiated staffing" (encouraging the hiring of a variety of both teachers and paraprofessional teaching aides, and assigning them to classroom tasks on the basis of their skills and interests) was little more than a vague term to most school staff. Its substantive meaning was actually assigned by school officials and teachers as it was being implemented. "The innovation was to be invented on the inside, not imported from the outside" (Charters and Pelligrin 1973).

So organizations often adopt not a specific blueprint for an innovation but a general concept whose operational meaning gradually unfolds in the process of implementation. Thus "innovation" in an organization may often amount to "reinventing the wheel."

EXTERNAL ACCOUNTABILITY

External accountability is the degree to which an organization is dependent on, or responsible to, its environment. Familiar forms of dependence are an organization's needs for funds and its personnel and clients, which it depends on outside sources to provide through exchange transactions with its environment. "An organization is dependent on some element of its task environment (1) in proportion to the organization's need for resources or performance which the element can provide, and (2) in inverse proportion to the ability of other elements to provide the same resource or performance" (Thompson 1967, p. 30).

But dependence can go much deeper, incorporating a psychological dimension. Organizations, like individuals, may have "reference groups." Each organization has a set of individuals, groups, and other organizations which it consistently takes into consideration in its actions and decision making. In operational terms, external accountability may be measured by which outside groups the organization allows to ask questions which it must answer (the *points* of accountability) and the subject areas which such questions may legitimately address (the *terms* of the accountability).

There are many possible measures of an organization's external accountability. One, used by Aiken and Hage (1968), is the number of joint programs conducted cooperatively with other organizations. The externally accountable agencies by this criterion, Aiken and Hage (1968) found, provided for "the involvement of [an organization's] staff in interorganizational relationships [which] introduces them to new ideas, new perspectives, and new techniques for solving organizational problems. The establishment of collegial relationships with comparable staff members of other organizations provides them with a comparable framework for understanding their own organizations."

The mechanism by which external accountability is translated into organizational action involves the formation of organizational expectations, which come from two main sources. The first source is the norms of the organization and its professionals. Over most classes of organizations, this source of expectations tends to be fairly constant over time. The other, less stable source of expectations is external accountability. In general, the greater the number of accountability relationships to which an organization is a party, the more expectations it will acquire and the greater the probability of its defining performance gaps. *Organizations with a higher degree of external accountability are more innovative.*

Most public schools and universities are "domesticated" in that they do not have to compete strenuously for clients and a certain level of funding and other necessary resources is guaranteed (Carlson 1964). Domesticated organizations do not have to adapt quickly to a changing environment; they have a low degree of external accountability, and hence of innovation.

Organizations must influence their relevant environment and have some degree of control over it (rather than simply react or adjust to it) if they are to be effective over time while incorporating innovations (Zaltman and others, 1973, p. 113). Organizations with greater perceived control over their environment will adopt innovations more rapidly (Danowski 1974).

The greater activity of innovative organizations in manipulating their environments was evidenced in a study of the steel industry. "The innovative organization inserts itself in its environment, accepts the dependency which it implies but attempts to manage it. Morever, it establishes units that become boundaries between the organization and the environment" (J. G. Miller 1971, p. 95).

Generally, organizations which try to control their environment rather than just adjusting to it, are more innovative (Chapter 3).

SLACK RESOURCES

Slack resources are resources that are not already committed to other purposes. The presence of organizational slack is important in the matching of an innovation with a problem. All innovations require an investment of at least some resources for their implementation. Thus the *presence of slack resources is presumably essential for the adoption of an innovation.* Slack may already exist within the organization, or it may be deliberately created. The amount of slack resources present in an organization at any given point (and all organizations have *some* slack at all times) is positively related to the probability that any given innovation will be adopted.

The concept of slack resources has been used by a variety of organizational analysts; it can be traced both to Cyert and March (1963, pp. 278–79) and to Dahl (1961). Unfortunately, it has seldom been operationalized with much depth or precision. It is a concept which is as much psychological as financial, and accordingly it must be approached through multiple measurements of its various facets. It is possible to measure a number of features of the organization which reflect the presence of various types of slack resources.

Among these might be the following.

1. *Financial slack—might be measured by:*
   Amount of long-term financial commitments
   Amount of shift between budget categories over time
   Amount of discretionary funds (as opposed to those allocated by formula) allocated each year
   Degree of difference between a budget request and final allocation
   Amount of total budget increase
   Amount of difficulty encountered in securing new funds
2. *Personnel slack—might be measured by:*
   Number of temporary or short-term employees
   Turnover or retirement rates
   Work overload or underload
   Number of professionals not working full-time at their profession
3. *Physical slack—might be measured by:*
   Unoccupied office space
   Accumulated office supplies and equipment
   Computer "down-time"
   Changes in service–demand patterns

While these measures tap only parts of the total concept, they function rather differently from less specific measures such as "size" or "total resources." None of the above measures is capable of being used alone as a total measure of organizational slack. Their importance lies in their combination with each other into more general indices, and in the pattern of relationships between the various types of slack resources.

We argued earlier that slack resources are essential for innovation to occur in an organization; a very high level of slack resources may even *create* a need for innovation. The perceived performance gap is then defined in terms of maximal use of slack resources. An illustration is the oil-rich Arab nations, who are purchasing satellite television broadcasting systems and other high-cost innovations.

ORGANIZATIONAL STRUCTURE

Organizational structure is the arrangement of components and subsystems within a system (Chapter 4). Much research attention has been given to correlating various features of an organization's structure with its innovative behavior (Hage and Aiken 1970; Gordon and others, 1974b; Kaluzny and others, 1974). Variables such as centralization, formalization, complexity, integration, and openness influence the way in which organizations perceive problems, search for solutions, and make decisions. Relatively low correlations with innovativeness have often been obtained in this research, suggesting that the other factors we have identified (such as environmental factors) may play a greater role in the innovation process.

Structural variables influence the problem definition process in an organization, and its outcome. We noted earlier that innovation is not an inevitable outcome of this process. Other possible outcomes are (1) *no change,* (2) *expansion* or *contraction* of present activities, and (3) *noninnovative change* (the rearrangement of existing organizational elements without the incorporation of identifiable innovative elements). Any model of innovation must also allow for these possible, noninnovative responses to the existence of perceived performance gaps.

STAGES IN THE INNOVATION PROCESS

The adoption decision is, for us, only the beginning of the innovation process, rather than, as in most previous models, the end point (or dependent variable). The first stage of the innovation process involves the matching of an organizational problem (a performance gap) with an innovation. This is essentially a decision that the potential innovation is, in fact, an appropriate possible solution to the problem. This decision may be made at different times in different parts of the organization; for example, the research staff may be convinced of the need for the innovation before management is. At some point an organizational decision is made to match the problem and the innovation with appropriate slack resources for adoption. At this point, we may say that the actual process of innovation has begun (we do not consider the problem definition process to be a stage of the innovation process but rather a precondition for it; the fact that noninnovative outcomes also result from problem definition makes it misleading to tie the two processes into a unidirectional sequence).

The organizational decision to match problem, innovation, and resources is the point commonly identified as the "adoption" of the innovation. It marks the shift from problem definition to innovation proper. The innovation process has a number of steps or subprocesses:

1. Adoption (or matching)
2. Testing, a limited implementation to assess the accuracy of the match and its possible effects
3. Installation, the process of connecting the innovation to the ongoing structure and activities of the organization
4. Institutionalization, the process of removing the status of "innovation" from the new element, thus making it an integral part of the system

At the completion of the process, the innovation is no longer identifiable to the organization as an innovation. It has become part of the organization's regular, ongoing activities, an integral part of its total functioning.

The innovation process is neither unidirectional nor uniform. There are differences between organizations, and with respect to innovations within the same organization, in the amount of time consumed by each phase, and in the degree to which each phase is in fact completed. At any phase, the process may be aborted or shifted to a new direction. Such shifts are governed by changes in the nature of the organization's agenda of performance gaps as time passes; such shifts are in turn a result of changes either in organizational expectations or in actual performance. Any model of the innovation process should consider this element of feedback and redirection. An analysis which stops at the first, or "adoption," step, is not very useful in imparting a complete understanding of innovative behavior. In fact, the consequences of adoption decisions have a direct bearing on future problem definition and further innovation. Thus our model must be able to follow the innovation process through its full course if we are to understand its real effects.

Figure 6–1 is a representation of the model of the innovation process which we outlined in this section.

FIGURE 6–1. Paradigm of the Innovation Process in Organizations

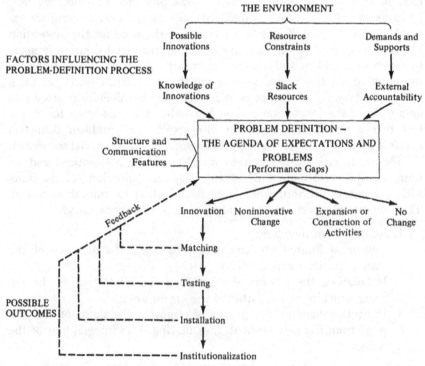

Communication, as we have described it in this book, is the key to the innovation process. Innovation is the result of an active process of sharing information—about performance gaps, about alternative innovations, about external accountability, and about available resources—among the members of an organization. Thus it is only in terms of an understanding of the process of communication in organizations that understanding of innovation is possible.

CONSEQUENCES OF INNOVATION FOR ORGANIZATIONAL EFFECTIVENESS

It is frequently assumed that innovation is in itself the dependent variable in a research effort; that is, that the adoption decision is the desirable outcome. As we have noted, this constitutes a rather limited perspective, at least in the context of organizations. (We criticize this assumption in more detail in a later section.) A more comprehensive variable of interest is organizational effectiveness, with innovation but an intervening variable.

Organizational effectiveness is the degree to which organizational purposes are achieved. The purposes may be defined in relation to individuals, groups, or larger aggregations, and thus there are many different perspectives from which the "effectiveness" of an organization may be assessed. The criteria applied, and the specific variables whose values are used to apply to the criteria, are a function of who is making the analysis of effectiveness and why it is being undertaken. For some purposes, the degree to which "output goals" are achieved is the most appropriate measure of effectiveness; for other purposes, the maintenance of system variables within steady ranges may be an appropriate index. No one perspective is uniquely valid.

In the interests of generalizability, we need criteria of effectiveness which are comparable between organizations, but which retain operational applicability to each specific organization we study. To this end, we may view the organization as a multipurpose system (Georgopoulos 1972). Organizations are seen as systems attempting to simultaneously meet a variety of demands. These demands, such as adaptation or change, allocation, coordination, integration, strain, output, and maintenance, are continually changing, and the problem of satisfying all of them with optimal solutions is difficult, especially over time. The degree to which they are simultaneously met at any given point may be called the "effectiveness" of the organization as an operating system at that point. In this scheme, formal goals, or defined and shared purposes, may be formulated in relation to any system demand. The absence of a particular formal goal, however, does not mean that the organization does not have to face that demand, and does not necessarily relieve the research analyst of the obligation to formulate criteria of effectiveness in that area if he is attempting to measure effectiveness in system terms. Since all organizations may be viewed as systems facing a basic set of demands, an analytical framework based on these demands allows us to make comparisons between organizations which may have different formal goals.

One broadly based effort to study organizational effectiveness was that of Mott (1972). Based on the system–demand model just described, Mott defined effectiveness as the ability of the organization to mobilize to meet demands in the areas of production, adaptability, and flexibility. These areas were broken into components, and an additive index, derived from questions administered to organization personnel, was constructed so as to reflect the overall effectiveness of the organization studied. Mott compared his assessments of effectiveness using this technique with various external assessments, and found that the results obtained from his method (based on judgments made by personnel inside the organization) were remarkably congruent with judgments formed by outside observers using their own criteria.

We see innovation itself, then, as only an intervening variable, leading in turn to the more ultimate dependent variable of organizational effectiveness. We are not interested in innovation per se, but rather as a means to the end of greater organizational effectiveness. The connection between the two concepts has too long been assumed to be self-evident, and has been far too little tested.

We conclude that *innovation in organizations is related to organizational effectiveness.*

INNOVATION AND BUREAUCRACY IN THE KINGDOM OF SIAM

The little that most Westerners know about Thailand often has a hazy basis in the book and film, *Anna and the King of Siam* (*The King and I*), the story of an English schoolteacher who tried to introduce educational innovations in the Palace School in Bangkok some years ago. So perhaps it is particularly appropriate to focus here on innovation in the Thai Ministry of Education. One of the authors (Rogers and others, 1969) studied how ten innovations that were promoted by the Minister of Education spread through his Ministry to the teachers in thirty-eight government secondary schools in the mid-1960s.

The concept of bureaucracy (described in Chapter 3) originated in the West, and was introduced to most of Latin America, Africa, and Asia by the colonial powers. How appropriate is the Western model of rational bureaucracy when implemented in governmental organizations in these countries? We set out to find the answer in the case of Thailand.

Thailand is an especially interesting locale in which to study this question because it is about the only Southeast Asian nation that did not come under Western imperial control. But there was extensive contact through trading with the English and French after about 1800, and Western ideas about bureaucracy and other matters started to come into the Thai government. Beginning about 100 years ago, an attempt was made by the King of Siam to pattern his governmental structure after the Western bureaucratic model. Today, observers have described Western bureaucracy in Thailand as a thin veneer atop the traditional Thai system of organization.

Western innovations, both ideological and technological, have passed upon arrival in Thailand through an informal cultural "customs." Those elements of Western educational theory and practice unsuited to the Thai cultural milieu simply did not find their way into the system. They were dropped at dockside, or soon thereafter.

It is facile and perhaps natural for Westerners to assume that the Thai Ministry of Education is dedicated solely to improvement in the human condition through change and development. But the Western bureaucratic model, adopted by King Chulalongkorn and Prince Damrong in 1892, has, since that day, been reshaped and redirected by Thai civil servants to meet the traditional and more broadly accepted need in their country for attainment and legitimization of personal power and prestige. The Thai civil service is seen by those within it as a structure whose primary function is the conferring of status, the legitimization of status, and the defense of status. While nearly all Thai bureaucrats would hold that some benefit to the public should result from their efforts, any suggestion that public service is the main goal of their bureaucracy would probably be greeted with good-natured tolerance. The Thai bureaucratic polity exists first and foremost to confer and apportion power, prestige, and status among those members of society who are fortunate enough to find positions within it.

"The Thai bureaucracy is not fundamentally resistant to innovation, provided the impetus comes from outside and the approval from above" (Siffin 1966, p. 247). The visibility of the adoption or nonadoption of an innovation affects its rate and likelihood of adoption. If the Ministry "powers" push adoption of school libraries or encourage formation of Boy Scout troops, the failure of schools to adopt these innovations is easily determined by visual inspection. Nonadoption of the discussion method of instruction, on the other hand, is more difficult to detect.

Gazing with an unpracticed eye upon the organizational structure of the Ministry of Education, the Westerner is prone to liken it to the administration of education in France. Both bureaucracies are headed by a cabinet minister who, by virtue of access to other national leaders and direct participation in national decision making, is in a position to co-ordinate educational management with socioeconomic development plans. Both countries establish nationwide school curricula, centralized control of teacher preparation, systems of frequent and standardized examination to control the promotion of students from grade to grade, and separate "tracks" for those intent on vocational and academic goals. In both countries, by virtue of their centralized control and clearly delineated lines of communication, authority, and responsibility, one would expect to find a more rapid diffusion of innovations than in decentralized systems such as those in the United States and England.

Appearance is deceiving, however, for the organization and administration of education in Thailand depart widely from organization charts and public statements of national goals. While some disparity between ideal and practice is found in every organization, in Thailand the form but not the substance of Weberian bureaucracy has been adopted.

Traditionally, Thai education was provided in Buddhist *wats* (temples); only during the the past forty years did any significant number of Thai youth attend government schools. We selected a random sample of thirty-eight such high schools and interviewed all of the teachers and administrators there as to whether and how they first heard about, and decided to adopt, ten innovations (ranging from the use of class discussion to the giving of objective tests, to the use of slide projectors). All ten innovations had been introduced in Thailand by the Ministry of Education, and all teachers had been formally ordered to adopt them.

Needless to say, most of the teachers had not done so. Some of the teachers had never heard of the ten innovations.

What are the main reasons that these educational innovations were not adopted very quickly in the Thai schools?

1. The decision-making criteria in the Ministry of Education are primarily political. The transfer of responsibility for elementary education from the Ministry of Education to the Ministry of the Interior was made by the Cabinet in 1966 on the basis of political calculations, rather than on the basis of advancing the goals of education, or of development. The professional educators who staff the Ministry of Education offices in Bangkok do not have much political power, so they are ignored in policy matters.

Meetings and conferences in the Ministry offices in Bangkok are abundant, but clear-cut decisions are rare. Political behavior frequently dominates such meetings, and decisions, when reached, tend to reflect friendship or an exchange of favors. The Thai humorously refer to this interchange as "whiskey–soda coordination."

On certain rare occasions, the political structure of the Ministry becomes activated to support an innovation, and then the innovation diffuses very quickly. An example is the spread of the Boy Scout movement in

Thailand. The King of Siam, while a young boy, became very enthused about scouting. In the early 1960s, the Ministry of Education began to encourage the diffusion of scouting, and within a few years almost every school child in Thailand was a Scout. All schoolteachers were expected to become Scout leaders, and all students were encouraged to wear their Scout uniforms to classes one day a month. In fact, each classroom of students rather automatically became a Scout troop, with their teacher as the troop leader. Classes were excused for a few hours each week for Scout activities, which were held at the school. With the Minister, the Ministry supervisors, the school principals, and the teachers all promoting the idea of scouting, it diffused very quickly. But another innovation, like objective tests or slide projectors, diffused slowly or not at all.

2. Communication channels for the administration and evaluation of education at the local level are weak and ineffectual.

Within the Thai Ministry of Education, as in any large organization, formal channels of communication transmit only a small proportion of the total communication load. Records maintained by offices at every level in the hierarchy carry perhaps the heaviest share of official information. While much useful information is transmitted via this channel, much of the record keeping represents only an attempt by subordinates to document compliance with directives from above, in case questions may later be raised. Generally speaking, the Ministry of Education in Bangkok appears to lack a mechanism for digesting and using the feedback data contained in the mountains of records and reports which it regularly receives from lower echelons.

Personal inspections are used by higher-ranking officials to seek feedback information. Thai civil servants often carry out such inspections, but more often to transmit than to receive information. Such government officials in the field tend to talk rather than listen. As a consequence, the Thai Ministry of Education tends to suffer from an insufficiency of feedback messages, especially those dealing with negative feedback.

One much-used communication channel, perhaps unique in the sheer volume and diversity of information (and misinformation) it carries, is the ubiquitous grapevine. This network, reaching from Bangkok to the remotest village, is a model of its kind in the world, and is abetted by the fact that Thais appear to be both keen observers and inveterate gossips. Within the Ministry, county education officers must come to Bangkok monthly for the purpose of picking up the pay of their school principals and teachers. This provides an ideal opportunity for the collection of information in the national capital for transmission back home to the provinces. The communication efforts of these officials are bountifully supplemented by those of traveling supervisors and other personnel from the central office.

In the nearly total absence of officially sanctioned means for expressing their frustrations and airing their problems, educational personnel in large numbers resort to the accusatory, anonymous letter. Such messages emanate in impressive numbers from every level in the bureaucracy. They are most frequently addressed to those occupying positions of high status in the Ministry—up to and including the Minister. Such letters undoubtedly provide these officials with considerable information about conditions in the field, and may constitute a channel of greater functional utility than the officially kept and duly submitted records.

3. County education supervisors are unwilling or unable to diffuse information about innovations or to assess the extent of their implementation; this important communication and feedback link between Bangkok and local schools, through which all administrative orders flow, carries few innovation messages. The typical education supervisor is responsible for about 100 schools and 3,360 teachers, and is allotted 10 *bhat* (U.S. $0.50) of travel funds per school. How can he travel to 100 schools on 50¢ apiece? He can't.

So there is very little official contact of any kind between the Ministry supervisors and the local school staffs. And when such contact does occur, it is mostly concerned with budget or other administrative matters. In fact, the supervisors are incompetent to transmit educational innovations to school staffs, because, with few exceptions, they do not know anything about education. These supervisors are general administrative personnel, who belong to the Thai civil service; their assignment to the Ministry of Education is only for a year or two, until they move on to another responsibility in another ministry.

Our research showed that the Ministry office in Bangkok had sent written orders to all supervisors, school principals, and teachers, urging them to adopt the ten innovations. But the supervisors from the Ministry did not personally follow up on these formal directives, and so little action occurred in schools.

In fact, the channel through which most teachers learned of the ten innovations was *not* a downward flow of new ideas from top executives in the Ministry, through the educational supervisors to school principals and teachers—(although the Weberian model of bureaucracy led us to expect such a downward flow). Instead, we found that most of the diffusion of the ten innovations occurred *upwardly* from teachers, especially those young teachers who were most recently trained, to principals and to Ministry supervisors! How can we explain this seeming paradox?

The answer lies in the ten teacher-training colleges in Thailand. All high-school teachers must graduate from one of these institutions, which lies outside the formal hierarchy of the Ministry. The professors who teach at these teacher-training institutes had learned of the ten innovations independently of the Ministry, such as by observing the use of class discussions and objective tests while attending graduate school in the United States. These professors used many of the innovations in their own classes at the teacher-training institutes. So the newly trained teachers entered Thai high schools with a stock of innovations superior to that of the more experienced teachers, or the principals or supervisors.

Thus the ten innovations entered Thai schools at the bottom and spread upward, in spite of the Ministry's hierarchy rather than because of it. And we see that a Western organizational model—Weberian bureaucracy—operates in a culturally distinctive way in Thailand.

Organizational Innovativeness

We begin this section by synthesizing research on organizational innovativeness in terms of the sources of data and the problem of "yesterday's innovativeness," individual versus organizational characteristics, the conceptual inadequacies of organizational size as a predictor of innovativeness, and structural characteristics in relation to the innovativeness of organizations. Then we discuss three questionable assumptions of traditional diffusion studies, and how they might be addressed in future research.

RESEARCH ON ORGANIZATIONAL INNOVATIVENESS

Our main concern in the present review is with the 373 publications reporting the results of research on organizational innovativeness, which are a subset of the some 2,700 documents dealing with the diffusion of innovations (Figure 6–2). Most of these 373 publications are relatively late on the diffusion research scene and were heavily influenced by their nonorganizational intellectual ancestors.[6] For example, almost none of these studies deal with the innovation *process* in the sense in which we have discussed it. "There have been few studies of the actual process of change in organizations" (Hage and Aiken 1970). In fact, in their book-length review, Hage and Aiken (1970) can provide only one illustration of this type of research. And there are very few others.

The large-sample survey researches which predominate among the 373 publications are properly studies of innovativeness rather than innovation. The researchers mainly compared the various organizations (their respondents) and searched for correlations between selected (and often rather stereotyped) independent variables and their measures of inno-

---

[6] Interestingly, a few of the very first diffusion researches, even prior to the Ryan and Gross (1943) study of hybrid corn, were investigations of organizational innovativeness. Examples are McVoy (1940) and Pemberton (1936). Then the organization was largely forgotten as a unit in diffusion research until about the mid-1960s.

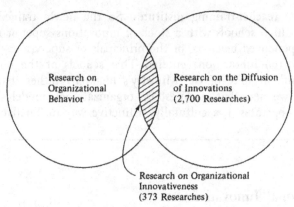

Research on
Organizational
Behavior

Research on the Diffusion
of Innovations
(2,700 Researches)

Research on Organizational
Innovativeness
(373 Researches)

FIGURE 6-2. The two "invisible colleges" of research on organizational behavior and on the diffusion of innovations come together in researches on organizational innovativeness. (*Note:* The exact number of publications on organizational behavior is not available, but could be estimated minimally at several thousand.)

vativeness. Unfortunately, then, these studies tell us very little, if anything, about the *process* of innovation itself.

SOURCES OF DATA AND THE PROBLEM OF YESTERDAY'S INNOVATIVENESS

In addition to manifesting inadequate concern with the innovation process within organizations, the traditional cross-sectional correlational designs used in studies of organizational innovativeness suffer as a result of the type of data that is typically gathered by the researcher. Usually he sends a mailed questionnaire to the top individual in the organization or, more rarely, interviews him personally. All data about the organization's innovativeness, its structural characteristics, and the leader's characteristics are obtained from this one respondent. As a result, the researcher gains a picture of organizational innovativeness only as seen from the top. Quite obviously, the perceptions and viewpoints of the various members of the organization cannot be incorporated in the analysis, because they have not been obtained.

One cannot adequately understand the process of innovation in an organization from just one member's viewpoint of that process. But the usual studies of organizational innovativeness do enable us to know "a little about a lot." A large sample of organizations can be studied when there is only one respondent for each organization. Such studies are relatively low in data-gathering cost per organization.

They do, however, pose special problems for the measurement of innovativeness, which is the most common dependent variable in these studies. Mohr's (1966) approach to operationalization is fairly typical. His ninety-three directors of local health departments were asked which of a number of innovative programs their agency had adopted in the past; innovativeness "points" were awarded to health departments according to the number of innovations they had adopted.

There is a logical difficulty in this use of retrospective data about innovativeness in an analysis including independent variables that are measured cross-sectionally: *in essence, one is correlating yesterday's innovativeness with today's independent variables* (Kaluzny and others 1974). Often the problem is worse; the correlations are between today's variables and the cognitive dissonance–reducing *perception* of yesterday's innovativeness. Success is more likely to be remembered than failure; the organization's files may even be purged of records of unsuccessful innovations. The past constantly tends to be reinterpreted in terms of the present or the anticipated future. As we noted earlier, innovation diffusion is a highly time-dependent process, and it is very difficult to analyze it with data gathered at only one point in time. However, the solution is certainly not to measure the dependent variable at time t_1 and the independent variables at t_2.[7]

A number of possible sources of data about innovativeness can be used:

1. Published records on the time of adoption of an innovation
2. Organization records, such as the notes kept from regular staff meetings at which innovation decisions are discussed
3. Personal interviews (or mailed questionnaires) with executives in the organization, and with all of the members
4. Observation and physical inspection of the innovation's adoption

These methods of data gathering are probably more accurate, but they are also more costly to pursue.

INDIVIDUAL "VERSUS" ORGANIZATIONAL CHARACTERISTICS AND INNOVATIVENESS

There are two broad classes of independent variables which have been used to predict organizational innovativeness: (1) individual characteristics of the organization's leader or leaders, and (2) organizational characteristics such as size, centralization, and system openness. "Many studies of innovation have focused on individuals rather than on organizations. However, individuals may have a substantial influence on the adoption of new means and goals by organizations" (Mohr 1966, pp. 20–21).

---

[7] Although the reverse procedure might occasionally be appropriate: viz., to measure the independent variables at t_1 and the dependent variables at t_2, as in Hage and Dewar (1973). An understanding of the meaning of the amount of time lapsed would seem to be mandatory in this case.

The research question that remains to be fully answered in future investigations is: to what extent is the degree of innovativeness of organizations a function of one or another of these classes of variables? Even though a full answer is not available, recent research offers some insights.

First of all, we must point out that the question of individual *versus* organizational variables is something of a phony issue in explaining organizational innovativeness. Obviously both sets of independent variables would be expected to vary with innovativeness, and the two are interdependent in their relationship with innovativeness. The interaction of structural and individual variables is illustrated by Mohr's (1966) study of health departments. "When resources are high [an organizational variable] . . . a unit increase in health officer motivation [an individual variable] . . . has about 4½ times the effect upon innovation, as it does when resources are low."

We essentially agree with Mytinger (1968): "Is [innovativeness due to] the man, the agency, or the place? No one of these can be said to play a singular role." The effects of individual and structural variables on the dependent variable of innovativeness seem to be complementary rather than competitive. Multivariate statistical tools should be utilized in organizational studies to untangle these joint effects.

Hage and Aiken (1970, pp. 122–23) conclude their study of innovativeness in sixteen rehabilitation agencies with the remark that "structural properties were much more highly associated with [innovativeness] than attitudes toward change [on the part of the executives]. This implies that the structure of an organization may be more crucial for the successful implementation of change than the particular blend of personality types in an organization." This conclusion may be somewhat overenthusiastic, considering that the relative contribution of individual and organizational variables to explaining innovativeness depends, in part, on precisely how such individual and organizational variables are measured. Hage and Aiken (1970) express a strong antipsychological bias in their intellectual position, and as both are sociologists, one might surmise that their measurement of structural characteristics would be more thorough than their operationalization of the individual variables.[8]

The question of the relationship between leader variables and structural characteristics is complicated by a serious problem—yet to be adequately addressed in research—of the interaction over time between the leader and his or her structure. Leaders tend to be modified by the

---

[8] In fact, other researches, such as Mytinger (1968), found that individual leader characteristics are of considerable importance in explaining organizational innovativeness. Most researchers report that the individual variables make at least some contribution to predicting organizational innovativeness, with the exact contribution depending in part on exactly which leader variables are measured. Considerable improvement could undoubtedly be made in both the conceptualization and measurement of individual variables related to organizational innovativeness.

organization in which they function, and they in turn shape and modify the structural characteristics of the organization. We expect, for example, that a leader with democratic beliefs will move the entire organization in a more participatory direction regardless of his or her or the organization's "natural" innovativeness. In practice, this might lead to a degree of innovativeness which some studies explain by "structural" variables and others by "leadership," but which results from a common phenomenon.

Naturally there are problems in these studies of classifying exactly which variables are executives' personal characteristics and which are organizational structural variables. For example, an executive's cosmopoliteness in the eyes of one researcher may be considered the organization's openness by another scholar.

These studies, and the ambiguities connected with them, point up the difficulties of using correlational analytical designs in the study of innovation. Such techniques can help identify relationships but can cast no particular light on the *processes* involved. We are left as much in the dark as ever about how and why structural, leader, and resource characteristics of organizations come together in particular ways. Only a process research strategy can come to grips with these questions.

ORGANIZATIONAL SIZE AS A PREDICTOR OF INNOVATIVENESS

A study of innovativeness in forty local health departments in California concluded that "size—size of community and size of [the health] department—is perhaps the most compelling concomitant to innovativeness" (Mytinger 1968). Similar evidence for the importance of size as a predictor of organizational innovativeness is provided by Mohr (1966), Kaluzny and others (1974), Mansfield (1963), and several others.

Why do researchers consistently find that size is one of the best predictors of organizational innovativeness? First, size is a variable that is easily measured, presumably with a relatively high degree of precision.[9] Hence it has been included for study in almost every organizational innovativeness investigation.

Secondly, size is probably a surrogate measure of several dimensions that are related to innovation: total resources, slack resources, organizational structure, and the like. What is called "size" is, in fact, usually operationalized as a resource measure of some sort (personnel, income, sales, budget) which complicates assessment of the relationships involved. The precise meaning of "size" apart from "resources" is not wholly clear. These intermediate variables have not been clearly identified, nor ade-

[9] Although if we regard the organization as a sum of *roles* rather than individuals—a point of view consistent with open system theory—the actual size of the organization is not necessarily equal to the number of individuals in it.

quately measured, in past researches. Undoubtedly these unidentified un-measured variables constitute a fundamental, and intellectually deceiving, reason for the size–innovativeness "relationship."

Few organization scholars have much theoretical interest in size as a variable. We urge that once its effects on innovativeness (through the intervening variables) are isolated and understood, size be dropped from further study, or at most relegated to the status of a control variable.[10]

STRUCTURAL CHARACTERISTICS AND ORGANIZATIONAL INNOVATIVENESS

A recent—and, we feel, healthy—trend in organizational innovativeness research is the inclusion of independent variables measuring certain dimensions of the organization's structure: centralization, formalization, openness. For our purposes, we divide these variables into *internal* and *external* structural characteristics (for example, centralization or formalization, on the one hand, or openness, on the other). Hage and Aiken (1970) have played a key role in specifying the main internal structural variables related to organizational innovativeness, and their concepts have been picked up by other scholars, such as Kaluzny and others (1974). Our discussion of the relationships of these structural variables to innovativeness was presented in Chapter 3 and previously in the present chapter.

THREE QUESTIONABLE ASSUMPTIONS OF DIFFUSION RESEARCH PERSPECTIVES ON INNOVATION

We conclude our review of research on innovativeness in organizations by identifying three questionable assumptions made in most diffusion research. These assumptions have generally been carried over into research on organizational innovativeness without much questioning or analysis.

ASSUMPTION 1: INNOVATION IS ADVANTAGEOUS FOR ALL ADOPTERS.

The classical diffusion model assumed that everyone should adopt innovations, that diffusion rates should be rapidly increased, and that rejection of an innovation was an undesirable and/or irrational decision.[11]

---

[10] Hall and others (1967) showed that size alone was a poor predictor of structural variables, but confirmed that it was associated with many other factors, and would thus play a surrogate role in any analysis in which it was included.

[11] A fundamental reason, we believe, for this pro-change bias in diffusion research is due to the tendency for diffusion researchers to look at the process from the source's viewpoint, rather than from the receiver's. This taking of the source's viewpoint in turn may stem from the sponsorship of most diffusion research by sources of innovations (that is, by change agencies).

This pro-change bias may have been justified in the case of many of the agricultural innovations that were originally studied; after all, hybrid corn was a highly profitable innovation for farmers.

But many innovations do not have universal usefulness, and such innovations may be appropriate only for adoption by *some* individuals, or by *some* organizations.

One approach to overcoming the limits posed by this assumption is to study a wider range of innovations, including some which are not suitable for adoption by all possible organizations. Diffusion research could thus shed some of its pro-change bias. Our focus should increasingly be on how innovation decisions are made, by whom, using what criteria, and with what consequences—in short, on the use of process models for the study of innovation. Our focus should include not just *how* innovative an organization is, but how *well* it innovates.

In suggesting that not all innovations should be adopted by all organizations, we imply that there are some criteria by which this judgment can be made, either by the organization studied or by the research analyst. Use of such criteria is intimated by Utterback (1974), who, in reviewing the major researches on industrial innovation, concluded: "The retrospective nature of nearly all of the sources [that is, research publications] discussed previously means that the [innovation] process has been viewed as much more rational and well-ordered than it is in fact."

ASSUMPTION 2: CROSS-SECTIONAL DATA GATHERING AT ONE POINT IN TIME IS SUFFICIENT FOR THE INVESTIGATION OF A PROCESS.

We stress that diffusion is a process, continuous through time, never ending and never beginning. For heuristic purposes of analysis, however, we sometimes find it convenient to "freeze" the action in this continuous "film" and isolate certain elements or variables in the process. Most social science research methods are better suited to obtaining snapshots of behavior than moving pictures, which would be more appropriate for determining the time order of the variables. Correlational analysis of one-shot survey data is overwhelmingly the favorite methodology of diffusion investigators.[12] Essentially, this approach amounts to making the innovation process "timeless." It is convenient for the researcher but intellectually deceitful with respect to the process he is investigating.

Speaking about studies of organizational innovativeness, Hage and Aiken (1970) critically note that: "The current state of knowledge about organizational behavior is based to a great extent on cross-sectional studies.

[12] There are more appropriate research methods for studying the process aspects of diffusion: For example, field experiments, longitudinal panel studies, and simulation. Such approaches rest on the necessity of gathering data from the same (or similar) respondents at several points in time. One of the few organizational innovativeness studies to gather data at even *two* points in time was Hage and Dewar (1973).

. . . They fail to sensitize the student of organizations to the ongoing process of change in organizations. Organizations seldom stand still."

A further problem with cross-sectional survey data is that they cannot answer many of the "why" questions about the diffusion of innovations.[18] The one-shot survey provides grist for description, of course, and makes possible a type of correlational analysis: various independent variables are associated with the dependent variable (usually innovativeness). But little can be learned from such a correlational approach about *why* a particular independent variable varies with innovativeness.

"Such factors (as wealth, size, cosmopoliteness, etc.) may be causes of innovation, or effects of innovativeness, or they may be involved with innovation in cycles of reciprocal causality through time, or both they and the adoption of new ideas may be caused by an outside factor not considered in a given study" (Mohr 1966). Future research must be designed so as to probe the time-ordered linkages among independent and dependent variables. One-shot studies can't tell us much about this.

ASSUMPTION 3: INNOVATION DECISIONS ARE MADE SOLELY BY THE CHIEF EXECUTIVE OF AN ORGANIZATION RATHER THAN BY VARIOUS GROUPS OF MEMBERS.

Almost all diffusion researches in the past have ignored the effect of *organizational structure*. When innovation diffusion has been investigated, it has not really been studied *within* the organization. Instead, the process has been investigated as if innovations diffused only from organization to organization and did not also have to be implemented *within* the organization. For example, most educational diffusion has been analyzed with the school system as the unit of analysis. So the school is considered as (or reduced to) an "individual" in past diffussion research. Certainly further research in innovation in organizations must obtain data from all of the actors in the organization that are involved in an innovation decision, rather than just from the chief executive (who may not even know the details about the innovation process). In this way, a more complete understanding of the innovation process can be obtained.

SUMMARY

The present chapter investigates organizational innovation in order to understand the nature of organizational structure and the communication processes involved in organizational settings. Communication is a necessary ingredient at every step in the innovation process.

---

[18] Although it may be possible to *infer* certain of the "why" relationships among variables that are measured cross-sectionally.

One might think that innovation is a rather rare commodity in the organizational arena, but in fact all organizations are changing and innovating at all times in varying degrees. But all organizations are not innovating at an appropriate rate.

An *innovation* is an idea, practice, or object perceived as new by the relevant unit of adoption. *Innovativeness* is the degree to which a given unit is earlier than other units in adopting innovations.

Innovations *of* the organization and innovations *in* the organization are two more general classes of innovation in organizations. The first type does not require different behavior on the part of organization members following the organizational decision. Innovations *in* the organization require changed individual behavior.

Most past research on organizational innovativeness has sought to determine the relationships among variables without going through the prior step of variable identification in exploratory case studies of the innovation process.

There are various ways to bring about change in organizations in addition to innovation: destroying the organization, altering the communication structure, reorganizing the system or its subunits, shuffling organizational members to different positions after retraining, or recruiting more innovative individuals as members.

We present a model of the innovation process in organizations. *Problem definition* is the process by which organizations define and specify their *performance gaps*, perceived discrepancies between the organization's expectations and its actualities. Four main classes of variables affect the problem definition process: (1) knowledge of innovations; (2) *external accountability*, the degree to which an organization is dependent on, or responsible to, its environment; (3) *slack resources*, those which are not already committed to other purposes; and (4) organizational structural variables such as formalization and centralization. The problem definition process does not always lead to innovation.

The process of innovation comprises the stages of: (1) adoption, or the matching of the innovation with the problem; (2) testing; (3) installation; and (4) institutionalization. We urge study of the consequences of innovation for *organizational effectiveness*, the degree to which organizational purposes are achieved.

We are critical of studies of organizational innovativeness which reflect the measurement problem of "yesterday's innovativeness," in which yesterday's innovativeness is correlated with today's independent variables. Both the personal characteristics of individual leaders and the structural characteristics of the organization are associated with organizational innovativeness.

Needed are "tracer" studies of the innovation process in organizations.

7. A Propositional Summary

In this brief epilogue, we summarize the main contents of this book in the form of fifty-two propositions about organizational communication. These propositions are something more (in their degree of truth claim) than just untested hypotheses, but much less than firmly supported principles. The propositions are listed approximately in the order of their appearance in the text so as to facilitate, for the reader, finding further details about each proposition and definitions of the concepts they contain.

Chapter 1: The Nature of Organizational Communication

1-1: The behavior of individuals in organizations is best understood from a communication point of view.

1-2: Organizational structure lends predictability and stability to human communication, and thus facilitates the accomplishment of administrative tasks.

1-3: Communication is the vehicle by which organizations are embedded in their environments.

1-4: Communication is an indispensable element in an organization's functioning.

1-5: Attention to feedback makes a communication system more effective.

Chapter 2: Three Schools of Organizational Behavior

2-1: The Scientific Management School did not accord a very significant role to communication, and it conceived of communication as limited to command and control through vertical, formal channels.

2-2: The Human Relations School saw communication as more important than did the Scientific Management school. It conceived of organizational communication as comprising not just management *talking to* workers, but also management *listening to* what the workers were saying.

2-3: The Human Relations School focused attention on informal communication among peers in an organization.

2-4: The Systems School viewed an organization as an open system that inputs and outputs information to its environment across its boundary.

2-5: The Systems School perceived information processing as the main function performed by all organizations.

Chapter 3: Open System Theory and Organizational Environments

3-1: Open systems theory assigned communication a high priority in understanding organizational behavior.

3-2: Open system theory shifted organizational communication research from individualistic to relational analysis, thus helping to put social structure back into such research.

3-3: Open system theory influenced organizational scholars to look outside the organization's boundary at environmental variables for fuller explanations of organizational behavior.

3-4: The greatest degree of uncertainty for an organization occurs when its environment is complex and rapidly changing.

3-5: Openness to its environment facilitates an organization's innovativeness.

3-6: An organization is more likely to innovate when its relevant environment is rapidly changing than when it is steady.

3-7: Organizations which seek to control their environment rather than adjusting to it, are more innovative.

3-8: Innovation in organizations is often motivated by performance gaps, which are more likely to occur in organizations with rapidly changing environments.

3-9: An organization's climate exerts a strong influence on its members' behavior.

Chapter 4: The Effect of Organizational Structure on Communication Behavior

4-1: Usually, organizational structure is a determinant of communication behavior; occasionally, it is a consequence of communication behavior.

4–2: One purpose of structure in an organization is to provide stability, regularity, and predictability.

4–3: The formal and informal communication channels in an organization are usually complementary and substitutable.

4–4: The informal communication structure is often a breeding place for rumors.

4–5: While the purpose of bureaucracy is to achieve rational efficiency in organizational behavior, bureaucracy is also a dirty word in that it may lead to inefficiency and to various human problems such as alienation.

4–6: A common misconception about communication problems in organizations is that the main problem is restricted flows, and that the solution is to unclog blocked communication channels.

4–7: One of the most important functions of organizational structure is to restrict communication flows, and thus decrease problems of information overload.

4–8: The solution to problems of information overload in an organization that restricts communication flows, such as gatekeeping, filtering, and queuing, tend to cause problems of distortion and omisssion.

4–9: Horizontal communication flows in an organization are more frequent than vertical flows.

4–10: Downward communication flows in an organization are more frequent than upward flows.

4–11: The content of upward communication flows in an organization is more likely to contain positive, rather than negative, feedback.

4–12: Officials near the top of an organizational structure may possess less operational information than do individuals nearer the operational level.

4–13: The existence of informal communication flows in organizations is evidence that the formal structure does not completely predict communication behavior.

4–14: Informal communication is always of some importance in an organization, whether or not the formal communication channels are functioning adequately.

4–15: The existence of specialized communication roles, such as liaisons and gatekeepers, indicates that an informal communication structure exists in an organization, and that the formal structure does not completely determine communication behavior.

Chapter 5: Communication Networks in Organizations

5–1: While the formal communication system in an organization (like the organization chart) is to some extent forced on the members of an organization, the informal communication networks emerge spontaneously.

5-2: Compared to the formal communication system in an organization, the informal communication networks are less structured, and hence less predictable.

5-3: The importance of networks in affecting the behavior of individual members of an organization is suggested by system effects.

5-4: The informational strength of dyadic communication relationships is inversely related to the degree of homophily (and the strength of the attraction) between the source and the receiver.

5-5: Open system theory shifted the nature of organizational communication research from an atomistic focus on individuals as units of analysis (1) to dyadic or other relational units in which communication relationships constitute the main research emphasis, and (2) to more systems-level concerns, often involving communication network analysis.

5-6: The degree of centralization in small-group communication networks (as in the "wheel" rather than the "circle") is related to high performance, a high error rate, and low member satisfaction.

5-7: Small-group laboratory experiments on communication networks provided information about the structural effects in communication networks, but the precise nature of the relationships among the variables involved remained largely unclear.

5-8: Most clique members in a communication network of the members of an organization are relatively close to each other in the organization's formal hierarchy, suggesting the similarity of the formal and informal communication systems in an organization.

5-9: The distinctiveness of liaisons stems not from such individual characteristics as their personal lifestyle, but from their unique communcation-bridging function in an organization's network.

5-10: Individual communication roles each represent a special function that needs to be played in a communication network: (1) the *gatekeeper* prevents information overload by filtering and screening messages; (2) the *liaison* integrates and interconnects the parts (clique) of the network; (3) the *opinion leader* facilitates informal decision making in the network; and (4) the *cosmopolite* relates the system to its environment by providing openness.

5-11 The degree of differentiation in a communication network is negatively related to (1) the rate of diffusion of innovations, and (2) productivity in accomplishing tasks requiring collaboration by the total system.

5–12: The degree of connectedness in a communication network is positively related to the rate of diffusion of innovations.

Chapter 6: Innovation in Organizations

6–1: Those structural characteristics of an organization (such as high complexity, low formalization, and low centralization) that facilitate *initiation* of the innovation progress by opening the organization to its environment make it difficult for the organization to *implement* the innovation.

6–2: Perception of a performance gap in an organization creates a search for new alternatives, including innovations.

6–3: An innovation is essentially reinvented by each organization that adopts it, as it goes through extensive revision in the process of adoption and implementation.

6–4: Organizations with a higher degree of external accountability are more innovative.

6–5: The presence of slack resources in an organization is essential for the adoption of an innovation.

6–6: Innnovation in organizations is related to organizational effectiveness.

References

MARK ABRAHAMSON (1965), "Cosmopolitanism, Dependent Identification and Geographical Mobility," *Administrative Science Quarterly*, 10: 98–106.

REKHA AGARWALA–ROGERS (1973), *Technology and Communication Behavior in an Organization: A Case Study in India*, Ph.D. Thesis, Allahabad, India, University of Allahabad.

REKHA AGARWALA–ROGERS (1974), "The Structure and Communication of a Manufacturing Company in India," *Indian Journal of Industrial Relations*, 9: 385–96.

MICHAEL AIKEN AND JERALD HAGE (1968), "Organizational Interdependence and Intra-Organizational Structure," *American Sociology Review*, 33: 912–930.

C. N. ALEXANDER (1964), "Consensus and Mutual Attraction in Natural Cliques: A Study of Adolescent Drinkers," *American Journal of Sociology*, 69: 395–403.

RICKARD K. ALLEN (1970), *A Comparison of Communication Behaviors in Innovative and Non-Innovative Secondary Schools*, Ph.D. Thesis, East Lansing, Mich., Michigan State University.

THOMAS J. ALLEN (1966), "Performance of Information Channels in the Transfer of Technology," *Industrial Management*, 8: 87–98.

THOMAS J. ALLEN (1969), "The World; Your Company: A Gate for Information! Who Guards the Gate?" *Innovation*, 3: 33–39.

THOMAS J. ALLEN (1970), "Communication Networks in R & D Laboratories," *R & D Management*, 1: 14–21.

THOMAS J. ALLEN AND S. I. COHEN (1969), "Information Flow in Research and Development Laboratories," *Administrative Science Quarterly*, 14: 12–19.

THOMAS J. ALLEN AND PETER G. GERSTBERGER (1971), *Report of a Field Experiment to Improve Communication in a Product Engineering Department: The Nonterritorial Office*, Cambridge, Mass., Massachusetts Institute of Technology, Sloan School of Management, Working Paper, 57a–91.

THOMAS J. ALLEN and others (1971), "The International Technological Gatekeeper," *Technology Review*, 36–43, 73.

EDWIN H. AMEND (1971), *Liaison Communication Roles of Professionals in a Research Dissemination Organization*, Ph.D. Thesis, East Lansing, Mich., Michigan State University.

MICHAEL ARGYLE (1953), "The Relay Assembly Test Room in Retrospect," *Occupational Psychology*, 27: 98–103.

CHRIS ARGYRIS (1957), *Personality and Organization*, New York, Harper.

CHRIS ARGYRIS (1960), *Understanding Organizational Behavior*, Homewood, Ill., Dorsey.

CHRIS ARGYRIS (1974), *Behind the Front Page: Organizational Self-Renewal in a Metropolitan Newspaper*, San Francisco, Jossey–Bass.

ROBERT B. ARUNDALE (1971), *The Concept of Process in Human Communication Research*, Ph.D. Thesis, East Lansing, Mich., Michigan State University.

JOHN ATHANASSIADOS (1973), "The Distortion of Upward Communication in Hierarchical Organizations," *Academy of Management Journal*, 16: 207–26.

HELEN BAKER (1948), *Company-Wide Understanding Industrial Relations Policies: A Study in Communications*, Princeton, N. J., Princeton University, Memo Report.

J. VICTOR BALDRIDGE AND ROBERT BURNHAM (1973), *The Adoption of Innovations: The Effect of Organizational Size, Differentiation, and Environment*, Stanford, Ca., Stanford University, Stanford Center for Research and Development in Teaching, Research, and Development, Memorandum 108.

LOREN BARITZ (1961), *The Servants of Power*, Middletown, Conn., Wesleyan University Press.

CHESTER I. BARNARD (1938), *The Functions of the Executive*, Cambridge, Mass., Harvard University Press.

DEAN BARNLUND (1968), *Interpersonal Communication: Survey and Studies*, Boston, Houghton Mifflin.

D. C. BARNLUND AND C. HARLAND (1963), "Propinquity and Prestige as Determinants of Communication Networks," *Sociometry*, 26: 467–79.

ALLAN H. BARTON (1968), "Bringing Society Back In: Survey Research and Macro-Methodology," *American Behavioral Scientist*, 12: 1–9.

ALEX BAVELAS (1950), "Communication Patterns in Task-Oriented Groups," *Acoustical Society of America Journal*, 22: 727–30.

HOWARD BECKER (1954), "Vitalizing Sociological Theory," *American Sociological Review*, 19: 383–84.

LUIS RAMIRO BELTRÁN (1972), "*La Problemática de la Communicacíon para el Desarrollo Rural en América Latin*," Paper presented at the Inter-American Association of Librarians and Agricultural Information Specialists, Buenos Aires.

WARREN BENNIS (1966), *Changing Organizations*, New York, McGraw-Hill.

DAVID K. BERLO (1960), *The Process of Communication*, New York, Rinehart and Winston.

DAVID K. BERLO and others (1970), *Organizational Communication: A First-Line Managerial Communication System*, East Lansing, Mich., Michigan State University, Department of Communication, Mimeo Report.

DAVID K. BERLO and others (1971), *Relationships Between Supervisor–Subordinate Communication Practices and Employee Turnover, Attendance, and Performance Evaluations*, East Lansing, Mich., Michigan State University, Department of Communication, Mimeo Report.

DAVID K. BERLO and others (1972), *An Analysis of the Communication Structure of the Office of Civil Defense*, East Lansing, Mich., Michigan State University, Department of Communication, Mimeo Report.

KENNETH BERRIEN (1968), *General and Social Systems*, New Brunswick, N.J., Rutgers University Press.

LUDWIG VON BERTALANFFY (1956), "General Systems Theory," *General Systems*, 1: 1–10.

LUDWIG VON BERTALANFFY (1962), "General Systems Theory: A Critical Review," *General Systems*, 7: 1–20.

LUDWIG VON BERTALANFFY (1968), *General Systems Theory*, New York, Braziller.

SAMUEL BETTY (1974), *Some Determinants of Communication Network Structure and Productivity: A Study of Clinic Staff Interaction in Two Philippine Family Planning Organizations*, Ph.D. Thesis, East Lansing, Mich., Michigan State University.

PETER M. BLAU AND MARSHALL W. MEYER (1971), *Bureaucracy in Modern Society*, New York, Random House.

ROBERT BLAUNER (1964), *Alienation and Freedom: The Factory Worker and His Industry*, University of Chicago Press.

WARREN BREED (1955), "Social Control in the Newsroom: A Functional Analysis," *Social Forces*, 33: 323–35.

JOHN BREWER (1971), "Flow of Communications, Expert Qualifications, and Organizational Authority Structures," *American Sociological Review*, 36: 475–84.

LYMAN BRYSON (1948), *The Communication of Ideas*, New York, Institute for Religious and Social Studies.

WALTER BUCKLEY (1967), *Sociology and Modern Systems Theory*, Englewood Cliffs, N.J., Prentice–Hall.

WALTER BUCKLEY, ed. (1968), *Modern Systems Research for the Behavioral Scientist: A Sourcebook*, Chicago, Aldine.

TOM BURNS AND G. M. STALKER (1961), *The Management of Innovation*, London, Tavistock.

MERVYN L. CADWALLADER (1968), "The Cybernetic Analysis of Change in Complex Organizations," in Walter Buckley, ed., *Modern Systems Research for the Behavioral Scientist: A Sourcebook*, Chicago, Aldine.

DONALD T. CAMPBELL (1969), "Prospective: Artifact and Control," in Robert Rosenthal and R. L. Rosnow, eds., *Artifacts in Behavioral Research*, New York, Academic Press.

DONALD T. CAMPBELL AND D. W. FISKE (1959), "Convergent and Discriminant Validation by the Multitrait–Multimethod Matrix," *Psychological Bulletin*, 56: 81–105.

NATHAN CAPLAN AND STEPHEN D. NELSON (1973), "On Being Useful: The Nature and Consequences of Psychological Research on Social Problems," *American Psychologist*, 28: 199–211.

ALEX CAREY (1967), "The Hawthorne Studies: A Radical Criticism," *American Sociological Review*, 32: 403–16.

RICHARD O. CARLSON (1964), "School Superintendents and Adoption of Modern Math: A Social Structure Profile," in Matthew B. Miles, ed., *Innovation in Education*, New York, Columbia University, Teachers College.

ROBERT M. CARTER (1972), *Communication in Organizations: A Guide to Information Sources*, Detroit, Gale Research.

ALFRED D. CHANDLER, JR. (1962), *Strategy and Structure*, Cambridge, Mass., Massachusetts Institute of Technology Press.

W. W. CHARTERS, JR., AND ROLAND J. PELLIGRIN (1973), "Barriers to the Innovation Process: Four Case Studies of Differential Staffing," *Educational Administration Quarterly*, 9: 3–14.

ELI CHINOY (1955), *Automobile Workers and the American Dream*, New York, Random House.

G. D. H. COLE (1917), *Reorganization of Industry*, Series II, Oxford, England, Ruslan College.

JAMES S. COLEMAN (1958), "Relational Analysis: The Study of Social Organizations with Survey Methods," *Human Organization*, 17: 28–36; also in Amitai Etzioni, ed. (1961), *Complex Organizations: A Sociological Reader*, New York, Holt, Rinehart, and Winston.

BARRY E. COLLINS AND BERTRAM H. RAVEN (1969), "Group Structure: Attraction, Coalitions, Communication, and Power," in Gardner Lindzey and Elliot Aronson, eds., *Handbook of Social Psychology*, Reading, Mass., Addison–Wesley, Volume 4.

DESMOND COOK (1967), *The Impact of the Hawthorne Effect on Experimental Design in Educational Research*, Columbus, O., Ohio State University, Report.

DIANA CRANE (1972), *Invisible Colleges: Diffusion of Knowledge in Scientific Communities*, University of Chicago Press.

RICHARD M. CYERT AND JAMES G. MARCH (1963), *A Behavioral Theory of the Firm*, Englewood Cliffs, N.J., Prentice–Hall.

ROBERT A. DAHL (1961), *Who Governs? Democracy and Power in an American City*, New Haven, Conn., Yale University Press.

JAMES A. DANOWSKI (1974), "An Informational Processing Model of Organizations: A Focus on Environmental Uncertainty and Communication Network Structuring," Paper presented at the International Communication Association, New Orleans, La.

JAMES A. DANOWSKI (1975), *An Information Theory of Communication Functions: A Focus on Informational Aging*, Ph.D. Thesis, East Lansing, Mich., Michigan State University.

James A. Davis (1961), "Locals and Cosmopolitans in American Graduate Schools," *International Journal of Comparative Society*, 2: 212–23.

Keith Davis (1953a), "Management Communication and the Grapevine," *Harvard Business Review*, 31: 43–49.

Keith Davis (1953b), "A Method of Studying Communication Patterns in Organizations," *Personnel Psychology*, 6: 301–12.

Keith Davis (1967), *Human Relations at Work: The Dynamics of Organizational Behavior*, New York, McGraw-Hill.

Richard H. Davis (1965), *Personal and Organizational Variables Related to the Adoption of Educational Innovations in a Liberal Arts College*, Ph.D. Thesis, University of Chicago.

Brenda Dervin (1971), *Communication Behaviors as Related to Information Control Behavior of Black Low-Income Adults*, Ph.D. Thesis, East Lansing, Mich., Michigan State University.

Karl W. Deutsch (1952), "On Communication Models in the Social Sciences," *Public Opinion Quarterly*, 16: 365–80.

Juan Diaz–Bordenave (1972), "New Approaches to Communication Training for Developing Countries," Paper presented at the Third World Congress of Rural Sociology, Baton Rouge, La.

John T. Diebold (1958), *Readings in Management*, Cincinnati.

William Dill (1958), "Environment as an Influence on Managerial Autonomy," *Administrative Science Quarterly*, 2: 409–43.

John Dimmick (1974), *The Gate-Keeper: An Uncertainty Theory*, Minneapolis, University of Minnesota, Journalism Monographs 37.

Marshall E. Dimock and others (1961), *Public Administration*, New York, Holt.

Anthony Downs (1967), *Inside Bureaucracy*, Boston, Little, Brown.

Robert B. Duncan (1972), "Characteristics of Organizational Environments and Perceived Environmental Uncertainty," *Administrative Science Quarterly*, 17: 313–27.

Robert B. Duncan (1974), A Contingency Approach to Designing Organizations for Innovation: Some Implications for the Organizational Designer," Paper presented at the Conference on the Management of Organization Design, Pittsburgh.

F. E. Emery and E. L. Trist (1965), "The Causal Texture of Organizational Environments," *Human Relations*, 18: 21–32.

Amitai Etzioni (1961), *A Comparative Analysis of Complex Organizations: On Power, Involvement, and Their Correlates*, New York, Free Press.

Amitai Etzioni (1964), *Modern Organizations*, Englewood Cliffs, N.J., Prentice-Hall.

William A. Faunce (1968), *Problems of an Industrial Society*, New York, McGraw-Hill.

Henri Fayol (1949), *General and Industrial Management*, London, Pitman.

E. Forsyth and Leo Katz (1946), "A Matrix Approach to the Analysis of Sociometric Data," *Sociometry*, 9: 340–47.

CARL F. FROST and others (1974), *The Scanlon Plan for Organization Development: Identity, Participation, and Equity*, East Lansing, Mich., Michigan State University Press.

JOHN W. GARDNER (1964), *Self-Renewal: The Individual and the Innovative Society*, New York, Harper Colophon.

WALTER GELLHORN (1966a), *Ombudsman and Others: Citizens' Protectors in Nine Countries*, Cambridge, Mass., Harvard University Press.

WALTER GELLHORN (1966b), *When Americans Complain: Governmental Grievance Procedures*, Cambridge, Mass., Harvard University Press.

BASIL GEORGOPOULOS (1972), *Organization Research on Health Institutions*, Ann Arbor, Mich., Institute for Social Research, Report.

BARNEY G. GLAZER (1963), "The Local–Cosmopolitan Scientist," *American Journal of Sociology*, 69: 249–59.

GERALD GORDON and others (1974a), "A Contingency Model for the Design of Problem-Solving Research Programs: A Perspective on Diffusion Research," *Health and Society*, 52: 185–220.

GERALD GORDON and others (1974b), "Organizational Structure, Environmental Diversity, and Hospital Adoption of Medical Innovations," in Arnold D. Kaluzny, ed., *Innovation in Health Care Organizations: An Issue in Organizational Change*, Chapel Hill, N.C., University of North Carolina, School of Public Health.

ALVIN GOULDNER (1954), *Patterns of Industrial Bureaucracy*, New York, Free Press.

ALVIN GOULDNER (1957), "Cosmopolites and Locals: Toward an Analysis of Latent Social Roles," *Administrative Science Quarterly*, 2: 281–306.

ALVIN GOULDNER (1961), "Metaphysical Pathos and the Theory of Bureaucracy," in Amitai Etzioni, ed., *Complex Organizations*, New York, Holt, Rinehart.

MARK S. GRANOVETTER (1973), "The Strength of Weak Ties," *American Journal of Sociology*, 78: 1360–80.

HAROLD GUETZKOW (1965), "Communication in Organizations," in James G. March, ed., *Handbook of Organizations*, Chicago, Rand McNally.

LUTHER GULICK AND LYNDALL F. URWICK (1937), *Papers on the Science of Administration*, New York, Columbia University, Institute of Public Administration.

D. GVISHIANI (1972), *Organization and Management: A Sociological Analysis of Western Theories*, Moscow, Progress.

JERALD HAGE (1974), *Communication and Organizational Control: Cybernetics in Health and Welfare Settings*, New York, Wiley–Interscience.

JERALD HAGE AND MICHAEL AIKEN (1969), "Routine Technology, Social Structure, and Organization Goals," *Administrative Science Quarterly*, 14: 366–76; reprinted in Richard H. Hall, ed., *The Formal Organization*, New York, Basic Books.

JERALD HAGE AND MICHAEL AIKEN (1970), *Social Change in Complex Organizations*, New York, Random House.

JERALD HAGE AND ROBERT DEWAR (1973), "Elite Values Versus Organizational Structure in Predicting Innovation," *Administrative Science Quarterly*, 18: 279–90.

TORSTEN HÄGERSTRAND (1971), "On Monte Carlo Simulation of Diffusion," in W. L. Garrison and Duane F. Marble, eds., *Quantitative Geography, Part I: Economic and Cultural Topics*, Evanston, Ill., Northwestern University, Studies in Geography 13.

EDWARD T. HALL (1959), *The Silent Language*, Garden City, New York, N.Y., Doubleday.

RICHARD H. HALL (1968), "Professionalization and Bureaucratization," *American Sociological Review*, 13: 92–104.

RICHARD H. HALL and others (1967), "Organizational Size, Complexity, and Formalization," *American Sociological Review*, 32: 903–12.

BRUCE HARRIMAN (1974), "Up and Down the Communications Ladder," *Harvard Business Review*, 52: 143–51.

RONALD G. HAVELOCK (1969), *Planning for Innovation*, Ann Arbor, Mich., University of Michigan, Institute for Social Research, Report.

H. G. HICKS (1967), *The Management of Organizations*, New York, McGraw-Hill.

ALBERT O. HIRSCHMAN (1973), *Exit, Voice, and Loyalty: Responses to Decline in Firms, Organizations, and States*, Cambridge, Mass., Harvard University Press.

GEORGE C. HOMANS (1950), *The Human Group*, New York, Harcourt, Brace.

GEORGE C. HOMANS (1961), *Social Behavior: Its Elementary Forms*, New York, Harcourt, Brace, and World.

EUGENE JACOBSON AND STANLEY SEASHORE (1951), "Communication Patterns in Complex Organizations," *Journal of Social Issues*, 7: 28–40.

MORRIS JANOWITZ AND WILLIAM DELANY (1957), "The Bureaucrat and the Public: A Study of Informational Perspectives," *Administrative Science Quarterly*, 2: 141–62.

ARNOLD D. KALUZNY and others (1974), "Innovation in Health Services: A Comparative Study of Hospitals and Health Departments," in Arnold D. Kaluzny, ed., *Innovation in Health Care Organizations: An Issue in Organizational Change*, Chapel Hill, N.C., University of North Carolina, School of Public Health.

DANIEL KATZ and others (1950), *Productivity, Supervision, and Morale in an Office Situation*, Detroit, Darel Press.

DANIEL KATZ AND ROBERT L. KAHN (1966), *The Social Psychology of Organizations*, New York, Wiley.

ELIHU KATZ (1957), "The Two-Step Flow of Communication: An Up-to-Date Report on an Hypothesis," *Public Opinion Quarterly*, 21:61–78.

ELIHU KATZ AND PAUL LAZARSFELD (1955), *Personal Influence: The Part Played by People in the Flow of Mass Communications*, New York, Free Press.

HERBERT KAUFMAN (1973), *Administrative Feedback: Monitoring Subordinates' Behavior*, Washington, D.C., Brookings.

A. KERCKHOFF and others (1965), "Sociometric Patterns and Hysterical Contagion," *Sociometry*, 28: 2–15.

A. KERCKHOFF AND KURT BACK (1968), *The June Bug: A Study of Hysterical Contagion*, New York, Appleton-Century-Crofts.

D. LAWRENCE KINCAID (1973), *Communication Networks, Locus of Control, and Family Planning among Migrants to the Periphery of Mexico City*, Ph.D. Thesis, East Lansing, Mich., Michigan State University.

CHARLES KORTE AND STANLEY MILGRAM (1970), "Acquaintance Networks between Radical Groups: Application of the Small World Method," *Journal of Personality and Social Psychology*, 15: 101–108.

THOMAS S. KUHN (1970), *The Structure of Scientific Revolutions*, Chicago, University of Chicago Press.

HENRY LANDSBERGER (1958), *Hawthorne Revisited*, Ithaca, N.Y., Cornell University Press.

J. T. LANZETTA AND T. B. ROBY (1957), "Group Learning and Communication as a Function of Task and Structure 'Demands'," *Journal of Abnormal and Social Psychology*, 55: 121–31.

RICHARD LaPIERE (1967), "Attitudes versus Actions," in Martin Fishbein, ed., *Readings in Attitude Theory and Measurement*, New York, Wiley.

OTTO LARSEN AND RICHARD HILL (1958), "Social Structure and Interpersonal Communication," *American Journal of Sociology*, 63: 497–505.

ERWIN LASZLO (1975), "The Meaning and Significance of General System Theory," *Behavioral Science*, 20: 9–24.

EDWARD O. LAUMANN (1973), *Bonds of Pluralism: The Form and Substance of Urban Social Networks*, New York, Wiley–Interscience.

EDWARD E. LAWLER AND LYMAN W. PORTER (1967), "The Effect of Performance on Job Satisfaction," *Industrial Relations*, 7: 20–28.

PAUL R. LAWRENCE AND JAY W. LORSCH (1967), *Organization and Environment: Managing Differentiation and Integration*, Boston, Harvard University Press.

PAUL F. LAZARSFELD and others (1948), *The People's Choice*, New York, Columbia University Press.

HAROLD J. LEAVITT (1951), "Some Effects of Certain Communication Patterns on Group Performance," *Journal of Abnormal and Social Psychology*, 46: 38–50.

HAROLD J. LEAVITT and others (1973), *The Organizational World*, New York, Harcourt Brace Jovanovich.

NANCY HOWELL LEE (1969), *The Search for an Abortionist*, University of Chicago Press.

DANIEL LERNER (1958), *The Passing of Traditional Society: Modernizing the Middle East*, New York, Free Press.

FRED G. LESIEUR (1958), *The Scanlon Plan: A Frontier in Labor–Management Relations*, Cambridge, Mass., Massachusetts Institute of Technology Press.

FRED G. LESIEUR AND ELBRIDGE S. PUCKETT (1969), "The Scanlon Plan Has Proved Itself," *Harvard Business Review*, 47: 109–18.

KURT LEWIN (1958), "Group Decision and Social Change," in Theodore M. Newcomb and Eugene L. Hartley, eds., *Readings in Social Psychology*, New York, Holt.

RENSIS LIKERT (1961), *New Patterns of Management*, New York, McGraw-Hill.

RENSIS LIKERT (1967), *The Human Organization*, New York, McGraw-Hill.

NAN LIN (1973), *The Study of Human Communication*, New York, Bobbs-Merrill.

GEORG N. LINDSEY (1974), *An Alternative Method for the Evaluation of Networks in Large Organizations*, M.A. Thesis, San Jose, Calif., San Jose State University.

SEYMOUR MARTIN LIPSET and others (1956), *Union Democracy: The Internal Politics of the International Typographical Union*, New York, Free Press.

WILLIAM T. LIU AND ROBERT W. DUFF (1972), "The Strength of Weak Ties," *Public Opinion Quarterly*, 36: 361–66.

DONALD MACDONALD (1970), *Communication Roles and Communication Contents in a Bureaucratic Setting*, Ph.D. Thesis, East Lansing, Mich., Michigan State University.

DOUGLAS McGREGOR (1960), *The Human Side of Enterprise*, New York, McGraw-Hill.

EDGAR C. McVOY (1940), "Patterns of Diffusion in the United States," *American Sociological Review*, 5: 219–27.

JAMES G. MARCH AND HERBERT A. SIMON (1958), *Organizations*, New York, Wiley.

ELTON MAYO (1933), *The Human Problems of an Industrial Civilization*, New York, Macmillan.

EDWIN MANSFIELD (1963), "Size of Firm, Market Structure, and Innovation," *Journal of Political Economy*, 71: 556–76.

PETER MEARS (1974), "Structuring Communication in a Working Group," *Journal of Communication*, 24: 71–79.

RICHARD L. MEIER (1963), "Communications Overload: Proposals from the Study of a University Library," *Administrative Science Quarterly*, 7: 521–44.

STANLEY MILGRAM (1967), "The Small World Problem," *Psychology Today*, 1: 61–67.

STANLEY MILGRAM (1969), "Inter-Disciplinary Thinking and the Small World Problem," in Muzafer Sherif and Carolyn W. Sherif, eds., *Interdisciplinary Relationships in the Social Sciences*, Chicago, Aldine.

JAMES G. MILLER (1955), "Toward a General Theory for the Behavioral Sciences," *American Psychologist*, 10: 513–31.

JAMES G. MILLER (1960), "Input Overload and Psychopathology," *American Journal of Psychiatry*, 116: 695–704.

JAMES G. MILLER (1962), "Information Input Overload," in M. C. Yovits and others, eds., *Self-Organizing Systems*, Washington, D.C., Spartan.

JAMES G. MILLER (1965), "Living Systems: Basic Concepts," *Behavioral Science*, 10: 193–237.

JAMES G. MILLER (1971), "The Nature of Living Systems," *Behavioral Science*, 16: 277–301.

JAMES G. MILLER (1972), "Living Systems: The Organization," *Behavioral Science*, 17: 1–182.

ROGER E. MILLER (1971), *Innovation, Organization, and Environment*, Sherbrooke, Canada, University of Sherbrooke Press.

J. CLYDE MITCHELL (1969), "The Concept and Use of Social Networks," in J. Clyde Mitchell, ed., *Social Networks in Urban Situations*, Manchester, England, Manchester University Press.

WILLIAM G. MITCHELL (1970), *Communication of an Educational Innovation in an Institution of Higher Learning*, Ph.D. Thesis, East Lansing, Mich., Michigan State University.

LAWRENCE B. MOHR (1966), *Determinants of Innovation in Organizations*, Ph.D. Thesis, Ann Arbor, Mich., University of Michigan.

PETER R. MONGE AND GEORG N. LINDSEY (1974), "The Study of Communication Networks and Communication Structure in Large Organizations," Paper presented at the International Communication Association, New Orleans, La.

J. D. MOONEY AND A. C. REILEY (1939), *The Principles of Organization*, New York, Harper.

JACOB L. MORENO (1953), *Who Shall Survive? Foundations of Sociometry, Group Psychotherapy, and Sociodrama*, Beacon, N. Y., Beacon House.

JACOB L. MORENO AND HELEN H. JENNINGS (1960), *The Sociometry Reader*, New York, Free Press.

PAUL E. MOTT (1972), *The Characteristics of Effective Organizations*, New York, Harper and Row.

NICOS P. MOUZELIS (1968), *Organization and Bureaucracy: An Analysis of Modern Theories*, Chicago, Aldine.

ROBERT MYTINGER (1968), *Innovation in Local Health Services: A Study of the Adoption of New Programs by Local Health Departments with Particular Reference to Newer Medical Care Activities*, Washington, D.C., U.S. Government Printing Office, PHS Publication 1664–2.

RALPH NADER (1966), *Unsafe at Any Speed*, New York, Simon and Schuster.

ANANT R. NEGANDHI AND BERNARD C. REIMANN (1973), "Correlates of Decentralization: Closed and Open Systems Perspectives," *Academy of Management Journal*, 16: 570–582.

JIRI NEHNEVAJSA (1960), "Graphic Presentation," in Jacob L. Moreno and Helen H. Jennings, eds., *The Sociometry Reader*, New York, Free Press.

TALCOTT PARSONS (1951), *The Social System*, New York, Free Press.

W. J. PAUL AND K. B. ROBERTSON (1970), *Job Enrichment and Employee Motivation*, London, Gower.

H. Earl Pemberton (1936), "The Curve of Culture Diffusion Rate," *American Sociological Review*, 1: 547–56.

Johannes Pennings (1973), "Measures of Organizational Structure: A Methodological Note," *American Journal of Sociology*, 79: 686–704.

Charles Perrow (1970a), *Organizational Analysis: A Sociological Perspective*, Belmont, Ca., Wadsworth.

Charles Perrow (1970b), "Departmental Power and Perspective in Industrial Firms," in Mayer Zald, ed., *Power Organizations*, Nashville, Tenn., Vanderbilt University Press.

Charles Perrow (1972), *Complex Organizations: A Critical Essay*, Glenview, Ill., Scott, Foresman.

John Pile (1968), "Clearing the Mystery of the 'Office Landscape' or 'Bürolandschaft,'" *Interiors*, 127: 94–103.

John Platt and James G. Miller (1969), "Handling Information Overload," *Ekistics*, 28: 295–96.

Ithiel de Sola Pool (1973), "Communication Systems," in Ithiel de Sola Pool and Wilbur Schramm, eds., *Handbook of Communication*, Chicago, Rand-McNally.

Derek J. de Solla Price (1963), *Little Science, Big Science*, New York, Columbia University Press.

Derek J. de Solla Price (1970), "The Scientific Foundations of Science Policy," *Nature*, 206: 233–38.

Diane S. Pugh and others (1971), *Writers on Organizations*, London, Penguin.

William H. Read (1962), "Upward Communication in Industrial Hierarchies," *Human Relations*, 15: 3–15.

A. Rice (1958), *Productivity and Social Organization: The Ahmedabad Experiment*, London, Tavistock.

William D. Richards, Jr. (1971), "An Improved Conceptually-Based Method for Analysis of Communication Structures of Large Complex Organizations," Paper presented at the International Communication Association, Phoenix, Ariz.

William D. Richards, Jr. (1974a), "Network Analysis in Large Complex Organizations: Theoretical Basis," Paper presented at the International Communication Association, New Orleans, La.

William D. Richards, Jr. (1974b), "Network Analysis in Large Complex Organizations: The Nature of Structure," Paper presented at the International Communication Association, New Orleans, La.

William D. Richards, Jr. (1974c), "Network Analysis in Large Complex Organizations: Metrics," Paper presented at the International Communication Association, New Orleans, La.

William D. Richards, Jr. (1974d), "Network Analysis in Large Complex Organizations: Techniques and Methods–Tools," Paper presented at the International Communication Association, New Orleans, La.

William D. Richards, Jr. (1974e), "Network Analysis in Large Complex

Organizations: Negopy—V.4.0—Program Description," Paper presented at the International Communication Association, New Orleans, La.

FRITZ J. ROETHLISBERGER (1941), *Management and Morale*, Cambridge, Mass., Harvard University Press.

FRITZ J. ROETHLISBERGER AND WILLIAM J. DICKSON (1939), *Management and the Worker*, Cambridge, Mass., Harvard University Press.

DAVID L. ROGERS (1974), "Sociometric Analysis of Interorganizational Relations: Application of Theory and Measurement," *Rural Sociology*, 39: 487–503.

EVERETT M. ROGERS (1973), *Communication Strategies for Family Planning*, New York, Free Press.

EVERETT M. ROGERS (1975), "Where We Are in Understanding the Diffusion of Innovations," Paper presented at the East–West Communication Institute Conference on Communication and Change: Ten Years After, Honolulu.

EVERETT M. ROGERS and others (1969), *Diffusion of Innovations: Educational Change in Thai Government Secondary Schools*, East Lansing, Mich., Michigan State University, Institute for International Studies in Education and Department of Communication, Mimeo Report.

EVERETT M. ROGERS AND REKHA AGARWALA–ROGERS (1975a), "Organizational Communication," in Gerhard J. Hanneman and William J. McEwen, eds., *Communication and Behavior*, Reading, Mass., Addison–Wesley.

EVERETT M. ROGERS AND REKHA AGARWALA–ROGERS (1975b), *Evaluation Research on Family Planning Communication*, Paris, UNESCO, Technical Report.

EVERETT M. ROGERS AND DILIP K. BHOWMIK (1971), "Homophily–Heterophily: Relational Concepts for Communication Research," *Public Opinion Quarterly*, 34: 523–38.

EVERETT M. ROGERS WITH F. FLOYD SHOEMAKER (1971), *Communication of Innovations: A Cross-Cultural Approach*, New York, Free Press.

IAN C. ROSS AND FRANK HARARY (1955), "Identification of the Liaison Persons of an Organization Using the Structure Matrix," *Management Science*, 1.

DONALD C. ROWAT, ed. (1965), *The Ombudsman: Citizen and Defender*, London, Allen and Unwin.

A. H. RUBENSTEIN (1957), "Liaison Relations in Research and Development," *IRE Transactions on Engineering Management*, 72–78.

BJARNE RUBY (1974), *Design for Innovation: A Cybernetic Approach*, Copenhagen, Institute for Future Studies.

BRYCE RYAN AND NEAL C. GROSS (1943), "The Diffusion of Hybrid Seed Corn in Two Iowa Communities," *Rural Sociology*, 8: 15–24.

HARVEY SAPOLSKY (1967), "Organizational Structure and Innovation," *Journal of Business*, 40: 497–510.

WILBUR SCHRAMM (1955), "How Communication Works," in Wilbur Schramm, ed., *Process and Effect of Mass Communication*, Urbana, Ill., University of Illinois Press.

DONALD F. SCHWARTZ (1968), *Liaison Communication Roles in a Formal Organization*, Ph.D. Thesis, East Lansing, Mich., Michigan State University.

PHILIP SELZNICK (1949), *TVA and the Grass Roots: A Study in the Sociology of Formal Organization*, Berkeley, University of California Press.

PHILIP SELZNICK (1972), "Coöption," in Merlin B. Brinkerhoff and Phillip R. Kunz, eds., *Complex Organizations and Their Environments*, Dubuque, Iowa, Brown.

CLAUDE E. SHANNON AND WARREN WEAVER (1949), *The Mathematical Theory of Communication*, Urbana, Ill., University of Illinois Press.

M. E. SHAW (1954), "Some Effects of Unequal Distribution of Information Upon Group Performance in Various Communication Nets," *Journal of Abnormal and Social Psychology*, 49: 547–53.

M. E. SHAW (1964), "Communication Networks," in Leonard Berkowitz, ed., *Advances in Experimental Psychology*, New York, Academic Press.

M. W. SHELLY AND J. C. GILCHRIST (1958), "Some Effects of Communication Requirements in Group Structure," *Journal of Social Psychology*, 48: 37–44.

F. FLOYD SHOEMAKER (1971), *System Variables and Educational Innovativeness in Thai Government Secondary Schools*, Ph.D. Thesis, East Lansing, Mich., Michigan State University.

ROBERT L. SHOTLAND (1969), *The Structure of Social Relationships at MSU: A Communication Study*, East Lansing, Mich., Michigan State University, Educational Development Program, Project Report 302.

ROBERT L. SHOTLAND (1970), *The Communication Patterns and the Structure of Social Relationships at a Large University*, Ph.D. Thesis, East Lansing, Mich., Michigan State University.

SAM D. SIEBER (1973), "The Integration of Fieldwork and Survey Methods," *American Journal of Sociology*, 78: 1335–59.

WILLIAM J. SIFFIN (1966), *The Thai Bureaucracy: Institutional Change and Development*, Honolulu, East–West Center Press.

HERBERT A. SIMON (1947), *Administrative Behavior*, New York, Macmillan.

HERBERT A. SIMON (1956), *Models of Man*, New York, Wiley.

HERBERT A. SIMON and others (1950), *Public Administration*, New York, Knopf.

C. E. SNOW (1927), "Research on Industrial Illumination," *Technical Engineering News*, 257–82.

ROBERT SOMMER (1967), "Small Group Ecology," *Psychological Bulletin*, 67: 145–52.

WILLIAM H. STARBUCK (1965), "Mathematics and Organizational Theory," in James G. March, ed., *Handbook of Organizations*, Chicago, Rand Mc-Nally.

SAMUEL A. STOUFFER and others (1949), *The American Soldier: Studies in the Social Psychology of World War II*, Princeton, N. J., Princeton University Press.

HAROLD SUTTON AND LYMAN W. PORTER (1968), "A Study of the Grapevine in a Governmental Organization," *Personnel Psychology*, 21: 223–30.

A. J. SYKES (1965), "Economic Interest and the Hawthorne Researches: A Comment," *Human Relations*, 18: 253–63.

ARNOLD TANNENBAUM AND STANLEY SEASHORE (n. d.), *Some Changing Conceptions and Approaches to the Study of Persons in Organization*, Ann Arbor, Mich., University of Michigan, Survey Research Center, Report.

FREDERICK TAYLOR (1911), *Scientific Management*, New York, Harper and Row.

SHIRLEY TERREBERRY (1968), "The Evolution of Organizational Environments," *Administrative Science Quarterly*, 12: 590–613.

LEE THAYER (1967), "Communication and Organization Theory," in Frank E. X. Dance, ed., *Human Communication Theory: Original Essays*, New York, Rinehart and Winston.

LEE THAYER (1968), *Communication and Communication Systems: In Organizations, Management, and Interpersonal Relations*, Homewood, Ill., Irwin.

LEE THAYER (1972), "Communication Systems," in E. Laszlo, ed., *The Relevance of General Systems Theory*, New York, Braziller.

JAMES D. THOMPSON (1967), *Organizations in Action*, New York, McGraw-Hill.

NOEL TICHY (1973), "An Analysis of Clique Formation and Structure in Organizations," *Administrative Science Quarterly*, 18: 194–208.

JEFFEREY TRAVERS AND STANLEY MILGRAM (1969), "An Experimental Study of the Small World Problem," *Sociometry*, 32: 425–43.

JAMES M. UTTERBACK (1974), "Innovation in Industry and the Diffusion of Technology," *Science*, 183: 620–26.

VICTOR VROOM (1964), *Work and Motivation*, New York, Wiley.

L. WESLEY WAGER (1962), "Channels of Interpersonal and Mass Communication in an Organizational Setting: Studying the Diffusion of Information about a Unique Organizational Change," *Sociological Inquiry*, 32: 88–107.

CHARLES T. WALKER AND ROBERT H. GUEST (1952), *The Man on the Assembly Line*, Cambridge, Mass., Harvard University Press.

R. WALTON (1972), "How to Counter Alienation in the Plant," *Harvard Business Review*, 50.

SANDRA ARDAH WARDEN (1964), *The Local–Cosmopolitan Dimension of Individual Value Orientation: A Study*, M.A. Thesis, East Lansing, Mich., Michigan State University.

W. Lloyd Warner and J. O. Low (1947), *The Social System of the Modern Factory*, New Haven, Conn., Yale University Press.

Roland L. Warren (1967), "The Organizational Field as a Focus for Investigation," *Administrative Science Quarterly*, 12: 396–419.

John Watney (1974), *Clive in India*, England, Saxon House.

Paul Watzlawick and others (1967), *Pragmatics of Human Communication: A Study of Interactional Patterns, Pathologies, and Paradoxes*, New York, Norton.

Eugene J. Webb and others (1966), *Unobtrusive Measures: Nonreactive Research in the Social Sciences*, Chicago, Rand McNally.

Max Weber (1946), *From Max Weber: Essays in Sociology*, transl. Hans Gerth and C. Wright Mills, New York, Oxford University Press.

Max Weber (1948), *The Theory of Social and Economic Organization*, transl. A. M. Henderson and Talcott Parsons, New York, Oxford University Press.

Max Weber (1968), *Economy and Society*, ed. Guenther Roth and Claus Wittich, New York, Bedminister Press.

Karl Weick (1969), *The Social Psychology of Organizing*, Reading, Mass., Addison-Wesley.

Robert S. Weiss (1956), *Processes of Organization*, Ann Arbor, Mich., University of Michigan, Institute for Social Research, Report.

Robert S. Weiss and Eugene Jacobson (1955), "A Method for the Analysis of the Structure of Complex Organizations," *American Sociological Review*, 20: 661–68.

Bruce H. Westley and Malcolm S. MacLean, Jr. (1957), "A Conceptual Model for Communication Research," *Journalism Quarterly*, 34: 31–38.

Thomas L. Whisler (1970), *Information Technology and Organization Change*, Belmont, Ca., Wadsworth.

Harrison C. White (1970), "Search Parameters for the Small World Problems," *Social Forces*, 49: 259–64.

T. N. Whitehead (1938), *The Industrial Worker*, Cambridge, Mass., Harvard University Press.

Martin King Whyte (1973), "Bureaucracy and Modernization in China: The Maoist Critique," *American Sociological Review*, 38: 149–63.

Martin King Whyte (1974), *Small Groups and Political Rituals in China*, Berkeley, University of California Press.

Norbert Wiener (1950), *The Human Use of Human Beings: Cybernetics and Society*, Boston, Houghton Mifflin.

Harold L. Wilensky (1967), *Organizational Intelligence: Knowledge and Policy in Government and Industry*, New York, Basic Books.

Joan Woodward (1958), *Management and Technology*, London, Her Majesty's Stationery Office.

Joan Woodward (1965), *Industrial Organization: Theory and Practice*, London, Oxford University Press.

Dharam P. Yadav (1967), *Communication Structure and Innovation Diffusion in Two Indian Villages*, Ph.D. Thesis, East Lansing, Mich., Michigan State University.

Gerald Zaltman and others (1973), *Innovations and Organizations*, New York, Wiley–Interscience.

Author Index

201

Subject Index

Note: *Italic* numbers indicate page showing definition

Alienation, assembly-line, 87
Attitudes, *13*
Authority, 78

Biases in communication research, 18–23
  against mutual causality, 20
  lack of process, 18–20
  psychological, 20–23
Black Hole of Calcutta, 86–87
Boundary, 62
Boundary-spanners, 67–68
Bridge, *130*
Bureaucracy, 83–89, 166–171, 182
  as a dirty word, 85–86
  elements of bureaucratic structure, 83–85
  hierarchy, 85
  in the Kingdom of Siam, 166–171
  Mao Tse-tung's antibureaucracy, 88–89
  rules and regulations, 84
  specialization, 85
Bürolandschaft, 25, 102–106
Bypassing, *94*

Centralization
  of networks, 120–122
  of organizations, 156–157, 183–184
Change in organizations, 153–155
  through reorganization, 154
  through training, 154
Channel, *12*, 169
  interpersonal, 12
  mass media, 12
Climate, 73, 181
Clique connectedness, *142–143*, 146
Clique dominance, *143*, 146
Clique integration, *143*, 146
Clique openness, *143*, 146

Cliques, *113*, 127, 129–131, 142–143
Closed system, *51*
Communication, 9, 180
  affected by structure, 89–106
  channels, 169
  effects, 13
  "hypodermic needle" model, 39
  informal, 38–39
  internal function of, 53–54
  models, 10–14, 15–17, 17–18
  nonverbal, 11
  process, 17
  problems, 90
  purpose, 18
  restricted flows, 90–92
  and structure, 1–2, 6–8
  synergistic process, 18
  systems view of, 55, 57
  and Taylorism, 34–35
  two-step flow, 39
Communication behavior, 181–182
Communication flows, sociometric
    measures, 109
Communication integration, *125*
Communication networks, 108–148, 182–184
  and formal structure, 110–111
  system effects, 111–112
Communication problems, 182
Communication process, main elements in,
    10–14
Communication research
  biases, 18–23
  component approach, 15–17
  laboratory experiments, 119–123
  nature of, 14–15
  network analysis, 24–25
  open system approach to, 50–52

205

Printed in the United States
By Bookmasters